Rebel without a Car

Surviving and Appreciating
Your Child's Teen Years

Fred Mednick

Fairview Press   Minneapolis

A portion of this book's proceeds will be donated to the Multicultural Alliance, a non-profit agency dedicated to the recruitment and training of, and support for, teachers of color.

Published by Fairview Press, 2450 Riverside Avenue South, Minneapolis, MN 55454.

Library of Congress Cataloging-in-Publication Data

Mednick, Fred 1954–
    Rebel without a car : surviving and appreciating your child's teen years / Fred Mednick.
       p.   cm.
    Includes bibliographical references and index.
    ISBN 1-57749-014-2 (alk. paper)
    1. Parent and teenager. I. Title.
HQ799.15.M43 1996
649'.125—dc20
                    96-19691
                    CIP

First Printing: September 1996

Printed in the United States of America
00 99 98 97 96   7 6 5 4 3 2 1

Cover design: Circus Design

Publisher's Note: Fairview Press publishes books and other materials related to the subjects of social and family issues. Its publications, including *Rebel without a Car,* do not necessarily reflect the philosophy of Fairview Hospital and Healthcare Services or their treatment programs.

For a free current catalog of Fairview Press titles, please call this toll-free number: 1-800-544-8207.

Contents

Acknowledgments

To my wife, Rosalie Frankel, who has provided wisdom, psychological intuitiveness, and encouragement. And to my two children, Alanna and Lora, who both humble and inspire me.

To my parents, both teachers, because they endured my own adolescence.

To Bobbie Becker, in memoriam, whose unabashed charisma and enthusiasm for life were inspiring. He taught me to love and appreciate the teenage mind. He told me adolescents have strength, spirit, and the capacity for wonder. I still believe him.

Many thanks to my colleagues and friends at The Oakwood School and at The Bush School, and to the students and parents who have provided me with both theoretical help and essential day-to-day, on-the-job-training. Thanks to the National Association of Independent Schools for its extraordinary scholarship in education, dedication to children, and support of teaching, and to the Los Angeles Unified School District and the Seattle Public Schools for their fabulous and inspirational teachers.

Special appreciation, affection, and acknowledgments for Jim Astman, Ph.D., Jeri Weiss, Ph.D., and Barbara Kornblau, Ed.D., my three mentors, to Rhoda Wasserman and to all colleagues who also live with teenagers, and whose collective experience and expertise and wisdom I have found immeasurable.

Thanks to Daniel Will-Harris, whose computer expertise, encouragement, and humor gave me the strength to complete this project: http:www.will-harris.com/mednick

Thanks to friends Vicky and Hummie Mann, whose intelligence and kindness have given me perspective and direction.

And finally, thanks to teenagers, everywhere, who have provided me with great joy, self-understanding, and a decent career.

How old would you be if you didn't know how old you was?
—Satchell Paige

"Ado, ado, adolescence,
I wince before your luminescence."
—Ogden Nash

"Could you get your sister to pass the salt?"
—a forty six year-old father of a teenager and a nine year old

A little more than a decade ago, you used to be able to sleep until 5:23 in the morning, when you would hear the pitter-patter of your little toddler's feet, waking you up to party. Now you sweat bullets and can't get to sleep until 5:23 in the morning, longing to hear some kind of noise, a key in a latch, preferably, as you wait for your child to come home from a party.

This book is best read while waiting up.

Introduction

We shall not cease from exploration
And the end of all our exploring
Will be to arrive where we started
And know the place for the first time.
—T. S. Eliot, The Waste Land

Allow me a few hours to guide you through the land of adolescence. Our tour will travel past some spectacular sights; we'll glimpse into the caverns and formations, the peaks and valleys of teenage life. I have a special orientation as your tour guide, for I have taken this trip several times as a junior-high and high-school principal. As an educator, I live with teenagers day-in and day-out, year after year. I observe them alone and in groups over the course of many years. In short, I live on the inside, in those provinces removed from parents.

I have come to witness this phenomenon we call adolescent culture, its capriciousness, its awkwardness, and its narcissism. I watch your kids from the place you drop them off (four blocks away from school). I watch them at the morning break, in the classroom, at the lockers; I know what and how they eat. I've listened to them in the counseling office and at the attendance desk. (The excuses for being late rate with the great Academy Award-winning performances. One day, a record number of grandmothers lost their lives, tragically.) I've read what they scratch onto their desks. I watch them right outside my office window, preening. I eavesdrop on conversations they think I can't hear, about drivers' training, the opposite sex, their "absurd" parents, peers, siblings, teachers, and clothes. My ears have adjusted to voices "marinated in whine," as one teacher put it, mixed with goofiness and pain and elation and helplessness.

Until now, most guides to adolescence were written from the perspective of doctors and psychologists, all of whom have extensive and invaluable experience with teenagers who come for help once a week or by special appointment. They use a therapeutic model; that is—your kid's got problems; you've got problems, let's work on those problems.[1] Psychologists may see teens for their psychopathology; I see them, for the most part, in their health, despite its fluctuations and irregularities. Although a psychological approach is invaluable and relied upon significantly in this book, I have a different perspective as an educator that comes from the role I play, every day, in mediating between your world and theirs.[2] My tour is up close and personal. It is an invitation to join the faculty meeting.

Tour guides usually speak in a garbled voice over the speakers about what lies ahead. Lost in your own thoughts, you may not be listening. You may be separated from the sights by panes of glass. You may or may not have an opportunity to step outside and stroll through the grounds, but you are asked to remain at a distance, particularly at dangerous regions (most likely for insurance reasons).

Most books about adolescence share such a distance by separating the parent from the adolescent as an object for study. In the end, they may even reinforce the generation gap which, for some, is the size of the Grand Canyon. Although your child is "out there" and separate, he or she is nonetheless your flesh and blood. Thus, some of you is out there, and some of your son and daughter is in you. There is a certain way in which the light strikes those tour bus windows, usually in the later afternoon, and they are transformed, for a moment, into reflective surfaces. Instead of looking out at the sights and being told what you are seeing, you might suddenly find yourself looking into a mirror. That later afternoon is your mid-life and part of what this book is all about, a back-and-forth journey between what you see in your teenager and who you are.[3] I hope to provide a new means of seeing adolescence in this light. We need both windows and mirrors.

In the world of science, no experiment is purely objective. In fact, scientists have often spoken of how the observer changes the experiment by his or her very presence, an additional factor that must be considered part of the phenomenon itself. So it is in this tour through adolescence. Teenagers cannot be seen as specimens, to be studied or "understood" in the abstract.

In another world, the world of Zen, you are asked to approach others as if they are all enlightened Buddhas and you are not. Therefore, you see those around you as people teaching you lessons about yourself and about adolescence you wouldn't otherwise understand. In this excursion, I am asking you to move past what you first see of teenage life to consider what it is that adolescents can teach you, how they can help you grow, how you can be enriched by what may seem threatening, how you may honor your obstacles, and how teenagers may even help you celebrate a deep and abiding sense of life. In short, this is a book to help you with your teenager and to help you with yourself.

When I was sixteen, I thought that college was a capitalist plot and decided to join the Young Communist League. The initiation was simple enough, then, a vow to work in factories to organize the workers, a promise to work toward the revolution, and a few dollars in monthly dues to pay for mimeograph supplies and stale cookies. I joined because, as a teenager, the world continued to floor me with its lack of justice, its racism, and its economic inequality. And I was intrigued by the rituals of political life, its sense of sacrifice and community, continuity and order, and its imminence and relevance.

I found work in a bagel factory, the graveyard shift. Raw bagels would descend to a floured, rotating plate, and I was required to place them on flat trays and deliver them to a large vat of steaming and bubbling water. I slipped four bagels around the fingers of each hand, plopped them in, and stirred them for five minutes with a soggy baseball bat.

The heat was intense from the lack of ventilation, from the water and from the oven set at 450 degrees, spewing hot air from its rotating shelves. I broke out into rashes. The boss poured baking soda on my head to ease the itching and hives, and the moisture from the vat of water turned the white powder into a paste that would cake into my skin. During breaks, I would hide in the bathroom and cry rather than propagandize the workers, and I wondered what was driving me. Most kids sleep during this time, or party, or hang out, I thought. Why was I trying to save the world?

Every dawn, liberated from work, I would punch out, catch a one-hour nap, and drag myself to school, where I really caught up on my sleep. School was stultifying and supremely impersonal. There was no connection to me, to the world, to any of the issues I was concerned about. I skipped school with great regularity and marched in anti-war rallies, committed to the rightness of it all. I wore buttons with inflammatory slogans to intimidate my teachers and to define myself for peers. Between my own exhaustion and the subjects' irrelevance, I did poorly.

My parents, though liberal, were frightened by my extremism, therefore making it that much more attractive to me. The tension in my house grew as I struggled to find a balance between my own need for unabashed joy and my sober and morose drive to correct every injustice I saw. I was struggling to find an identity. It was impossible for my ideas and those of my parents to be compatible. The very process of finding my own point of view, of determining my own will, meant that I had to reject theirs. In short, I was an adolescent, trying on various selves, like masks, longing to be an independent being.

At one heated moment (I cannot remember the catalyst; one rarely does.), I slugged my father, hard, in the solar plexus. He doubled over in pain, clutching the edge of a chair. I still remember the time of day, the light, the exact position where we stood, and the look of anguish, bewilderment, and physical pain on my father's face. Although he had always been the kindest, most self-sacrificing man I have ever met, I was incapable of seeing his virtues. At that that moment, he had simply become the enemy. He was to represent all that was corrupt in American society, all the phony adults, all that was not right. I was caught between guilt and anger, love and hate, dependence and independence. He was the father and I was the son; we were both in pain. For years, we could not acknowledge that incident.

Soon afterwards, and without prompts or threats, I hung up my apron one last time, dusted off my floured hands, and walked out of the bagel factory, never to return. I decided to go to college after all.

Seven years later, my father visited me in graduate school. We strolled in the woods, at which point I was struck by my overwhelming feelings of love for him. These thoughts were swimming in my head, almost unbeknownst to the rest of me, when I said, "I'm sorry, Dad." After I recounted the incident, he said, "I guess we were just learning. You were learning how to be a young man, and I was learning how to be your father. Something was driving us both. Something made us come to blows. We both made a lot of mistakes."

What a wonderful thing to say, for he acknowledged his part in my own adolescence. His own introspection allowed him to see that his struggles and mine were somehow intertwined. We were both wrong and we were both right.

In retrospect, I know I am better for having struggled to find a political voice. I still work, in my own way and with moderation, to make the world a better place. (I certainly have enormous respect for bagels and the workers who make them.) Most of all, I have come to see adulthood, like adolescence, as a process.

It seems as though I had been traveling in a strange country and had caught an unknown disease when I was a teenager. This book explores that country and that disease. We'll travel into the world of contemporary American teenage life. We'll explore sexuality and morality, parenting and schooling, life in the 1990s, and the new pressures adolescents face. And, of course, throughout, we'll look at schools.

I'll tell you this up front: we need to be straight with each other. And I'll offer you a deal: I'll believe half of what your kid says to me about home if you believe half of what your kid tells you about school. School serves as the off-site parent for much of a child's day, so it is essential that you hear how an educator views this period of life and how parents and teachers can be partners in caregiving.

This partnership is an imperative, for adolescents are virtually transforming right before our eyes socially, physically, and intellectually. They enter school as children and, by the time they graduate, they are adults physically capable of having their own children. Adolescence tests the parents' will. A parent once told me at commencement exercises, exhausted: "Thank you for the lovely education you have provided my son. Now please send him to a good four-year institution—in Antarctica." Teenagers use their intelligence to push buttons, to reopen wounds parents thought were long since healed, the same wounds these parents experienced as children. They remind us that we are middle aged (as if we don't have enough reminders already).

Adolescence is biological. It's psychological. It's sociological. It's political. It's loud. And it's tough. Adolescents need to make our lives miserable, we have all been told; this is their way of becoming individuals distinct from their parents. The Freudians say that the achievement of early childhood is mastery over the body and the achievement of the latency period is mastery over the environment. When it comes to adolescence, they claim, the achievement involves mastery over emotions. So, when your teenagers fight with you about cleaning up their rooms or not doing their homework, it may be a safe excuse to engage in a battle, any kind of battle, to work out their discomfort and their push for independence. They've all read what I call the unwritten developmental textbook. At last, you may say, excellent reading comprehension!

They engage in behaviors that previous generations would reserve for delinquents. They slam their books down (if they brought any home) and retreat to their rooms without a word or start an argument over an absurdity, just to get a rise out of you. You'd slip them a ten-dollar bill if they'd only speak in complete sentences. Incredulous, you have to ask them to turn the volume down on their Walkman headphones. They slump into a stupor on the couch. When you want to engage them in conversation, they appear as accessible as a gas-station restroom. They can astonish you with their lack of gratitude, their rudeness, their slovenliness and hostility, their impulsivity and manipulation. But, then again, so do most politicians.[4]

I once asked a bookstore clerk to direct me to the section on parenting of teenagers. She looked at me incredulously and asked, "Why?" It is true, I must admit, that adolescence in America needs an image consultant.

But take a moment to answer these questions: How would you feel if your life depended upon looks and your face was as pock-marked as Beirut? How would you feel if you were a fourteen-year-old male with an erection about to give an oral report in class? Do you remember your own adolescent version of hell?

It may have been easier during our generation. The dress code was strictly enforced. Authority was scarier, clearer, and we basically complied. Moral tenets were less fluid. Street violence was less evident; though we did have drills in case of nuclear attack, we did not feel personally in danger on a daily basis. Now, drive-by shooting drills are a great deal more frightening than the amorphous political scare of the Russians. According to a poll by *Newsweek* and the Children's Defense Fund, "one in six youths between the ages of ten and seventeen has seen or knows someone who has been shot."[5]

Modern adolescence is gritty, erratic, and precipitous. "Increasingly, they are left to fend for themselves in a world of hostile strangers, dangerous sexual enticements and mysterious economic forces that even adults find unsettling."[6]

It simply isn't kind or gentle out there. Teenagers are barraged by the features of the contemporary landscape that bear on the very nature of life itself. They experience what one parent called a "100-channel paralysis," choices upon choices that confound and incapacitate them. Teenagers exist within a culture that marginalizes and trivializes them even as it exploits them for their advertising attractiveness. They're naturally confused and made more so by the world in which they live. This generation is taking an entirely different trip, and it's no vacation. There are rough spots along the way and strange sights that are hard to absorb.

I can't provide any guarantees or your money back, but I do promise to be helpful, clear, and entertaining. My observations and conclusions may very well touch a responsive chord. In addition to many years of experience with teenagers and virtually thousands of interviews, I have conducted a wide array of research to augment my own experience. Although this book will discuss normal adolescence (a bit of an oxymoron, I must admit), you will also gain a sense of when you and your child have entered areas where you need extra help.

There is no primer, no basal reader, no textbook, no teacher's manual to adolescence. I cannot guarantee a map to the territory, with all the highways laid out. Many such maps are arbitrary and artificial, and may lead you astray into areas far removed from the land teenagers inhabit. I *can* provide a compass, a general and helpful direction, and I can guarantee that you will have seen interesting things and have met engaging people along the way.

1
Adolescence Is a Syndrome

"There is no present or future, only the past,
happening over and over again, now."
—Eugene O'Neill

Adolescence is not just a stage, the way we have traditionally described this period; it is also a syndrome, a word defined as the concurrence of several symptoms in a disease. Teenagers "catch" something on their journey through life. A disease, in this sense, is associated more with dis-ease than with an illness; to dis-ease is "to make one uneasy, to put to discomfort or inconvenience; to trouble, to annoy, incommode, molest."[1] In fact, the word syndrome comes from the Greek word *syn*, meaning "with," and *dramein*, meaning "run." Running with? A perfect match. Teens seem to be running a perpetual fever, but you can't seem to identify the cause.

I see adolescence as a temporary disorder, a departure from "normalcy." Anna Freud has called adolescence a "developmental disturbance."[2] A teacher once observed: "It's a time when one has lost one's mind in order to come to one's senses." It is not as depressing as it sounds; there *is* a happy outcome. I want to provide a framework for living with your teenager to understand and work with, and even enjoy, the adolescent syndrome. To do so, I'll describe its features and how you—as parents and teachers—fit in.

Adolescence as a syndrome is different from adolescence as a stage. A stage is gone, never to return. If it were only a stage, a chronological peak, we could all breathe a collective sigh of relief. It's just not so.[3] A syndrome of this sort is an indication of something larger, something more intangible and fluid. Educators and psychologists often think of human development as a cycle or spiral rather than a ladder. In *Theories of Adolescence,* Rolf E. Muuss questions "the widely held assumption that adolescence is a distinct stage in human development that has its own unique characteristics and requires its own set of theoretical explanations. No fundamental qualitative differences exist among childhood, adolescence, and adulthood."[4]

Syndromes are managed, not cured. Adolescence can't be *fixed;* all attempts to do so are futile. It's often a matter of degree, and the "treatment" cannot be rushed. Adolescence may require simple first-aid—a few well-placed words of advice, a few strategies, a diversion here and there. Some families experience more symptoms than others; some may require a plan of attack, involving direct intervention by professionals. At these crucial moments, unambiguous action is required; questions having to do with whether your child is safe—emotionally or physically—immediately should be directed to qualified counseling professionals. But that's crisis mode. For the most part, adolescence arrives and must simply run its course.

Adolescence is contagious. Teenagers may pick it up at school, a fertile breeding ground of peers, who gather and rove in large groups, like cells. Adolescence seems to take over. In fact, it may change the pulse rate and blood pressure of the entire family. Sometimes the problems every family experiences can be solved by a rational approach; however, adolescents may turn the normal bumps and grinds of modern life into occasions that are insufferable, leading to another family member's acute crankiness or sudden urge to eat a half-gallon of Häagan-Dazs Vanilla Swiss Almond. Adolescence is certainly developmental and physiological in its individual forms; it is also infectious.

The syndrome of adolescence takes on the general qualities of other diseases. The cases may be chronic (slowly starts but lasts a long time), acute (suddenly starts and ends quickly), benign (has relatively few complications, and will probably turn out okay), or malignant (if left alone, in time, it may be terminal). Adolescence may go into remission for a while, but when you least expect it, the rash can spread all over the family. Progress begins when you see the syndrome as a matter of degrees.

Diseases may come from within the host organism or from the

outside environment. Much of adolescence is generated from within each child and from early childhood and experiences. Since this is a childhood syndrome, we are all predisposed to its eventuality. Other parts come from beyond the child, things over which he or she has little control. And these days, there are a number of environmental hazards out there. Life has changed considerably since the time when we experienced adolescence. There is more stress in the streets and at home in the family, and the settings traditionally considered safe—the home, the church, the local club, the schools—have been its victims. The rules about how to cope and succeed have changed, too, yet no one has bothered to consult, or even inform, the kids. Today's economy does not provide a particularly optimistic picture for teens, who have expressed an increasingly disparaging look at the future. Such factors may contribute to an adolescent's ongoing sense of loss, alienation, rebellion, and desperation. In short, there is a connection between "internal turmoil and external disorder."[5]

The syndrome of adolescence, like other syndromes, can reappear. It's a childhood disease for which we cannot develop an immunity, a kind of measles that can pock our face once again. Certainly, adolescence in America centers around the teenage years; however, the syndrome of adolescence, I believe, can come back to haunt us as parents. It has just lain dormant. At this point in your lives, you may be experiencing some of the same symptoms of the syndrome as your kids. The form may change, but the content stays the same. Gail Sheehy, the best-selling author of *Passages* and, more recently, *New Passages* calls this notion "middlescence." She writes: "Welcome to middlescence. It's adolescence the second time around. Turning backward, going in circles, feeling lost in a buzz of confusion and unable to make decisions."[6] You are essentially sharing the phenomenon, for adolescence may be taking place at the same time in the same house. In short, a mid-life crisis may simply be a different form of adolescence; it just comes later. Your ulcer may be only slightly different in form than your child's stomach pains. And you never knew you had something in common?

You may be suddenly faced with old, unresolved issues from your earlier bout with the syndrome. You may have repressed conflict with authority or with your parents, with your environment or your siblings or your childhood friends. It may be very difficult, then, to remember your own adolescence or empathize with the pain your child is exhibiting. There is the popular notion that when you're in bed with someone, there are about six other people with you—your mother and father and your first love, and your lover's mother and father and first love. Living with an adolescent is not much different. Standing next to you and living in your house is your adolescent and your own earlier adolescence, like a set of wooden Ukrainian dolls, each one inside the other. On some level, we are all diagnosed Adolescence Positive.

Many parents have not completely faced their childhood issues (nor is it reasonable to assume that one can put the past fully behind them to grow), and so the trials and the errors are inevitably heightened when parents see themselves in their own kids. They lose this essential perspective. That's why adolescence is especially difficult for everyone who experiences it. I know this to be true because I work with teenagers during the morning and parents in the late afternoon and evening, and am often struck by the similarity in their struggles, the mutuality in feelings.

Such tensions are exacerbated in a society that attempts to blur the generations—although the tensions between the two have not dissipated—in clothing, in food tastes, in entertainment, in advertising appeals, in language or manners or personal philosophy, in access to explicit sexuality and crime, in the permission to throw a temper tantrum or the incessant demand for immediate gratification.[7] Others have talked about how we rush our children's childhoods because it may get in the way of our careers or our economic survival; with two parents out of the house, children are often left to assume the roles of adults. Adults, in turn, may long for—even mimic—the carefree, halcyon days of youth.

Adolescence, therefore, can no longer be reduced to the teen years; sadly enough, I have seen teenagers act in more adult ways than their parents. But, in the end, you as parents are responsible for the life of another. Parenting of a teenager requires the essential recognition that one's age, one's experiences, one's strengths and frailties, and one's maturity can give one the general wherewithal to create a healthy framework in which another, younger human being can grow.

You're still the parent, the grown-up. And you must be in charge, even if you vacillate from charity to hysterics. Put it this way: when both you and your teenager were once much younger and both disabled by the flu, you were the one who had to get up to get the orange juice.

The syndrome of adolescence is accompanied by its emotional effects: depression and anxiety. Depression is characteristically a reaction to loss. For adults, it may be a loss of one's childhood or the separation from that once-adoring child. For your teenager, depression is also a loss of one's childhood and the vivid memories of dependent love and uncomplicated abandon, captured on a clunky video. Anxiety is a normal reaction to the unknown. You may not know where your teenager is going nor, for that matter, where you are headed. You may not know if the disease is going to get worse, or if it is a mild case. You may want to push another set of buttons and slam the entire videotaped experience in reverse— your teenager takes the joint *out* of his/her mouth or buttons up a fly or blouse or comes home. For your teenager, anxiety reflects aching questions: Who am I? What will I become? Am I going to survive this syndrome?

Your child's adolescence is unavoidable; you can't control or avoid adolescence through the elimination of contact. Classic forms of prevention include selective breeding or the introduction of some form of inoculation to ensure immunity. But because no Nobel Prize winner has come forward with such a solution, we must admit that no family is immune; there is no inoculation or anesthesia available. In fact, attempts to create one will result in complications at a much later date. In fact, fixing or preventing adolescence robs young people of the opportunity to be young. Though the forms of adolescence change, the teen years are to be lived, an essential part of human life to be felt fully and respected. What parents can do is work toward coping and gaining insight and regenerating themselves for the years ahead.

Adolescence requires a mutual understanding of symptomatology. New models of behavior in the medical profession suggest a more interactive relationship between doctor and patient. The patient certainly needs the doctor's expertise, judgment, and direction. The doctor needs the patient to provide information, feedback, and the will to heal, even to live; the patient must be an active player, not a victim, in the recovery process. This new model in medicine should serve as a metaphor for parenting an adolescent.

Try to avoid adding other strata to this syndrome; a primary one to avoid is sclerosis of the attitude. You've got to stick to your guns, but teenagers react to rigidity with resistance and can undermine all your best efforts. Other strata include lockjaw, in which adolescents and parents cannot communicate, or the common cold (shoulder), in which parents abdicate their responsibility and take an emotional or physical cruise away from their responsibilities.

Adolescence is a fairly easy syndrome to spot, with a wide range of behaviors you can recognize. And when it gets a bit rough, let me prescribe another bit of advice: take in two movies and call some-one—anyone—in the morning. That may all you need to come back—renewed and ready to keep going.

Time, along with patience, is a big help, too. Besides, think of it this way—you won't have to take them to birthday parties at Chuck E. Cheese anymore. After all, it's only a ten-year chunk of your life. There are more decades where that one came from.

Remember, too, that you are not the first parent of an adoles-cent who will—I promise—live to tell about it, fondly. If you think you're alone in this, take a number. In the meantime, since you're hassled and up late, waiting for your teenager to get home, this book will help you through all the muck and mayhem. The bottom line is this: here is an opportunity to hone your skills for insight, for common sense, humor, love, and the truth of your own intuition. One last dictionary definition: adolescence comes from *adolescere,* "to grow," and *olere,* "to nourish." It is an opportunity for nourish-ment. And if adolescence has its crisis, try to remember that the Chinese word for crisis is a combination of the characters represent-ing danger and opportunity.

We educators stay in the business of working with teens because of the clear conviction that, behind much of the anguish is a soul breaking free and defining itself; behind the anger and sullen-ness is an individual trying to make sense of change; lurking under the surface of raw feeling is the emergence of leadership; behind the occasional confusion in school and its accompanying self-depreca-tion is a budding intelligence. We who teach can appreciate that wide range of "normal" behavior, year after year. We can love them when you are having a hard time liking them. We know that those values that go underground have only lain dormant, and we watch those values reemerge—trust me. We know that most turn out well—the ones that have given you a hard time, the ones that were filled with fear, and the tentative and nerdy and abrasive ones, too. We know that this syndrome, if appreciated, can even feel good, especially during those serendipitous occasions when you find yourself engaging in a real conversation. We know that when they are believed in and when their feelings and thoughts count for something, they are capable of greatness.

2
Let's Get Cranky—
Adolescence Is Contradiction

"Sometimes the world has a load of questions.
Seems like the world knows nothing at all.
The world is near, but it's out of reach.
Some people touch it, but they can't hold on."
—*Talking Heads*[1]

"If you don't like people, they will like you"
—*a 13 year old*

The syndrome of adolescence involves its own unique form of schizophrenia.[2] The internal system is simply out of whack. The organism finds itself fighting off an infection of new body hair and bigger parts and new ideas. They're caught between the zit on their chin and a deep contemplation of the cosmos. Unfortunately, there are days when they can't decide which is more important. Adolescence is Janus-like; each issue they confront has two faces. They're chameleons.

Although adolescence takes place formally within the teen years, the symptoms may be difficult to pinpoint, precisely because of their change and flux. Chronological age may be one thing; a child's developmental age may be something else entirely. They may look one way and act another. As a principal, I spend a great deal of time thinking about where they are *now*, rather than where they should be.

In short, *adolescence is filled with contradiction.* As the old saying goes: they're too old to say something cute and too young to say something sensible.

Psychologists talk about how adolescents acquire (sooner or

17

later) powers of what the extraordinary Swiss psychologist, Piaget, called "formal reasoning," or the ability to think in more abstract terms. Parents may often be the subject of that newfound intellectual scrutiny. Teens become morally self-righteous, and they make sudden "discoveries" about you and may then treat you with abject scorn. They find your flaws and magnify them.

And then they may regress. A mother once reported that her daughter's persistent dinnertime expression of disgust and rancor over everything was destroying any semblance of civility in the family. Later one night, that same kid asked to be tucked into bed with a teddy bear and her tattered copy of *Goodnight Moon*.[3] Mom felt duped—put-down and manipulated and needed at the same time. The key issue here did not rest solely with the erratic and exasperating quality of her daughter's venomous or saccharin moods, but also the degree to which her daughter had control over her mother's reactions. The daughter's adolescence clearly *infected* the family.

This newfound sense of reasoning may be an inspiration one day and a devastation the next. They may have an *Aha* experience in school and a capacious sense of unlimited career possibilities, and then suddenly—without warning—they may see the world as a cesspool. As one educator put it: "They caramelize the world on one day and awfulize the world the next."

Another psychologist, Erik Erikson, has written about the social and emotional struggles teenagers face as one of "identity" rather than "role confusion." They're attempting, in their life course, to develop a new and coherent whole. As children, they never wondered who they were, but as adolescents, their newfound sense of self competes against conflicting messages about what role they are to play and who they are to become. They're no longer children, but they're not yet adults (neither are they acknowledged nor respected as such by society). So, they form cliques to find an identity. They're suddenly accepted, then rejected, and they do the same to others. Erikson believes that kids resolve their identity crisis when their role in life is made clear; however, the time at home or at school may be in disarray.

The eleven-year old with strange new formations (Bounty paper towels, perhaps?) under her blouse makes your life miserable because she wants to date a boy who wears a leather flak jacket and has hair like the lead singer of Green Day. The thirteen-year old boy suddenly embraces a strong position against your "crass" material-ism, but obsesses about the latest Game Boy or a pair of shoes that look like they'd fit a circus clown.

Their passions are tentative. Teenagers may be obsessed with the guitar and may find ways—through a part-time job and the manipulation of funds from you (grand larceny)—to purchase this icon of American culture, only to chuck it with disdain a few months later, when they can't jam like Hendrix. They still don't know the value of a dollar, though they are desperate to buy some-thing they can't live without, something dear that they'll forget or abandon.

Adolescents are extraordinary litigators, armed with a domi-neering and boorish pseudo logic and overbearing—courtroom demeanor. Unaware of their own contradictions, they put their intelligence to use trying to expose the flaws in yours. They chastise you for your conformity, but they consider the peer-group as a blood pact. In this same blood pact, of course, they are capable of ripping one of its members to shreds, yet may plead for advice and council from this "mortal enemy" the very next day. They serve both as the prosecution and the defense—capital "M" manipulators.

They have a visceral distrust for authority, especially yours. They find chinks in the armor and drive in a wedge. They still don't trust anyone over forty. At the same time, there is a slavish acquies-cence to authority figures of choice, such as rock stars easily old enough to be their parents. In fact, recent articles have pointed out an increasing fascination with and dependence upon cult leaders, many with authoritarian, even fascist tendencies.[4]

They are caught between independence and dependence. They want to leave your "terrible" home, but covet their own rooms as their sanctuary. My favorite eavesdropped conversation went like this: "Even the floor plan of our house is the same as everyone else's—bedrooms and bathrooms, bathrooms and bedrooms." In drafting class, of course, that same cynic sketched out the architec-tural renderings of his dream house which has—you guessed it—numerous bedrooms and bathrooms which looked surprisingly like those to which he returns after school.

Their newly formed and deeply passionate political beliefs make them capitalists and communists, democrats and republicans. Behind it all is an antiauthoritian spirit, idealism, and a free-floating anger at life's own inconsistencies. They won't clean up their rooms, but they'll receive the Kiwanis Club Community Service Award for their errantry at a neighborhood graffiti cleanup. They won't sit and eat a meal for more than five minutes, but are capable of joining friends and a beloved teacher to cook, serve, and clean for a homeless shelter during Thanksgiving. They may not give a friend the time of day, but can be seen in their room chatting for hours with a nameless friend on the Internet. I see this selfish/selfless disparity all the time. Sometimes they're heartless: "Well, besides that, Mrs. Lincoln, how was the play?" and at other times, if touched in the right way, they respond with extraordinary acts of compassion and sacrifice.

They consider awkwardness to be a cardinal sin and appearance everything (notice the obsession with mirrors or any other reflective surface, for that matter), but declare with alarm that parts of their body are growing out of proportion, like a chapter from Dr. Seuss. They proclaim that you have given birth to a freak and that you need to make an appointment for immediate reconstructive surgery or liposuction. They demonstrate super-human power and can watch late movies until 3:00 in the morning, yet even after long periods of rest, they can slip into overwhelming fatigue. On some days, they know how to be supremely mature and can astound you with articulate conversation, yet they pick the most inopportune moments to regress. If the boss is over for dinner, it's a toss up whether your child may clear the dishes without asking or emit a rippling fart.

There's a shift in emotions from the outside world to the inside. Sometimes they implode; sometimes they explode. We may think a significant event in our child's life is worthy of a particular emotion—anger or depression or elation—and yet they react in bizarre ways; they'll not be phased by a "D" on a Geometry test, yet they'll throw themselves into a rage if their locker combination doesn't work. "The adolescent lives with a vibrant sensitivity that carries to ecstatic heights and lowers to almost untenable depths."[5]

They have contradictory concepts of time. They may rush through a homework assignment or obsess on a single fact they can't seem to memorize. They may act as if there is no tomorrow, or they may worry needlessly about the future. They may baffle you because they seem to live only for the moment. And when you most expect them to appreciate the present, they live between now and later, a second before or after the moment, frustrated because they can't seem to close the gap.

They feel lonely all the time, but at the mall move in packs, laughing and grazing and discharging guttural sounds, oblivious to their impact on those around them. They want to hide, yet may find themselves being interviewed by a national television news network at a protest.

And I haven't even talked about sex. That's a chapter by itself. A large chapter

They won't complete a key paper for an English class, but will spend late evenings writing reams of poetry. You finally see them studying intently at the kitchen table, only to realize it's the handbook from the DMV.

And here comes the mother of them all, the contradiction between freedom and responsibility: They'll resist their parents' limits on their freedom as eloquently as a spokesperson for Amnesty International, but feel abandoned if such limits are really genuinely loosened. It is frightening for an adolescent to be truly free. They're trying to hold on to their childhood, where the world was ordered and freedom meant a romp in the playground, while their mother sat on a bench, peeling an orange for their lunch. The adolescent knows that with freedom comes responsibility, and that is a daunting proposition. They feel invulnerable and want to take risks, but they also want to be safe.

Freedom and responsibility *appear* as contradictions a great deal wider than your house; these issues expand to society at large and they're complicated. Teenagers are nothing more than a mirror of life in the U.S.A. They absorb the worst and the best parts of American culture. The worst: narcissism and greed, irresponsibility (without a change in facial expression), alienation, and discontentment. The best: selflessness when touched, energy and strength, frankness, optimism, a sense of fairness and a hatred of injustice. This same apparent contradiction between freedom and responsibility may come at a time when parents themselves may want more freedom from their responsibilities of child-rearing.

Adolescents are children and adults all rolled up into one, trying to find themselves, yet feeling lost all the time. They want to prove themselves sexually, but are often not able to act on their impulses. They want to prove themselves financially, but often make only the minimum wage. They want to prove themselves socially, but stumble on their words and the furniture. They want to sing out loud, but their voices crack. Nathan Ackerman writes: "Fear of being a child pushes the adolescent forward. Fear of being an adult pushes him backward."[6] They're all dressed up with no place to go. Now that's contradiction. A teacher once commented on how an eighth grade student of hers, unable to act on his urges, is "a rebel without a car." Adolescence is immobilizing and awkward and awesome.

The adolescent is a master at nothing, yet he or she wants to be the master at everything. No wonder it feels like World War III at home. (And, by the way, it can at school, too.) You say up; they say down; You say black; they say white. You say jump, and they say, "Why?" A parent told me about her child, "I don't know where she's at from day to day. It's as if I'm living in a nightmarish marathon of Mutual of Omaha's Wild Kingdom.

Some kids act like angels at home and devils at school. Others act like angels at school and devils at home. Some are angels or devils at both. I have seen the "good" kids—the ones that study hard, act in deferential ways toward teachers, and help with the dishes—become "bad," because they feel they must do so to become a separate human being. It may happen while they're teenagers, or it may be delayed until their twenties.

I have watched "bad" kids—the ones who cheat their way through school (and who have not yet been caught), who dismiss chores, who consider teachers to be just another set of obnoxious adults—become "good," because they've seen the other side; they've gotten it out of their system. Adolescents, like airline fares, are subject to change without notice. It's enough to make you batty.

Even battier when you think of the ways in which prodigious societal changes have complicated and confused an already unsettling time. We are witnessing a steady rise in the rate of divorce and gang violence, not to mention the AIDS epidemic and its effect on young people's notions of invulnerability and immortality.

Economists predict that this will be the first generation of young people who will not enjoy the same advantages of their parents. Adolescents see the territory before them, but there are no maps, no signposts along the way, no significant models urging them on. They don't see opportunities ahead of them as much as they see limits. You've got to acknowledge the immense toll this takes. Some adolescents are not sure all the struggle is worth it. Because there is less promise despite immediate access to the information sources that lure them toward false notions of success, they are having a harder time coping. I hear this in one form or another, every day—either in my office or by the lockers—and from every other principal I know.

Adolescence throws young people out of balance. You will most likely observe this phenomenon in every chapter of this book. Psychologists call it *disequilibrium*. They're in the ozone somewhere, trying to land. "Mutual of Omaha" meets the "Twilight Zone" meets "Star Trek." Some of it can be positive, because they are growing into a higher-order intellectual plane, where they can analyze, think about their thinking, come to conclusions, and distinguish themselves from their parents. Yet, more often than not, it's confusing.

When adolescents were much younger, their teachers spent a great deal of time helping them make the unfamiliar become familiar. Letters and numbers became real. In adolescence, the familiar becomes unfamiliar. Letters become symbols in algebra. Water is not just something one drinks, but a combination of hydrogen and oxygen molecules. That's why they look at *you* so strangely. Students who are on the cusp between concrete thinking and more abstract thinking experience this disequilibrium. It can be frustrating, and when there is a successful resolution, when they experience some kind of gestalt, it can be exhilarating.

Now for a little mirror—our own contradictions. We pretend to talk with our kids, but we end up talking at them. We claim that we are listening to them, but we don't hear what they have to say. If they are college bound, we tell them that they can make their own decisions, but we also say, "If you're smart, you'll take my advice." We stress independence, but we cannot let go; we push them out and pull them back in. We talk to girls about abstinence and then ensure that they have a renewable prescription for birth-control pills. We ask kids not to drink but tell them to do it in a controlled setting. We admonish them against the use of drugs, but may talk about our prescription for the latest cosmetic psychopharmaceutical. We tell them to enjoy life to its fullest and we punish them when they take risks.

We extol the virtues of brotherhood and sisterhood and condemn racism, yet we are concerned that our children may visit a friend in a neighborhood of which we don't approve. We obfuscate the truth about our own pasts, and with a little twinkle in our eye, confess that we, too, were "a little wild and crazy" once. Then we simultaneously switch, chameleon like, to a position of moral superiority that makes the contrast to our earlier tone stark and unconvincing. We ask them to do what we say, not what we do.

Adolescents are quite capable of exposing our emotions and our weak moments. Remember Holden Caulfield and *Catcher in the Rye?* "Adults are all phonies." Alan Packer, author of *Bringing Up Parents,* believes that parents have taken some kind of "hypocritical oath." He writes, "As an adolescent in search of truth, justice, and the American lay, this drives you bananas. Your father, who smokes two packs a day, nearly killed you for coming home smelling like an ashtray. Your mother, who has three martinis (extra-dry, olives) every evening, grounded you for a week for coming home drunk from a party."[7]

An awareness of our own contradictions does not mean that we should spend an enormous amount of energy rectifying them. In fact, in many cases, parents need to have the courage of their own contradictions, especially when it comes to limit setting. After all, you do have the right to stay out late, even when your kid does not. What is essential, in all of this, is an equal awareness that your own contradictions, if extreme, will be used against you.

• • •

There is lots of room for doom and gloom, but a teenager's first adolescence is eventually resolved; balance *is* restored. Kids end up finishing that unwritten developmental textbook. (Thank God they've at least finished something.) They separate from you and—statistics show—they do so basically intact. Very few turn into Manson girls or join the Billionaire Boys' Club. They develop a viable and distinct identity. They get jobs, establish and maintain personal moral systems, and enter into longer-lasting relationships; they spend less time in front of mirrors and they clear the dishes. I've even heard them say "please" and "thank you" in the school cafeteria. Those animal desires are in check or at least appropriately suppressed. There is some form of balance.

The ancient Greeks, exasperated by their youth, inscribed all sorts of mottoes on their buildings about the need for balance, so it's a notion that has been around for a long time. And if you keep this in mind, if you demonstrate your own balance in your responses to your teenager, you will do more to center the ship on course than any master plan or recipe or week at Esalen. Work toward balance and lighten up.

3
Let's Get Hysterical—
Parenting

"We'll no more meet, no more see one another,
but yet thou art my flesh, my blood, my daughter."
—*King Lear*

"Oh, to be only half as wonderful as my child thought I was, and only
half as stupid as my teenager thinks I am."
—*a parent[1]*

Think back, way back, even B.C. (before children), when you went out, when you spoke in complete sentences, when you actually displayed affection toward each other spontaneously. Then came children. Between the costs of the movie and the baby-sitter, going out became a major investment. You could not utter a word before being sidetracked by your toddler's use of raisins as an adhesive, by sibling skirmishes or screamfests over late carpools or gum in hair.

Despite moments of exasperation and fatigue, you felt you were in charge. Now that your child has entered adolescence, those may have now become the good old days. Your household may transform itself into the garbage can of teenage angst, and something seeps in the door, too, the left-over parts of your own youth. Some parents may react with horror and try to become best friends with their child. Others so mistrust their adolescent children (with whom they may, in fact, identify) that they intrude with excessive vigilance for fear that their child will become a serial killer. And some vacillate between the two in a frenetic search for middle ground. Parents may claim that they, too, were wild and crazy, but some of those same actions today are downright dangerous. Many say, with mixed emotions: "But I want to trust my kid."

I must emphasize again how the syndrome of adolescence is revisited on the parents—at the same time—and requires self-examination. The germs are everywhere. I see the mid-life crisis as a modified version of life as a teenager. The symptoms simply recur. In middle life, identity, sexuality, direction, confidence, competence, character all come into question. I believe that this confluence of similar thoughts and feelings is the source of serious tension. Adolescence arrives in parents' lives as they reach a crucial life-adjustment period of their own. There is a relapse and regression. When you've got two or more people in the same house—parents or kids—experiencing adolescentitis, you've got some ugliness to deal with.

A great deal of the time, at home, is characterized by mutual feelings of frustration, envy, rage, and fear (to name four). Parenting can quickly be reduced to a battle of intertwining wills. Each is frustrated that the other is not living up to his or her expectations, as low as they may be. Each is envious of the other—the child of the parent's independence, the adult of the child's vitality. Each is angry that the other is so inflexible and stubborn; both believe themselves to be reasonable and the other obstinate. Because teenagers are capable of thinking about their own thinking, they're capable of evaluating your thinking as well, pushing your buttons; they force intense self examination. As they vacillate between apathy and anger, they may characterize you as incompetent adults, as failures, as charlatans. And just as you are forced to live with them and their limitations, they have to live with you and your limitations, too.

The more kids grow, the more complicated their issues become. It's no longer a simple question of dealing with a fear of the dark, easily "fixed" with a Barney night light. But lest you get too depressed about this, you're in good hands. You're not crazy. Surveys show that parents of adolescents feel overwhelmed by their responsibilities a significant percentage of the time.

Although there are interesting variations, the most characteristic task of classic American adolescence—to form a separate identity—can be painful. When separation issues are dominant, some therapists have mentioned that both teenagers and their parents describe dreams of death or war or bloodshed or loss.

The separation game requires two or more players. We were born into a culture that values autonomy. Students have said, "My father deals with it by saying that, when I leave, he'll finally turn my room into a gym." Others comment: "He practically threw the suitcase at me and started packing." Still another: "My mom is suspiciously mellow these days. I'm worried about her, and I don't trust it." You may not be totally in control any more. You may want them out of the house, but at the same time, you may also want to reassert your control.

Adolescents may deal with separation by withdrawing from the emotional relationships they have with their parents. Some maintain a "good" image to get their folks off their backs, yet may live a creepy club-life late at night. A very high percentage lock themselves in their rooms. A parent once told me that a teenager is a person who enters his or her room, turns on the music, and comes out four years later. They live the dual life: part hedonist, part monk.

This emotional withdrawal takes its toll on parents, who find themselves shut away from the intimacy in which they once found such solace and special joy. You may find yourself feeling as if you and the phone are viewed as interchangeable sources of comfort, with the phone winning most of the time. You may struggle with maintaining your own ego as you work toward reinforcing the ego of your son or daughter.

When separation is painful, families often struggle to locate the reasons why. Blame takes on mythical proportions. The parents' blame runs something like this: the school and teachers are insensitive; the pediatrician is out of touch and doesn't care about my kid; the peer group is destructive; the neighborhood is too seedy; your mother (or father) is too lenient or too dictatorial. On another level: "You were sick as a child, and all that care made you too dependent and whiny;" "the house was tense when I lost my job, and we had to pay more attention to survival than to parenting." It may degenerate: "You were always a handful. Why can't you be like your sister?"

Factors of modern life may complicate the natural urge of adolescents to become individuals and explore the world. You worry about where they are, with whom, and about the lateness of the hour, the outside contagion which may exacerbate the disease. In large part, the normal battles between parents and teenagers may be additionally complicated. For parents, adolescence involves living with helplessness. You may say, "Go west, young man," but probably add: "But not in that part of town." In this generation, the move to independence must be combined with extra prudence—it's just not safe anymore.

Out of the realm of educational practice, psychologists spend an enormous amount of energy in family therapy sorting out these issues of will, of power, and of separation, for good reason; in working to discover the motivations for reactions, therapists hope to allow families the opportunity to see themselves more clearly and to understand each other's point of view. Many therapists work toward an understanding of the intricacies, the family dynamics.

Models of Parenting

As an educator, I am not in a position to engage in this sorting-out process. I prefer to comment on my experience with the families I see at school. Nevertheless, both the therapist's and the educator's points of view can help clarify the picture.

Each day, every year, I watch families struggle with these issues of individuation, separation, and emancipation. I have seen the entire family system blossom, bending and weaving but holding fast to the roller-coaster ride, and other families on a self-destructive collision course of repetitive, escalating power struggles and disenfranchisement.

I learn a great deal when parents first enter my office. I look at how they dress, where they sit, and who does the talking.

The cool and hip ones descend to the level of their adolescent children, dressing like them, talking like them, and completely losing their children's respect, for teenagers do not want you looking better than they do. A little twist to the Patty Duke Show: you may talk alike and walk alike, but you're not "two of a kind." These parents don't want to make the same mistakes their own parents made, yet they end up perpetuating family dynamics they themselves experienced—distance, anger, and cynicism. They hold a remnant political notion of the 1960s: that kids need unrestrained freedom so that their minds and spirits can grow. These are permissive parents who don't want to discipline, because they want to avoid being authoritarian. They are consumed with the idea of respect for each child's independent judgment. In fact, kids are taught that their rights are as important as the rights of their parents—rights to happiness and amusement, for example. Democracy and Equality take on mythic proportions. These same kids become suddenly irate and uncontrollable when those "rights" are infringed upon.

Strangely enough, the result is colossal competition. After all, parents may feel "new age," but they look middle-age. Somehow, their own narcissism turns parenting into an act of convenience, like a microwavable dinner. The kids themselves may see their parents as best friends for a while; ultimately, however, each betrays the other. Teenagers talk behind their parents' back at this feeble attempt to reverse time.

"The intrusion of permissive parents takes the form of a sentimental overprotectiveness rather than coercion and punishment."[2] Permissive parents often infantilize their children with excessive amounts of sheltering. Teenagers who live in such families are often consulted about, and therefore feel entitled to, decisions about everything. Many such children believe that adults must earn *their* respect. "In making them feel so trusted and believed, we have not only bridged the generation gap, we might have overlapped it."[3] There is a sloppy, permeable boundary between parents and their kids, and the kids do not know where one ends and the other begins. Parents adjust themselves totally to their child, who run circles around them. Strangely enough, the parents seem emotionally unavailable to listen even as they obsess over the family dynamics. They wonder why there is so much surly disobedience, whining, and lack of motivation.

I once heard a lecture about the consequences of nonjudgmental, new-age parenting by Robert Bly's retelling of *Jack and the Beanstalk* in modern terms.[4] In the story, a single mother asks her fairly doltish son to take their few remaining coins and buy a cow so that they can help sustain themselves as a family. The boy separates from his mother for a while and embarks upon his journey. He gets sidetracked along the way and ends up purchasing beans and a few idle promises. His mother calmly expresses her concern to Jack. "Now Jack," she explains patiently, using a 1990s politically-correct language intended not to hurt, "I am concerned about your choices. I believe that this now presents an issue for us to solve—together. Let's put the beans in a jar, and place them on the shelf, and as we struggle through this, we can decide how to deal with the situation." The beans are enshrined on the shelf and Jack senses a seething anger in his mother, whose act burns into his memory his inadequacy. In fact, when the mother dies, one can see Jack taking the beans to his new home as a negative memory he cannot overcome.

Of course, the original story is not written that way. It has a rougher edge. In every version I have read, mama is furious and, seeing the beans, grabs them from Jack and tosses them out the window. Case closed. She does not use psychobabble. Jack knows where he stands. His mother has made her nonnegotiables clear. She gave him some opportunities, she made very clear her expectations, and she expressed her disappointment. And, most important, the beans grow. In the new-age version, if Jack symbolizes the beans themselves, he goes nowhere. He does not grow.

At their most extreme, permissive parents can be accused of neglect. Itching to get on with their lives or even start new families, they ignore him completely. He feels lost and out of control, acts up at school, sleeps at various friends' homes, doesn't give his parents any indication of trouble because he feels dismissed, and thinks they don't care anyway. Secretly, he is falling apart.

At the opposite extreme are the drill sergeants—the ones with icewater in their veins. These are the authoritarian parents. Children have little voice and are forced to adapt unalterably to their parents. These parents condescend to their children. They believe in the good ol' days, in law and order. They react to adolescent behavior with retaliation, restriction, and recourse, yet these same parents end up wondering why they don't get Mother's or Father's Day cards. In fact, one student reported: "I wanted to say just one thing, and my folks cut me off at the groin." Some psychologists report that much of the impulse for authoritative parenting is tied up with parents' unresolved issues with authority. Whereas permissive parents may vow not to repeat the experience of their fascistic parents and may go overboard with freedoms, authoritarian parents don't leave any room for negotiation

At both extremes, both the permissive and the authoritarian parent are suffocating. There is middle ground, however. Authoritative parents represent balance. They listen, communicate clearly, and display warmth. They don't shelter or smother or overpower their kids, but they also don't let them feel lost, victimized by life.

They don't stand for emotional blackmail, but they keep blame and power struggles to a minimum. They look at the long term, in the interest of developing independence, and self-esteem based upon self-reliance, responsibility, and self discipline. They're firm, fair, and friendly. They tell the truth clearly and with love.

Parenting (and, of course, teaching) involves flexibility and listening. However, as *Jack and the Beanstalk* demonstrates, responsive parenting doesn't mean that you turn into mush. Nonnegotiable points of view need to be laid out. Moral authority, clarity, clear boundaries need to be established. There is a needlepoint sign on a Chicago high-school principal's office wall that reads: "If God had wanted permissiveness, he would have given us the ten suggestions."

Parenting of adolescents involves a delicate balancing act between rules and reasonable alternatives. In short, authoritarians do not negotiate with terrorists and may even use similar arsenal. Permissives give in to terrorist's demands, for it is too much to bear; alas, these parents resent it later. Authoritatives have been paying attention; they draw a line in the sand with an eye toward negotiating a peace treaty. A student once told me, "I loved my new bicycle when I was a kid. My parents were around, running alongside. And then, I would take off, knowing that my training wheels were there to keep me up. Well, I'm fifteen now. I don't need them hovering around so much. But I really feel bad for those kids that don't have their parents around at all. I don't want the training wheels completely taken off, just loosened a little."

What Gets in the Way of Effective Parenting?

The first mistake is operating out of a set of assumptions on how children are supposed to be, particularly your children. You might have assumptions about your child's capabilities, for one, that are not being realized and can be a source of enormous tension, but is particularly problematic with yuppie parents, who may insist that their child is "gifted." They can't stand the notion that their child may experience limitations. They may send a series of anxiety-producing messages to their children, who may end up not feeling smart enough to meet those expectations. In fact, some children, quite bright and able, may fail in school because they just can't keep up with some obsessive or unreasonable demands or because they wish to punish a parent for having set expectations high.

You might operate under a set of assumptions about how kids are supposed to act.[5] Here, too, the gap between theory and reality must be narrowed. The Gandhis and Martin Luther King Jr.s are rare in young people. Studies illustrate a series of percentages matching a child's approximate developmental level with the degree to which he or she can demonstrate true responsibility. For very young children, the percentage is quite low. In the case of teenagers, it's fifty percent. In other words, they are capable of taking out the trash every other time. It's maddening, but it doesn't give you permission to give up. Rather, by building real tasks with real responsibilities and consequences, they may take the trash out, in time, without thinking.

In short, you may assume too little or too much, thus setting expectations that your kids may achieve. You may believe your child is hopelessly immature, and therefore send that message in a myriad of ways without giving him or her an opportunity to prove you wrong. Or, you may think your child is so bright that he or she would never "huff" an inhalant or climb out a window, and therefore you prevent yourself from seeing the truth. The balance necessary during the various symptoms of the syndrome requires frequent temperature taking.

The second mistake is operating out of a set of revised memories of your past. The "when I was your age" lecture is worthless. And even if you think you are young and hip, your children may not think so. Though adolescents will pay attention to the stories you tell about your own childhood, the meaning or the message will not resound long, even if they are acutely similar to your child's current life, because a child must construct his or her own story. A memory is not just the event itself; it is also its recollection and its re-creation. A great deal of historical revision goes on. I sense, often, that parents distort their past. This distortion is interpreted for their children, I believe, to teach lessons. However, this past generation has witnessed so many subtle revolutions—in technology, in the pace of life, in the openness of graphic violence and sexuality—that it has little in common with your generation, except for high anxiety.

In the end, the more we struggle not to be like our parents, the more we tend to become like them. A *New Yorker* cartoon shows a man, slightly balding, at St. Peter's gate, hands at his side, ready for his judgment. St. Peter is holding some kind of scroll in his hands, from which he looks up, stares at the frightened man and declares: "What about that day in 1922 when you said 'shut-up' to your mother?" This is the hardest part of parenting—being able to see your child with perspective, for people often lack insight about their own growing up. Why is this so, in particular for parents of adolescents? Because their own childhood is tapped at the same time—its crises, its unfulfilled aspirations, its fears. Much of this baggage is dropped on our kids, on top of their own.

What Makes for Effective Parenting?

A few guiding principles should help

• Be still. Kids freak out at the most unpredictable moments, not necessarily connected to anything real. They feel a sense of impotent rage from time to time. The fact is they really are power-less in our society. Because they can't vote or place a newspaper ad or make any real and significant decisions in their lives, they often feel claustrophobic and trapped. My advice: keep still and listen to your child. Your anxiety is not going to make your child's anxiety any better. Much of the time, they just want to vent. They don't want you to blow the hot air back in their face. They just need a lis-tening post. Don't fix anything—yet.

Think back to this commonplace scene: your child was two and a half years old and you sat at a bench in the park, watching him play. He is climbing all over the jungle gym and digging holes in the sand and running around the perimeter of the play area. Once in a while, he calls your name to watch him or he comes up to you and pats you on the knee and then goes off again. Johnny just wants to know that you acknowledge him; he wants to know you're there. You're that steady presence, there on the bench; that's all he needs, and if he bumps his knee, he needs more emotional than medical attention. In the same way, that's what your teenager needs, too. Some parts of this syndrome simply heal themselves. Don't pick at the scabs.

Certainly, an adolescent crisis is more likely consequential than a skinned knee at the park. Teens are able to articulate their fears and disappointments or simply express their frustration and fury and vulnerability. Sometimes kids feel that they have no skin; everything that touches them hurts. You may not be able to stand your child's pain, but if you end up overinvested in what you hear, going nuts as they go nuts, you do no one any benefit. I observed a sophomore wailing into the pay phone that the teacher just failed her on a test. "Mom, she, like, failed the whole class. She's out of control. She's the teacher from hell." Trust me. She did not fail the class. It was just a hard test.

• Allow your kids to feel pain, suffer the consequences, deal with set-backs. This is a notion foreign to most modern parents. In our desire to protect our children from the harsh realities of life, we shield them from an essential coping mechanism, the ability to come to terms with failure. Bailing our kids out may rob them of the opportunity to recoup their losses. These parents may spend an inordinate amount of time worrying about all the bad influences in the world. They see life as one big minefield, and will do anything to prevent their child from feeling sad. Some may even view the school—as an institution—as some kind of invidious adversary; they'll be damned if their child will experience any form of suffering or injustice. Some parents will march into school to fix the situation; the teacher gets six "While You Were Out" messages, the principal gets a few calls, and then the fecal matter hits the air conditioning. In essence, parents end up colluding with their kids to transfer all that pain someplace else, in this case onto the school or an individual teacher.

However, there is a price, because these same children, though they are appreciative that their parents are fighting their battles for them, develop little self-reliance. They are incapable of handling suffering. Some educators have commented that—rich or poor—this kind of response is a form of "affluenza" and may cause complications for the adolescent syndrome. There is a qualitative difference between working in a child's service and working in a child's best interest. The former may help for a while, but only builds dependence. The latter may hurt for a while, but ends up building independence. It may be in a child's best service to solve the problem now, to demand that the teacher explain the grade, for example.

Yet such an approach may not be in that child's best interest, namely the necessity that a child learn the life skills of coping—talking with the teacher alone, for instance, or working on the means by which he or she can improve the grade next time.

We must view the failed test, the abandoned relationship, the hurtful glare as an opportunity for growth and for conversation. Kids are bound to suffer—its the effect of the syndrome—but we can help them with tools to solve their own problems.

• You win some, you lose some. You should not feel guilty about sticking to your non-negotiable rules and limits. Kids cannot run your life. However, in the struggle for separation and power, parenting also involves the art of negotiation. A kid has to win sometimes. The overall intention is to help them reach independence in constructive ways. That means giving in a little. Freedoms are essential for kids, along with limits. Kids have to be part of the process of running their own lives, within the context of your home and at school. Although they can't run the show, they need to be heard. Although feeling compromised is destructive, compromises are essential. Walking the fence that runs between the two is tricky, for there will be times when your best efforts to give a little are betrayed, and you get nothing in return. Wait; you will eventually.

In the desire for clarity, some parents do not let children win—anything. John Holt's famous book for teachers, *How Children Fail*, could easily be written for parents. He writes:

> Instead of trying to whittle down their fears, we build them up, often to monstrous size. For we like children who are a little afraid of us, docile, deferential children, though not, of course, if they are so obviously afraid that they threaten our image of ourselves as kind, lovable people whom there is no reason to fear. We find ideal the kind of "good" children who are just enough afraid of us to do everything we want, without making us feel that fear of us is what is making them do it.[6]

• Parenting is a relationship. If one of the primary issues between parents and teens is control, parents cannot possibly operate under the assumption that their actions can have the results they wish. In parenting, as in adult life in general, you are doomed if you think that pushing the right button will get you what you want. In parenting, as in work, developing relationships will lead more toward mutually satisfying rewards than anything else. That which strengthens the relationships within the family, or between teachers and students at school, will yield more mutually satisfying results than either capitulation or force.

• Set rules and regulations. I suggest that you keep them short and clear, and that you establish them together, provided that you have ultimate veto power. Curfew is a big one and a good example. They may pitch 4:00 in the morning; you may pitch 10:00 P.M. Depending upon the age of your teenager and the parameters of safety with which you feel comfortable, you should both agree. Then your kid can be held to them. Freedom, then, is earned.

Limits for a teenager are not that much different from limits for children at other ages. Teens are just smarter. They are also more intimidating and convincing. You may have put this same child in time-out or sent her to her room when she was two years old. She cried. She yelled. She protested. And, when it was over, love was suddenly restored. The same holds true for teenagers. Love simply doesn't go away when limits are set. In fact, setting limits is a way of expressing that love.

Consistency is important here. One parent exclaimed, "I'm trying to be consistent 60 percent of the time. Once in a while, I blow up and ground my son for four years. And then I realize how ridiculous that is to enforce. So, each time, I learn how to modify my responses and keep them consistent. But it is absolutely impossible to be consistent all the time. If I can shoot for a high percentage, perhaps he will get the point that the odds are in my favor that I will follow through."

Logically, consequences for infractions need to follow the "crime." In a North Carolina high school, in 1886, swearing received eight lashes; lies, eight lashes; wearing long fingernails, two lashes; quarreling, 4 lashes; and neglecting to bow when going home, two lashes. Obviously, we can't do that anymore, nor should we. Nevertheless, more than a century later, discipline and consequences are on everyone's mind. Consequences must be reasonable. In the words of Shakespeare, disorder is an "untended garden." It is essential that manners be "cultivated" and consequences meted out with this in mind. Both the extreme measures of cultivation by bulldozer and toothpick are ineffective.[7]

• Stand united. The barracuda syndrome comes into play here. Adolescents are sophisticated enough to run to Mom when they don't get what they want from Dad; they'll also take it a step further and turn inconsistencies into a chasm. Parents end up feeling that the entire problem is theirs. Be careful. When and wherever possible, go for the united front. Let's say that you disagree with your spouse whether or not to allow your son to drive forty miles in the rain to a club named "The Grunge Room." When clarity and resolution cannot immediately happen (and it inevitably won't), stay in the room during such conflicts and try, despite your cynicism, to work things out with your spouse so that you come to some form of agreement, in front of the kids. Kids need to see adults confront problems and work to resolve them. Many children experience the tension and the anger, but they're often shut out during the time when parents reconcile behind closed doors.

In earlier generations, parents protected their kids from everything—politics, scandal, and inner turmoil. Nevertheless, the kids detected all the permutations and combinations. They felt the Arctic draft in the room. All cannot be presented as peaches and cream. It's too suspicious. In recent generations, however, the opposite is equally destructive. Kids have been privy to everything, even the sexual and emotional parts of parents' relationships. I cringe when I hear kids talk about their family's intimate secrets. The problems you may experience in the natural course of your own relationship may not be resolvable in ways you might want your child to emulate. Kids cannot possibly resolve these conflicts; they cannot act as therapist or intermediary, for they can easily end up feeling a significant measure of panic, helplessness, and anger. If there are deepseated problems—sexual, emotional, relational—parents need to get some assistance.

• Hold your temper. It is entirely appropriate to get angry. Adolescents do not have the market cornered on histrionics. Remember Jack's mother in the beanstalk story. There is room for screaming at kids to ensure immediate compliance. In fact, teenagers have asked me, "Why don't my parents yell at me? Why are they always so appropriate and understanding? They should flip out. Maybe they just don't care enough." Shrieking does work at selected moments.

I suggest, however, that you use this strategy sparingly. All too often, the syntax of conversation is reduced to angry commands: do this; don't do that. There is the Gestapo interrogation sequence: who, what, when, where, how, and why? The conditional: if only you did this; if I were you, I'd do that. The definitive: You don't have a right to think that. And finally, the judgmental: Were you raised by wolves?[8]

• Stick around. Even when it feels as though you may want to run screaming from the room or need to be physically restrained from the intent to cause great bodily harm, it is essential that you keep an active interest in your teenager. In the end, you are the adult and, even if you forget (or want to forget) this fact, you must pay attention to the reminders. You come home from work where you have spent the day being mistreated, then you're mistreated by your own kid. Your kid comes home from having been mistreated at school, and is mistreated by you. A cycle begins, nothing short of a major power struggle. A teenager may ask for something—clothes or money for a compact disc. You say "no." Your child's response runs something like: "You don't give me anything. If you don't give me this, it will show you don't love me."

Some of your child's own anger is related to the issue at hand; a great deal of it may be an accumulation of tensions, and so this may not be rational time to have a discussion. Each side has tallied a secret list that now supersedes any other point. The issues bend and weave and resentments simmering on the back burner resurface. You may then cross the boundaries and touch upon a sore spot; unintentionally, perhaps, you strike a major blow. Middle-age adolescence meets teenage adolescence, and the home looks like a form of international conflict requiring U.N. peace-keeping forces.

There are some ways to try to prevent World War III: Pull your troops back; find a demilitarized zone. Power struggles only escalate, and in that mode nothing constructive happens. If you've weighed your points carefully and they seem rational, state your case and find a way out of the fight.

Let's make a distinction between a reaction and a response. A reaction is immediate, and though there's a place for reaction, parents often regret it later. A response is more measured. It involves time to think, to process things through, to count to ten. Whatever happened the night before, parents need to lead the way with a response. Teenagers need to know that parents have deliberated on the subject, that they have given some thought about each person's role in the conflict. The ensuing conversation, the discussion about what happened, is an instrumental part of building a relationship. Kids need to know your thinking. They need an explanation and, when necessary, an apology. Though the conversation feels like a monologue for a while, you will be heard. And you might be surprised by the results.

• It's okay to be vulnerable. Kids are vulnerable; parents are vulnerable. More often than not, however, parents keep it a big secret. Many parent conferences in my office go nowhere because they are turned into diatribes of each parent's obstinate points of view. I am not asking for sloppy emotionalism and certainly think it destructive to turn kids into your personal therapist to "include them" in your problems. But it is important for parents, from time to time, to let down their guard. In fact, an occasional expression of your own vulnerability may be just the permission kids need to speak about their own. Successful parenting involves an interchange of the truth of one's story.

• Hold them close, then let them go, and stay in touch. You loved them with all your heart. Now it is time to let them move on. You've given them roots, now help them with their wings. In a myriad of ways, separation is happening before your eyes, in increments, until the time when they actually leave home. Those with a mild case of adolescence have a reasonable separation. For many, it's inner turmoil. Some make sudden changes to convince themselves that this is the right step. You may want to call it moodiness, yet that description alone—however accurate—may not be sufficient. It is, more specifically, a great desire for self-understanding in the midst of independence.

A school head tells the following story: Imagine that you and your teenager are at the airport, ready to say good-bye to each other. Your child has been preparing for this new opportunity for quite some time, when he or she is ready to embark on an independent life; the bags are packed. The moment is awkward, because much is left unsaid, and the conversation takes on a perfunctory tone. All of a sudden, over the public address system, the family hears its name called: "Mr. and Mrs. Smith, white courtesy phone." You learn that the flight has been delayed, and now there you all are, prepared to say good-bye, but forced to make small talk in the airport coffee shop, over cardboard pizza, waiting for the next flight.[9]

Separation is inherent in every chapter of this book because it is bound up with the very process of reproduction and the generation and sustenance of a new life. I observe this in kindergarten classes in September and in senior classes in June.

Driving is a quintessential example of separation. The car is a metaphor for speed and distance, for escape, for maintaining one's own engine, for choice. It's their physics class realized on the road. Driving taps parents' fears about their child's safety and about the unknown. It wrests control over their child's whereabouts. It makes parents feel supremely vulnerable. You can stall this off, if you feel that your child is not ready, but it is an eventuality. You just need to know when to trust and when to let go. Simply check under your child's hood for testosterone and, if need be, take away the keys.

But as you let them go, in increments, don't get too comfortable. Don't let this new sense of independence (yours and theirs) serve as a means for abdicating your responsibilities. You may feel that they are ready to separate, but the white courtesy phone announcement is a reminder that parenting is not over; rather, it requires an evolving definition of how to remain a parent under new circumstances.

In fact, the dominant culture in American society overemphasizes separation. New studies on mothers and daughters show that the focus on separation is based primarily on a male model—the severing of ties with the family to strike out for new, uncharted territory. A female model assures the essential need to separate and to establish self-sufficiency and independence, but it does not eliminate connection and relationship in the process. "Self-determination is allowed to coexist with actions that take others into account. Although our language implies that independence is the polar opposite of dependence, women tell us that these are not mutually exclusive experiences. Separation and connection are linked."[10]

Conversations with boys at school seem to emphasize a physical distancing. Some may want to isolate themselves in their room or just "go away and be alone." Girls may express separation in terms of confrontation and argument, which nonetheless implies an interaction. Though you may see both qualities in your children, such observations may help you cope with the process in its various forms.

Wherever they are in the separation process, they need you.

There is always that critical moment when the mutual acknowledgment of separation takes place. Just remember the child who does not want the training wheels taken off, necessarily, just loosened, even when she is squealing that they're too tight.

• Quantity versus quality time: more is better. In the 1980s, quality time was invented to make parents feel less guilty that their busy lives prevented them from spending time with their children. The down side of such time management is that kids end up feeling managed, slotted in, like a hair or teeth or nail appointment. I've seen kids and their parents compare those bulky leather organizers. Of course, such appointments are subject to change without notice. Teenagers tell me all the time that, though they may go out kicking and screaming, the frequency makes them feel that their parents care. They're really not interested in something fancy, organized, or "fulfilling." They want you and your time.

• If you feed them, they may talk. Somehow, teenagers seem oblivious to parents when they're eating and talking with their friends. If there's food around, they tend to congregate and ignore you. Take this as a good thing. Certainly, all this eating taxes refrigerators and microwaves, but it allows you to see them and to hear snippets of their lives, and to put your two cents in. You will be surprised at how much is said in front of you that you weren't really supposed to hear.

• Parenting often happens in the nooks and crannies. No longer are kids beholden to the notion that they are to fill their parents in on their day. If there is a problem, when they experience, in Hamlet's terms, "the thousand natural shocks which flesh is heir to," an adolescent may astound you by going to a friend, regardless of how open and trusting a relationship you may have. However, parenting opportunities often reveal themselves—in the car, while watching television, or when you least expect it, not dissimilar to the times when, as a five-year old, your child asked—out of the blue—some profound questions about God or mortality. Advice, then? Don't barrage your child with questions, but ask sparingly and in creative ways.

• Try to build a little voice of conscience in the back of your child's head. Whether you are using carrots or sticks to motivate the behavior you want, the most success comes when teenagers act in appropriate ways because intuition told them it was their idea.

That's the goal. Our narcissistic society cultivates a lemming-like sense of personal advancement and aggrandizement. The more you can strengthen a voice that says "No," the more successful you will be.

• Relax. You're never going to be perfect. You are going to make many of the mistakes of your own parents. You're going to do the best you can to be good enough. That is all you can ask for; that's all kids expect.

Fathers and Mothers

Although there is plenty of room for variation, I have noticed a number of patterns in the fathers and mothers I see at parent conferences and in special parenting groups I have run and observed.

Control

Many men expect to be in charge, to lead, and to be thanked for their efforts. They spend an enormous amount of time in social and work settings establishing and maintaining an identity and working toward augmenting and supporting their sense of self. Of great importance are values such as reliability and competence. They feel that they need to report to higher authorities, and they expect to be reported to by those below them. They do not want their emotions to get the better of them, for they feel that they will lose their control. They do not want to be put on the defensive. Fathers, in particular, have a great deal of trouble expressing vulnerability. It is interesting to note, however, that a father and mother may finally get a breather and go out to dinner, whereupon the mother, now in the role as wife, listens as the father talks in vulnerable terms about his life—"this jerk at work really makes me crazy" or " is that all there is to middle age?"

In terms of children, control issues often center around limit-setting, an establishment of nonnegotiable rules in the house, and a belief that problems can be overcome. If grades slip, for example, fathers want to take control of the situation and ensure that such a setback does not happen again. "How was school today?" may, for fathers, serve as a thinly-veiled way of assessing how successful the child was. If a child gets into trouble, the measures the father takes at home support the belief that such an out-of-control experience will not happen again.

Such a point of view has enormous value, especially when kids need strict parameters and accountability; after all, ambition and drive are integral parts of the American work ethic and this approach is also a form of expressing love. The degree of a father's love is therefore no less than that of the mother. However, an obsession with such control may remove fathers from the delicate balancing act adolescents walk between achievement and aimlessness.

Different Points of View

A father may be suspicious of a child spending an enormous amount of time in his or her room, but understands the need; the mother may also be suspicious, but may stand by the door and want to talk. The man may consider a child's education in terms of the product he or she creates first, and the process second. The mother may concern herself with the process first and the product second. Men may rely on the intellectual and the rational mind exclusively. Women may use their intelligence to guide their intuition.

Women have a wider range of conversation starters and possibilities. A week before running a father's group, I would worry about the agenda for the meeting—its focus and its outcome. As I paced about the kitchen floor, my wife would ask me, "What is the purpose of the evening?" I would respond, "To get them to talk and to know and learn from each other." She would say, "Just throw out a word, like *supervision* or *anxiety*. If that is the purpose, women would just get together and talk. No over-planning necessary."

Deborah Tannen's book, *You Just Don't Understand* establishes an important distinction between *report* talk and *rapport* talk. She believes that men believe in the report; women, in rapport. In relationships, men talk for information and reporting; fathers may quiz kids about course material or their whereabouts or about the legitimacy of an act. They may trot out the journalism questions: who, what, when, where, why, and how. Women talk for interaction and rapport.[11] Mothers may ask kids about their experiences at school, the people they've met, or their sense of themselves.

One must be careful not to generalize; one cannot reduce such approaches to matters of gender. Although the research does lean toward certain characteristics identified more with one sex than the other, these categories and observations are more descriptive than prescriptive. No one approach is better than the other. In fact, mothers and fathers would do well to learn from each other.

If you think, for a moment, about issues at home—dating, homework, preparation for the future, as examples—such approaches take on concrete forms. The boy comes to the door for a date. One parent may want to make a decision about that boy's character. The other may want to find out about the boy's interests. A homework assignment is given. One parent may want to read the books alongside the teenager to connect with the subject to determine its appropriateness or fairness, or to ensure the child's accountability. The other may want to read it to draw out the child's interest in the subject and to talk about the ideas. After a day at school with a career guidance counselor, a child decides that he or she would like to pursue a certain profession. One parent may argue its merits vis à vis the salary; the other would probe its validity in terms of the child's passion. Again, both points of view contribute to the whole picture.

Whatever your orientation, reach back down into your earlier adolescence—when you needed an understanding word and when you also needed a kick in the pants; when you needed someone just to listen to your teenage angst and when you needed someone to give you a deadline; when you were honest and above board and when you were devious; when you needed to be dependent and when you needed to be independent; when you were vulnerable and wanted to be taken care of and when your dependence was just a crutch. Adolescence is neither predictable nor rational, and extremes don't work; balance does. It is the balance that both men and women bring, a balance that comes from introspection.

In Their Own Words

Below is a distillation of responses from years of asking the same two questions of freshman and seniors: *What do you want to say to your parents right now, at this point in your lives? And what do you want your parents to tell you?*

What do you want to say to your parents at this point in your lives?

The Freshmen

"There is nothing for you to know."

"Talk with me about school life more and stop quizzing me about grades."

"Leave me alone! Give me more money!"

"I want to say that there are no secrets in my house. Do you think I am unconscious?"

"Why tell you anything? I'd rather tell my brother. I tell you only what you deserve to know."

"Stop controlling me. It won't even matter. I'm still going to make the same mistakes you made."

"Give me more freedom."

"Leave me alone. I don't need the sheltering any more. Accept my mood swings. I love you even when I don't want you around."

"Getting Bs is okay. And another thing: why do you say that it does not matter if I get a bad grade, but when it happens, you get upset?"

"I want to tell you that, believe it or not, you may not always be right."

"That I appreciate you."

"I want you to know I love you. You're good people. Sometimes I'll go through the day and I'll think, 'I said hi to dad today, right?'"

"I want you to know that I'm in between being open and closed. It's weird."

"I want to tell you that I've done pot."

"I want to tell you that I'm having trouble in science. You think you can help me, but you can't. I complain about the teacher, but the teacher isn't the problem, really."

"That I am less of a goody two-shoes than you think I am."

"It's hard to tell you things because you want me to be perfect. And I'm not as perfect as my sister."

"Stop rambling. Talk rationally."

"I want to tell you that you don't know how to talk to me. Instead, you just restrict me. You punish first, just in case, and then talk later."

"That I'm not ten years old any more. Stop being paranoid about older boys."

"I want to tell you that fitting in is everything."

"I want to tell you that I am tired of comparing myself to your coolness."

"That divorce sometimes tears me apart."

"That I got a 59 on a recent test. I promise—it won't happen again."

"That you are open with me but not with each other."

The Seniors

"Grant me a formal declaration of independence. If you don't, you'll have another American revolution on their hands."

"I want you to say: "Don't worry; you'll handle it.""

"I want you to *ask* me to do errands—not *tell* me."

"Mom, stop the endless jokes about how happy you'll be when I'm gone—how you'll turn my room into a gym. You think you have a good sense of humor, but these jokes hurt."

"I want you to take care of me, even when I can't let you in, even when I am a total jerk. Sometimes I just can't help it."

"I want you to know that my life will not fall apart if I don't get into *your* first choice college."

What do you want your parents to tell you?

The Freshmen

"We love you, even when we forget to tell you."

"Be careful out there. Don't count on others for your life. Count on yourself. Believe in yourself. Don't be afraid of making a mistake—we won't scream at you if you do."

"Don't be envious of others. Others are envious of you—so why play that game?"

"Stop telling me you'd like to talk about sex and drugs, and just come out with it. I can at least deal with it."

"Take care of yourself, first."

"I want them to ask me—in a straightforward way—how far I've gone with guys."

"They're trying to say to me that they're scared. They tell me that I have a good head on my shoulders, but they won't let me use it. I want them to admit this."

"I think they want to tell me that they did drugs when they were kids. I mean, after all, their generation practically invented all the interest. But they won't. And then they say, 'Come, talk to me, we want to hear from you.' Well, if they won't tell me the truth, why should I tell them?"

"I think they're jealous that I'm getting a much better education than they got. I want them to support me and to tell me that I'm doing a good job."

"It's my dad, really. He just can't bring himself to talk about sex. My mom talks about it all the time."

"They want to tell me that they think I have bad judgment, but they're scared. I want them to tell me that I can handle myself."

"They act as if I'm leaving tomorrow. I'm only fourteen, for Chrissake. Can't they tell the difference? I want them to tell me that they'll take it easy and watch me grow up."

The Seniors

"I would like them to tell me that I no longer have things to do, this relative to see, that errand to run. The more they bug me, the more I won't do it."

"I want them to say, 'Go—you're free, write us, see you soon. Our job is over. You take the next steps, alone. We love you.'"

"I want them to be able to tell when to be there and when to go away. I am a woman and a little girl at the same time. I want them to know when to figure out when I am one and when I am the other. I know it's impossible, but it's also impossible being a teenager."

My parents don't want to tell me anything. That's part of the problem. I want them to talk with me! I want them to say not that they're proud I've done anything in particular, but proud of who it is I've become and what I have done.

"School is not everything."[12]

These young people are saying significant things about themselves and their families. They want to be seen as individuals, yet crave the crowd; they want to express love but cannot find the vocabulary, and fear appearing too vulnerable; they want freedom and limits, and expect parents to create a perfect balance between the two; they are confused about their changes but do not necessarily want anyone to explain it to them. These are true voices—voices from the inside—and therefore I urge you to "hear" them. Try to recognize your child and develop strategies (described in this book) accordingly.

The Changing Family

Families, which have served as a consistent tradition, are undergoing a historic transformation. Some say the family is breaking apart; others claim that the family is finding new forms as society changes. In Los Angeles, the local public television station published a poster entitled, "Family Diversity," in which different types of families were catalogued in an intricate web and array of shapes and colors: step families, foster families, nuclear families, domestic-partner families, immigrant families, lesbian-and-gay families, interracial families, multigenerational families, guardianship families, families with disabilities, cross-cultural families, single-parent families, and extended families.[13]

Many may take issue with these categories. A *Los Angeles Times* report discusses the importance of examining families less in terms of traditional boundaries and more in terms of what role they play in children's lives. "Gay households have become so commonplace that many experts now list them under the 'nuclear family' umbrella. This means a widening acceptance of the kind of nonbiological family ties that occur when older people who are widowed choose to live together, or when single parents affix an additional adult to their household."[14]

It would be both fruitless and time-consuming to attempt to characterize each one, and it would be both inaccurate and destructive to make judgments as to the quality of care in each. I have seen gay and lesbian families have a great deal of explaining to do, but provide warmth and consistent attention, and clear limits—in short—authoritative parenting. I have also observed intact families embroiled in a web of intrigue, in invidious, draining, and destructive relationships. Research is not yet clear or comprehensive enough to indicate the degree of effect such new family constellations have on adolescence, but there's a huge body of information about one: separation and divorce.

Separation and Divorce

During the syndrome of adolescence, teenagers want to separate from their parents, but not really. Then, all of a sudden, their parents may separate. Really. There are even cases reported in the newspapers in which teenagers are divorcing their parents. Families are confused. At one of our open houses, a teacher cynically whispered in my ear: "Well, I see that all the primary custodians and their significant others are here."

I will never forget a parent conference I called because a child's schoolwork had been taking a nose-dive. The mother and the father both came late, having driven separately, and sat at opposite ends of my office. Wearing a look on her face that alternated between righteous indignation and disinterest, the eighth-grade girl slouched in a chair. Her parents' body language did not take her into consideration. The tension mounted between Mom and Dad, as the young woman, pretending not to listen to all their invective rhetoric, the simmering jealousies and midlife rage, lathered her nails with multicolored, American flag nail polish. The child's academic difficulty served as nothing more than ammunition for an impending divorce. At one point, the father stood up, announced the official end of the conference by shouting, "Well, Fred, now you see our sick family. *You* decide custody!"

Some claim that the massive divorce rate this current generation of teenagers has had to endure has contributed a great deal to a sense of aimlessness and deteriorating rates of adolescent health. Kids of divorce or separation are bound to face some form of rejection from one or the other parent. Some sociologists link the family dynamics of divorce to a range of reactions, from low self-esteem and shyness to sexual promiscuity, alcohol, and drug abuse. This characterization is a bit extreme, and recent research has indicated that (1) a child able to develop skills in resilience may not be permanently damaged by divorce and (2) divorce may not necessarily be the *cause* of problems, but more the *symptom* of difficulties that may have begun in the family and with the child before the divorce actually takes place. Certainly, not all children of divorce are condemned to a life of emotional difficulty, but the message is clear: parents in a divorce need to know that their children have additional issues with which they must face. Certainly the divorce itself may be hard, but naiveté or lack of attention to the kids makes the situation worse.

Though divorce is upsetting at all ages, and can affect a child's development and attitude toward relationships, divorce can be particularly traumatic for a pre-teen or teenager. Just at the time when kids are separating from parents to form new attachments, they are watching established attachments fall apart. Although many adolescents have developed resources to cope with change, including independent extracurricular activities and greater dependence upon their peer group for emotional support, they have little time to adjust to the changes before the emancipation of college or the work place emerges.

Our culture has habituated to divorce; institutions have become inured to it. In school, divorce is omnipresent. The symptoms I see most are daydreaming, nervousness and irritability, noncompliance to rules, withdrawal, aggression, regression, and disrupted peer relationships. At younger grades, it may be manifested in requests to go to the nurse's office with complaints of stomachaches or headaches. Their normal mood swings are more pronounced; a teacher may be in the middle of bisecting an angle and discover a kid in tears. Some kids may choose to get into trouble by seeking attention at any cost.

I have seen kids who drag themselves to school, burdened by unusual amounts of criticism at home. In the midst of their parents' divorce, they are blamed or they live in an environment in which blame is a primary mode of communication. Many have been put in the middle between fighting parents. They are asked to take sides. Some are even bribed—overtly or covertly—to provide a source of information about one parent or the other. I have seen divorced parents divide parenting roles; one may be permissive and, in reaction, the other becomes authoritarian. Some are induced into colluding with one parent against the other. Some teens may take momentary glee in manipulating both parents, who, at this time in their lives, do not have the time or energy to find out the truth. In trying to make sense of their own lives and loyalties, some may choose to switch homes, at which point they will have to adjust and the parents may experience new forms of loss.

Others may take on magnanimous roles as surrogate parent, "the man" or "the woman" of the house who intends to "fix" the situation, restore the family, and take charge. Still others are placed in the awkward position of serving as therapists or placaters.

I don't care how sensitive and wonderful you are, children in the middle of a divorce often feel abandoned physically, geographically, and emotionally. Adolescents may be incapable of separating their problems from the problems of their parents. No matter how mature a teenager is, he or she may interpret the situation in the following way: You either love me or leave me. If you leave me, you don't really love me.

From the perspective of the school, the biggest difficulty of all occurs when teenagers find their parents increasingly remote. A separation or divorce may come as a surprise. There may be a number of changes in structure or in the pattern of daily life, but the kids' emotional needs are ignored. Kids may feel lost and unsupported while their parents try to work out their emotional turmoil. Accessibility becomes a problem—after all, you're busy getting your life together and you've got a surly teenager on your hands. However, they want to be close as they push you away. They want to feel your presence. Certainly, you may want to prevent yourself from being an emotional wreck in front of your children, but—once again—vulnerability, conversation, a constructive look at the future, and an active interest in your children can help enormously.

Teachers often take on extra importance; they serve as consistent, nonemotionally charged adults. They may be asked advice about the impending change. They may observe a great deal of anxiety on Fridays, when living arrangements may switch. They may see writing in class which directly or indirectly reflects this tumult. They may hear melodramatic or inflated versions of the truth about home. My advice is this: if you are about to separate or divorce (or, for that matter, if there is an issue that affects your family dramatically), call the school. Enlist the school's help in providing you with observations about your child's behavior and work. Since your child's school serves *in loco parentis* during the day, its own role may change; it may be invested with new powers of influence. In a time of crisis, the truth is distorted. The more communication, the better.

To Keep in Mind about Divorce

1. If a separation or divorce is about to take place, try to present the news together. At school, I have heard teenagers talk about the divorce as one parent's fault or mission. Whether the marriage is falling apart because one or the other is having an affair, or one is having an affair because the marriage is falling apart may not matter. What matters is that the family address the breakup as a unit. The family may not be intact again, but this last conversation should be, for your teen will remember it.

2. Go for the fewest amount of changes possible during this period. Don't give them too many choices, in the name of providing a sense of inclusion and choice. They may decide which of two fast-food restaurants will provide dinner, but not which parent they want to have dinner with. There should be a regular and predictable time and place for kids to complete their homework. In newly constituted homes, the rules may change. Such rules must be clear and should, for the sake of the children, be consistent.

3. Many teenagers are obsessed with their own sexuality. Remember that they are taking their lessons from the sexuality and courtship practices of their parents, whom they see dating. You need to be aware that you are being watched.

During such periods, I have observed the adolescent syndrome in parents quite clearly. With a newfound "liberation" or painful loneliness, parents are experiencing many of the same emotions as their teenage kids: questions about identity, about sexuality, about the future. Parents attempt to make themselves more attractive. I see a lot more leather. Teenagers are keenly aware of these permutations and combinations. They may even be gleaning some lessons.

When a New Parent Enters the Picture

For teens, a new family constellation may pose an additional set of difficulties, because adolescents are themselves in the process of separating. Teenagers may find it too confusing, complex, and confining to establish new attachments. They're worried about maintaining the same kind of emotional commitment they experienced when they were younger. They are desperate for real, rather than tokenistic, reassurance. They do not want to be forgotten just because their mother or father has found a new mate and is much happier.

A teenager may wake up in the morning to have breakfast with a step-sibling he/she didn't choose. If a stepparent has a child, an adolescent may feel ignored, especially if that child is younger and requires more attention. A teenager may have a complicated relationship with the stepparent, who might want some form of immediate family intimacy a teenager simply cannot provide. Teenagers may watch a mother or father show affection to these new family members, and may feel measures of embarrassment and revulsion. Such homes may initially experience rebellion or rivalry resentment.

Counseling can reveal these feelings and may help parents and children deal with issues of discipline, power, control, separation, and loyalty. Therapy may help them develop skills for more effective communication. Self-help groups can assist here, too, in the process of learning how to cope both with change and with a new constellation of family members—primary issues at play here, and in adolescence, generally.

The most important piece of advice I can give is this: Pay attention to your teenager. Note the moods; engage him or her in conversation. Time heals.

Divorce, separation, and remarriage indicate enormous change. More than anything else, kids want balance and normalcy. They need to know that, though these qualities cannot be achieved immediately, they are of paramount importance. Here, again, in the midst of it all, the models of parenting come into play. Authoritarian parents may spend so much time trying to control, that they won't acknowledge their kids' emotions and struggle. The permissive parent, on the other hand, may be too self-absorbed to serve as a source of love, safety, and limits. Balance requires authoritative parenting—warmth, solid structure, flexibility, and a listening ear.

• • •

Parenting an adolescent requires enormous will. It tests our resolve. We are forced to look within and to note the tensions we see there—between our desire not to repeat the mistakes of our own parents and the realization that we have become them; between our desire to straighten out and revise our own teenage years and our realization that, though they came from our loins, our kids are distinct human beings; between our desire to escape the incendiary conversations and slamming doors and the realization that time is precious and fleeting.

We are left with intuition, memory, and common sense. Some of you may have talent, yet may need some skills to get by. Some of you may have picked up all the skills along the way, but may feel that you don't have the talent for this parenting thing. In examining the issue of parenting, the famous psychologist Bruno Bettleheim's book title, *A Good-Enough Parent,* speaks for itself; you must do what you can to pick up the clues around you, to survey the scene, to describe what your child is experiencing and what way your own forms of adolescence may serve as contributors to the issue at hand. You can only do your best. That may just be good enough.

And you can talk with your children (if they'll let you). I talk all day long with them, and occasionally in my office. We talk in the cafeteria, in the public park, on a bench, at their lockers, at the parking lot. Conversation is the way in. It may be hard and your child may be particularly inaccessible. You may say that you have tried, but to no avail. Interactions that are meaningful rarely happen in response to formalized approaches like: "Let's have a talk." But conversations, even of trivialities, reveal that you still care.

If you can't talk, then write. If the tête-à-tête is too intense now, perhaps a letter's sense of distance, yet emotional power, may be just the catalyst for the kind of reflection you must model for your child. I've made this suggestion for both parents and teenagers, and have been shown letters, filled with clarity and love, expectation, darkness, fear, and vulnerability. A letter may allow both a mirror and a window—looking within to see out.

Your child may look like a hulking monster, but he or she is still a child, caught in a body that doesn't feel like it fits, caught in a society that idolizes teenage life but gives it no respect, caught between the desire to be free of one's childhood and the fear of adulthood—contradictions, once again, that make adolescents feel out of control. And the easiest way for them to come to terms with it all is to dump it in your lap. They tell me time and time again, in the words of one tenth grader: "Even though I give them such hell, I wish they didn't have to take it so personally. It's so hysterical at home, sometimes I think they forget to love me."

A colleague once recounted a story about the great Polish educator, Janusz Korczak, who arrived for a lecture at the Institute of Special Pedagogy in Warsaw in 1912, dressed in his Polish officer's uniform, leading a somewhat bewildered young boy by the hand. Apparently, Korczak announced that the class would move to the X-ray room of the Children's Hospital. There, as the child was placed behind a fluoroscope, the lights were extinguished and the class could observe on the screen the child's frightened breathing and heartbeat. "Look and remember," said Korczak. "In the future, sometime when you are tired or angry, when children become unbearable and distract you from your thoughts, when you lose your temper and begin to shout and punish, remember what a child's heart looks like."

4
Let's Get Physical—
Sex, Lies, and More Lies

*"Life is made into a nonstop, commercially prepackaged
masturbational fantasy."*
—*Allen Bloom,* The Closing of the American Mind

"It's ten o'clock. Do you know where your kids' hands are?"
—*a teacher*

Talk about a subject filled with contradiction, sex is riddled with it.
A *Time* magazine cover, "Kids, Sex, and Values," reads: "Just Do It.
Just Say No. Just wear a condom. What's a kid supposed to think?"
Add to those conflicting messages an adolescent's irrepressible
desire to feel something—anything—intensely, and the result is
this: the brain, moral training, the basics of common sense, and
good judgment go out the window. Sex is no longer under the
purview of good judgment. It's political. It's vocal. It's public. And
it's everywhere. The kicker is that this subject in particular strikes at
the core of parenting because, well, it's what made us parents in the
first place. It's enough to give you a headache.

The syndrome of adolescence includes acute horniness. It's one
big day in the life of a hormone. A teacher once commented, "With
boys, the little head becomes more important than the big head;
they have testosterone poisoning. With girls, cleavage is everything." It's simply an X-rated world. We know it. They know it. And
here's a little statistic to make your day: Adolescents watch up to
twenty-four hours of television, on the average, per week. Instead of
doing their homework, teenagers are doing TV, and what they see is
sexy. According to the American Academy of Pediatrics:

In a given year he sees more than 14,000 sexual references or innuendoes on TV. A lot of that sex is casual, without consequences, and outside of committed relations. On the afternoon soap operas, which many teenage girls watch avidly, 94 percent of all sexual relationships are between unmarried partners. And if Mom or Dad are at work or are otherwise unavailable to help teenagers put what they see in perspective, young people are likely to believe that what they're seeing is the adult norm.[1]

This, of course, does not include video, the hottest selling of which are, you know, sexy. Here's an experiment to conduct with your child: Watch MTV with the sound turned off for a few minutes. Then close your eyes, turn the volume back on, and try to decipher the lyrics. (Your child can help here.) Discuss your experience with your child.

Last but not least, the access to extraordinarily explicit, graphically sexual material is frighteningly accessible on the Internet. As *Time* reports, "Porn is immensely popular. It is ubiquitous. Perhaps because hard-core sex pictures are so widely available elsewhere, the adult Internet market seems to be driven largely by a demand for images that can't be found in the average magazine rack: pedophilia (nude photos of children), hebephilia (youths), and what the researchers call "paraphilia"—a grab bag of 'deviant material.' "[2] In short, there is no more room for fantasy. It's all available and it's all overwhelming.

When teenagers take a break between sexy soap operas or suggestive sit-coms or, increasingly, a sexy modem-friendly newsgroup, there's always the telephone, which, I might also add, can also be libidinous. Psychoanalysts have claimed that the teenage obsession with the phone is not limited to its use for gossip and connection, dealmaking and datebreaking; it's an erotic symbol, too. Think of it this way—someone is always talking in your ear, sometimes in whispers. It's a form of 100 percent safe sex. And, most of all, it's intensely private.[3] Try walking into the room, by accident of course, and test this theory. It's almost as if you walked in on someone naked.

Adolescents show their emerging sexuality in a variety of ways—your daughter suddenly looks sexy; boys talk about their fathers' *Playboys* or videos.[4] Some view sex as a means of satisfying emotional needs. Sex may be a form of revenge, a way to say thank-you, a means of feeling grown up, a single-minded demonstration of love, an act against authority.

Some kids are paralyzed by these new feelings and try to stop them cold. I've seen them at one point in the year engaged in all sorts of coed social activity. Then, when such activity takes a vaguely sexual turn, they turn suddenly into Styrofoam—stiff and non-communicative. They simply don't know what to do. Their thoughts are connected to their own loss of control (literally), to fantasies, to wildly changing images of themselves. They live in an incessant blend of curiosity, self-mockery, confusion, and panic. Now you go ahead and try to teach Algebra, knowing that the only obtuse angles on Johnny's mind are shifting about in a nylon dress in the front row.

Because development occurs at different rates, some adolescents are clueless. For these young people, it is only a matter of time and they should not be rushed—either into heavy conversations or graphic sex-education presentations. A parent once told me about how she responsibly introduced a sex talk to her son because she thought that such a conversation *should* take place at thirteen. After a short period of intense listening, the young man cupped his hands over his ears and sang loudly so that he wouldn't hear.

There is a window of opportunity for conversation about sex. It is up to you, however, to determine when that time is. This is where the clock is more important than chronological age. Though thirteen may be appropriate for some, it is too early—or even too late—for others. Some will react with prurient interest, others with disdain and disgust.

For the most part, long before they give you that stupid stare as you both sit down uncomfortably on the couch for your dissertation on the birds and the bees, many adolescents are serious scholars of the subject; I see them studying right outside my office window. They're consumed by it—sex on television, in the movies, on billboards, in the parks, not to mention that ongoing, pornographic blockbuster motion picture raging in their minds, complete with close-ups and sound effects. They insult each other sexually; they talk about how they saw a couple wax (have sex) each other on cable the night before; they trot out dirty words and show soft-porn magazines to each other; they hug each other a great deal and for too long; they squeeze themselves into their jeans with a shoe horn; they channel surf late at night looking for lingerie commercials or men in tight shorts; they dance to sexual music; they play *tonsil hockey,* referring to deep tongue kissing. Why do you think they call TV the "boob" tube?

At early stages of the hormonal rush, they say things like, "We're going to take a *testes* in math today," or "There is a *vas deferens* between 7th grade and 8th grade." On the museum field trip, some of the youngest ones have to be tugged away from the Rubens paintings or the mad Renaissance scenes, cherubic angels hovering about naked, muscular figures engaged in ecstatic abandon. You may think that they are missing essential research skills in the modern junior- and senior-high school, but you would be surprised how hard they're working on this particular subject in the library; in the spring, there's a run on National Geographics. The authors of *Everybody's Doing It: How To Survive Your Teenagers' Sex Life (And Help Them Survive It, Too)* write:

> Our children see Wilt Chamberlain, interviewed on the publication of his autobiography, talking about sleeping with twenty-thousand different women. "The world revolves around sex," he says, and who could argue after listening to him? They hear Magic Johnson, who says he slept with only a thousand women, more or less, revealing that he is HIV-positive, and Woody Allen justifying his sexual relationship with Mia Farrow's daughter.
>
> They watch Anita Hill accusing then-Supreme Court nominee Clarence Thomas of sexual harassment, William Kennedy Smith charged with date rape, Mike Tyson found guilty of rape, and naval officers accused of sexual assault in the Tailhook scandal.
>
> They're exposed to ads for Camel cigarettes featuring dromedaries whose faces strongly resemble male genitalia, in spite of the company's denial of any similarity. They hear songs on the teen hit parade with titles like "I Want Your Sex" and "I Want to Sex You Up."[5]

It takes place in class. Since you are not allowed to have access to their classrooms, I hope the following classroom interaction will help you see how pervasive this really is. At my school, we teach the same poem to seventh graders and twelfth graders and can therefore monitor their abilities to develop abstract thinking. Here's the poem, by William Carlos Williams.

This Is Just To Say

I have eaten
the plums
that were in
the icebox

and which
you were probably
saving
for breakfast
Forgive me
they were delicious
so sweet
and so cold[6]

I observed the following two conversations. The seventh graders giggled and talked about taking something that is not theirs and apologizing for it, half-heartedly. They provided their own examples. The twelfth graders talked about the loss of virginity; some even discussed the poem in terms of date rape. The poem is, in one interpretation, a Hallmark card written, young man to young woman, about eating the plums (the cherry?) that were supposed to be saved for marriage and that special morning afterward. The plums were in the woman's "box," cold and entered for the first time. There was mention of the possible transference of the HIV virus. The experience itself was sweet, but without feeling, and now, upon reflection, is filled with mixed emotions—elation and guilt, sweetness and coldness and fear.

But sex is not an academic exercise, and the sexual harassment to which the students allude in the poem happens regularly in schools. A study of sexual harassment in schools indicated that four in five girls had been placed in a situation in which someone had "made sexual comments, jokes, gestures or looks; written sexual messages or graffiti; spread sexual rumors about you; touched, grabbed or pinched you in a sexual way; spied on you as you dressed or showered at school; pulled your clothing off; forced a kiss; 'mooned' you; or forced you to do something sexual, other than kissing."[7] It happens in rest-rooms and locker rooms, in the hallways, between classes, on the athletic field, at the school dance. And it starts at an early age. Boys talk about the necessity of "making the grade" before they graduate. And scores of articles have appeared about the Spur Posse, the Southern California group of boys who tallied lists of their sexual conquests.

Though you may have had to endure similar injustices as a condition of growing up, research is indicating the damaging impact on its victims. Some young people have stayed home; many have lost their motivation to do schoolwork. Women's groups indicate such a problem as an epidemic. I agree. In fact, a ruling by a U.S. district judge in San Francisco, states that "students harassed by peers can win damages from districts under Title IX of the Educational Amendments of 1972, which bars sexual discrimination in schools receiving federal funds."[8]

• • •

We know that adolescents *talk* about sex all the time; but lest you feel that you need to quarantine your child, you should know that they're not all *doing* it. One of the key features of adolescence is that they talk a good game. At school, they may talk like sex kittens or studs. One twelve-year old writes: "At school, it's perfectly all right to talk about it happening, but there's no way of coming out and asking your friends how it happens. It's one of those things that everyone thinks about, but no one's able to admit it. It was not okay to ask a friend, you had to squeeze it out of a conversation. So no one is going to come out and ask, How do you get a girl to have sex with you? Or, How do you start having sex?"[9]

The problem with such talk is that we don't always know what to believe, because lying is raised to an art form. They lie to us; they almost have to. We lie to them. And they lie down with each other. According to a 1992 Centers for Disease Control study, the number of 9th graders who say they have already had sex is 40 percent."[10] And if three-quarters of them have had sex by the time they are twenty, the chances are fewer and fewer that they have escaped the experience. It's enough to make an aging liberal freeze, especially the most ardent free-love advocate of 1968. The problem is that, when we acted irresponsibly as teens (Didn't I see you with your top off at Woodstock?), we may have had to deal with pregnancy or a strange itching feeling. Acting irresponsibly now could mean death. We never had to remember phrases like "HIV-negative is positive and HIV-positive is negative." We had our fantasies and suggestive poetry. Contemporary teens are smothered with MTV and songs with parent advisory lyrics.

The subject is too personal, too meaningful, too filled with emotion to be confined to the home. Sexuality is simply an issue that forces parents—all of us, in fact—to face helplessness. It is the symbol, the very epitome of separation from parents and connection to someone else. Because parents experience the syndrome of adolescence, too, the issues are confusing. Your kid is emerging into sexuality, unclear where it will all lead. And now, in middle age, you may also become unsure of your own sexuality. They're having a pre-age crisis; you're having a middle-age crisis. After all, think of the natural process of separation in sexual terms—they're pulling out and pulling away.

It takes careful listening. Just take it from your school's nurse, generally someone non-threatening, who has developed a fine-tuned ear. Sometimes, nurses hear open confessionals—"Am I pregnant?" and at other times, it is more subtle: "Uh . . . I keep on getting this stomach flu, like when I . . . uh . . . like wake-up." Or, "Could you explain, again . . . kinda what, like, wet dreams are all about?"

Pointers

For many young people, the "talk" comes too late; the hormone festival has already arrived. While this may be true, it is worthwhile to keep the following advice in mind, for any talk:

1. Don't plan a day and date for "the talk"; such a buildup will only result in false expectations, hype, and mutual disappointment. I saw a cartoon once of a boy at his father's feet, by the easy chair. The father is smoking a pipe, providing a sense of great import for the momentous occasion. The boy interrupts his father, half-way through: "I know all that, pop. Let's get on to the perversions."

2. Don't say anything that makes you holier or seem more moral than they are. Nonetheless, you need to have a discussion that deals

with morals—about the connection between sexuality and intimacy, about making responsible decisions, about abstinence. When your son thinks of a virgin as "hymenically challenged,"[11] you can rage or you can use it as an opportunity to talk about humor and when jokes can hurt.

3. Don't be a hypocrite. You can't expect your son or daughter to buy into the "Do as I say, not what I do" predicament. All too often, I have seen irresponsible parents lecture their children on responsibility. Don't continue a hypocrisy of the double standard as well—girls still hear they need to be chaste; boys do not hear it as often. Finally, be real. Tell the truth. You were not an asexual being. Take a trip down memory lane—that wasn't a banana in your pants; you *were* really glad to see that special someone.

4. Be clear about curfews. You'll need to establish a clear protocol when your kids go out. There is a kind of witching hour out there on dates to the prince's ball, and there is a chance you can get your daughter home with both shoes on before that certain hour. I have seen a correlation between the lateness of the hour and trouble. You need to know where they are and to be able to have phone contact with them.

5. Try to see sex education as a natural process, not an artificial construct. Sex wasn't invented yesterday. The torch has been blazing for millennia. God made sex feel good to keep the idea of propagating the species a good concept. That's a "fact of life."

6. Allow your child room to come to terms with what you are saying and what he or she experiences in the media and at school. They'll amaze you with how quick they are to learn, as well as to pick up the wrong information. If you correct everything, they'll feel embarrassed. Fill them in on a few of the essentials and let time take its course.

7. Don't do all the talking. The "talk" should be replaced by conversation, by dialogue—casual, formal, or whatever form it takes. You don't have to feel as if you are doing your job by lecturing. When you least expect it, an opportunity to talk may arise.

8. Don't keep pressing the subject; kids do not want to be hounded by parents who, in the interest in being responsible, do a great deal more alienating than enlightening. Don't make threats, either. Threats bring up a gag response.

9. Emphasize abstinence by addressing both the scientific and

social and emotional what-ifs: what if you don't use a condom? What will you feel inside about yourself if you "do it"? What if you get a sexually transmitted disease? What if you get pregnant?

10. Have some answers available, if you need to be fortified in advance, by picking up a brochure and doing a little boning up. AIDS cannot be picked up from a toilet seat or from a kiss. Know about STD's. Your local library, school, and medical clinic have brochures. Legitimate Internet web sites provide up-to-date information. You can't corrupt a kid with information.

11. If you have a daughter and decide that she should use birth control, then follow through with the instruction manual that comes with the pill or the device. Talk about the consequences of such a choice; enlist the assistance of her gynecologist. Your job is not over once you have broached the subject. The condom issue requires more extensive conversation, for it is still the case that girls consider condoms a good thing and boys consider it a bad thing.

12. Don't assume that you are making yourself clear. They may nod their head or tell you, with characteristic bravado, that they know this information already. But *assume* nothing; it makes an *ass* out of *u* and *me*.

And another thing: even though you did all the right things when your teenagers were toddlers, adolescence changes all that. It's unpredictable. You don't need to do this portion of parenting particularly well; in fact, the smooth delivery of such a rough subject is cause for suspicion. Admit the discomfort; vulnerability is okay. I've seen countless numbers of smooth, yuppie parents with as big an ax to grind as the repressed old-school parents. Sexuality is weird for everyone.

A note here, free for the price of admission: Bringing up the subject does not mean that you are encouraging risky behavior, nor does discussing intimacy mean giving tacit permission to teenagers to engage in "sexy" stuff. My experience in schools shows me that students who have a relationship with their parents that allows for meaningful exchange, where physical facts and moral and social and emotional issues are brought out into the open, fare better in terms of personal judgment and good common sense than those families who avoid it.

At the other end of the spectrum, teenagers alienated from

authority because of extreme harshness or absolute freedom are, in my opinion, more likely to engage in those risk-taking behaviors or enter into all the physical features of their relationships and may end up with some strange bedfellows. Parents have the difficult task of determining when to hear the uncomfortable things kids have to say, and in what situation to assert themselves and to set limits.

At last count, approximately 33 percent of teenagers have talked about sex, but not birth control, with their parents, and 35 percent have talked about both sex and birth control. But the issues surrounding sexuality as a topic between parent and child have always been strained. In my research for this chapter, I asked a series of consultants, educators, psychologists, and sex therapists not for a contemporary rendering of their opinions about post-modern sexuality; rather, I asked them to open up their teenage diaries for me. The revelation was something akin to the opening of the missing Pentagon Papers—a great deal of fanfare, then straight intuition. The themes were (a) I love this person (b) I want to go all the way (c) I'll die if my parents know. Sound familiar?

The School's Part

The Disney animated menstruation movie of the early 1960s has been replaced by a more realistic, less condescending treatment of the subject. It's hard to imagine a 'toon with a period. Kids now need the real thing, and educators have finally caught on. Nonetheless, the debate over appropriateness or degree of information disseminated in schools rages on, thus sex education ranges wildly from school to school.

The comprehensive, they-need-to-know school of thought uses a wide range of techniques to bring the subject to bear—role-playing; board games; direct talks on reproductive biology, sexually transmitted diseases and contraception; and discussions of sexual values. Programs in schools provide straightforward information, "answers" to the burning questions (and the burning sensation), combined with a great deal of conversation and the expression of feelings within a safe place. Such schools maintain that in a culture that abides by "If it feels good, do it," there had better be opportunities to talk about it.

In greater detail, the comprehensive program goes something like this:

1. Adolescents get the facts—tab "A" goes in slot "B." It's far more graphic now. No longer confined to the reference desk, sex education books are more explicit. They talk about the sex act. They put condoms on bananas. This is the most difficult part for parents to face, for, in the words of one twelve year old, "They showed us a film about the in and out."

2. They define and explain sexually-transmitted diseases; they inform students about how 2.5 million teens are infected with a sexually transmitted disease each year—one-fifth of the nation's STD cases,[12] how many strains are resistant to medication, and how teenagers are particularly vulnerable, particularly girls, who are becoming more sexually active earlier. Students learn not only that STDs are prevalent, but also that some of them, like herpes and genital warts, can make young people susceptible to HIV. They talk openly about HIV and hepatitis B; about how one in five sexually active teenage girls who contract chlamydia become sterile. Schools talk about the difference between "safe" sex—petting without intercourse—and "safer" sex—the use of a condom during intercourse. They address the fact that there are many STDs for which a condom provides no protection. It's not easy talking about how blood or sexual fluids should not enter the mouth or the penis or the vagina or anus, but AIDS changes everything.

3. They discuss birth control. The trend has been: "If you choose sexuality, here are condoms and other birth-control devices and how they work."[13] Although AIDS gets all the press, teenage pregnancy is an enormous issue—one that impacts the self and society—emotionally, socially, and economically. "Each year, one in eleven American girls aged fifteen to nineteen has a birth or abortion, as compared with fewer than one in twenty in Canada, England, or France."[14] The failure rate for condoms has been determined to be as high as 31 percent. Research is indicating that, although teenagers are attracted in large numbers to the Norplant contraceptive device, they may therefore choose not to use condoms and remain unprotected from STDs, so education in contraception must continue to be thorough, despite the scientific advances.[15] The facts about birth control are combined with discussions that focus on the extent and nature of responsibility and care

for another life. In some programs, kids are asked to carry around eggs or other fragile objects to bring "home" the need and affect of such vigilance.

4. They discuss sexual orientation and make it clear that if you are consistently attracted romantically and sexually to someone of the same sex, you should be prepared for some confusing times ahead.[16] Here, sex education is intertwined with a series of conversations about fitting in.

5. They discuss intimacy. Kids need to be involved in discussions about the differences between sex and love, about commitment, about care. Schools hold discussions with teenagers about the relationship between sexuality and love and about the commitments of pregnancy. They discuss issues such as a girl's desire for intimacy and boy's desire for victory. The message is often this: if you're a girl, you should understand this but protect yourself; if you're a boy, you should understand this and be sensitive. In a society where sexuality is mostly narcissistic rather than giving, these issues become delicate and require enormous skill.

Comprehensive sex-education programs provide room both for the straight facts and for discussion. Proponents believe that sexual intercourse can only be dealt with responsibly and effectively when kids learn the skills of *social* intercourse. Are such discussions devoid of judgment? Some are and some are not. At times, judgment simply needs to be suspended for the sake of open conversation. And though it may make parents uncomfortable, the fact is that schools are not obligated to advocate any particular beliefs.

At the other end of the spectrum, some schools take a much more restricted approach. They are aware of their role as educators, but feel they can only go so far. Aware of the prevalent set of contradictions and volatile pressures in and about schools and families and neighborhoods, they take the *safe* sex route—chastity. These courses focus more on overt moral admonitions and pleas and less on the graphic facts of life. Kids repeat phrases like: "Do the right thing, wait for the ring" or wear T-shirts that read: "I'm worth waiting for."[17] They may hit the high points of plumbing in health education, but leave the heavy petting talk to the parents.

School officials express concern about the correlation between liberal thinking and the decline of western civilization, along with the concomitant decline in standards of morality. They express alarm at non-judgmental approaches that do not challenge students to confront their own assumptions and to understand the moral credos by which they are expected to live. They believe that the comprehensive approach is hypocritical when it comes to the issue of abstinence because the abstinence-is-best-but-if-you-can't-hold-out-here's-a-condom approach is too permissive and contradictory. Some buy the prepackaged abstinence programs that consider the detailed promotion of sex education to be destructive.

In fact, the issue of abstinence remains central in most school approaches, but the value system behind it must be understood. Based upon a set of moral and religious obligations, some schools may pitch abstinence as a principle. One simply shouldn't "do it." In other programs, abstinence at all costs is seen as alienating; instead, it is discussed as a decision for safety and/or self-respect. There is no national standard for sexuality education, so the degree and level of such programs vary from school to school.

Sex education requires an enormous balancing act. Programs can only go so far. At each extreme they may underestimate teenagers' abilities to make informed decisions, and therefore they overdo it, turning kids off. I suggest that you familiarize yourself with your child(ren)'s school program and ask about the approach: You might want to start with two specific questions. First, "How do you treat the question of abstinence?" Second: "What *don't* you talk about in this program?" The answer to these questions will tell you a great deal about the value system behind and approach to their sex education program.

Once again, I urge a balance between information and judgment. We must be straightforward, both about the kind of factual detail that can *answer* questions, yet we must not rest there; we must also be straightforward about the kinds of issues associated with ethics, relationship, and commitment that can help *raise* questions.

Such balance must also take into consideration the similar and different needs of both males and females. In the 1950s and through much of the 1960s, boys and girls were separated for sex education talks. In the 1970s and 1980s, this point of view came under attack as too artificial. What occurred then, in subsequent coed meetings, were some interesting interactions, along with a great deal of discomfort. It's hard for boys to talk about getting . . . uh . . . well . . .

er . . . you know . . . hard, in front of girls. It's equally hard for girls to talk about menstruation or their own sexuality in front of boys.

In the 1990s, many schools have chosen the particular circumstances in which to integrate and which to segregate girls and boys for sex education. In selected sessions, where hearing the same information—the facts—is useful, girls and boys are kept together. In other sessions, boys and girls are segregated—mostly for discussion. In still other sessions, they are brought back together to talk about common themes, to share feelings. Researchers into junior and senior high-school women's lives have shown a great deal of evidence supporting the notion of separate ways of seeing.[18] It has always been my belief that separate moments for each gender are helpful for consolidation and for comfort, but cannot be ends unto themselves. It is perfectly appropriate for boys and girls to have their own moments noting and celebrating differences—to be together, more responsibly, at a later time.

Dating and Sexuality

We've all seen the scenario. That same boy, the one with the leather flak jacket and hair like the singer from Green Day, shows up at the door to take your princess "out." The lines of tension are clearly readable on your face and neck. You know you will be lied to, because you lied to your parents. You immediately condescend to this "little twerp."

By no means does this scrutiny focus on boys alone. Girls are asking boys out with greater frequency. And though, to a large extent, girls want conversation and intimacy, boys are often confused. They don't know what to do. They just feel their pants tightening.

Try not to make cast-in-concrete, political positions about "the date" or "dating," without looking at your kid first. Disregard the time frames you've heard regarding the *appropriate* time to date. Spend more time thinking about the maturity level of your kid, his or her ability to handle difficult situations, and the ways in which he or she thinks about girls or boys. The more a parent protests, categorically, the more resistance there will be. Kids still climb out of second-story windows or sneak out the back. And the intrigue and drama of it all can lead to danger. One parent reported: "I used the iron hand, and she ended up taking off the velvet glove."

It is important to have conversations about the dating experience—to explore scenarios, like: "Let's say you're alone, and he . . ." Because kids often feel invulnerable and oblivious to time, they need to come to the conclusions, themselves, that they are in charge of their own fate and their own sexuality. They need to be in control of their own relationships. More and more, kids are choosing to date in groups. Some of the younger ones say they choose an even number, so that no one is left alone. The pack formation may help them avoid the tension of intimacy. There's safety in numbers. It is far better for a child to conclude, "Maybe a few of us will get together and we'll go to the mall all together. I think I'll feel safer then," or "If we go to a public place, then maybe I won't get into any of those situations. I don't think I'm ready yet."

Rape ("No" Does NOT Mean "Yes")

Listen to those parent-advisory lyrics; they'll chill your bones. I have heard numerous debates in classrooms over the influence of music on teenagers, on free-speech and censorship, and on music as social commentary. However you slice it, rape is out there in serious numbers:

1. A rape is reported every six minutes.
2. A rape often involves drinking or drugs.
3. Four out of five teenage rape victims are assaulted by someone they know.
4. In half of reported rapes, the victim, the offender, or both, are teenagers.[19]

It can happen on a dark corner or behind a store or in one's own bedroom. In public pools, teenage boys surround young girls and "whirlpool" them—moving through the water, pulling off their bathing suits and molesting them. It can happen on a date which starts out wonderfully and then ends in disaster. Girls in school report about dates who grab, kiss, and fondle them. They report that boys suddenly change behavior when they hang around in groups, taunting girls and treating them like meat.[20] They report feeling betrayed by someone they trusted and that they feel pressured by boys who taunt them: "You're such a tease, babe, why not finish what you started?" Girls have spoken about how their own mind has raged out of control in a blitz of horror and confusion as they try to determine whether to scream and run and hit, or comply to avoid getting hurt. Alas, some even worry about not wanting to hurt the feelings of the assailant.

This is where teachers, secretaries, and nurses must enter the picture as significant figures in teenagers' lives, because the incidents of attacks on women have skyrocketed, and kids need safe people with whom to talk about it. When such a subject comes up in school, many counselors are encouraged to help young women with communication. For girls, this involves assertiveness and a dependence upon one's instinct, as well as a clarity about limits. Young women are also involved in role-playing exercises where they see how peer pressure can completely obfuscate judgment. They are encouraged to demand that no means no.

On a larger scale, on college campuses, rape-education seminars and large rallies have become the norm.[21] Such activities have put the movement against rape in the limelight of political activism. But while the debates rage on about appropriate definitions of rape, parents can work toward a home-grown education in common sense.

Should you learn that your child has been sexually attacked, there are direct avenues you can take. Whether or not the child has injuries, she or he must be seen by a doctor. Next, a counselor must enter the picture. Many counselors are sensitive to cultural or ethnic differences and are capable of understanding special needs. Finally, you can always look in the yellow pages, under "Rape."

Most important, experiences such as these underscore the importance of keeping the lines of communication open. Kids are capable of enormous insensitivity and cruelty; however, in times of crisis, they need sensitivity and kindness. They need that spirit of openness to feel they have permission to tell you the necessary details of their ugly experience.

Sexual Abuse

Abusers come in all shapes and sizes, all socioeconomic groups, all religious orientations, all ages and ethnicities and appearances. The lecherous old fart in a raincoat who flashes girls in the park may be replaced by the business associate. Abused kids usually know their abusers; they can even be family members. There is no child-molester profile, except for the statistic that the overwhelming majority of abusers are men (although some researchers claim that women abusers are an underrepresented minority). Either way, child molesters entice and they entrap.

Studies are tracking abused kids of all kinds as they grow up, and it's not a pretty picture. Many draw parallels between abuse and subsequent sexual dysfunction, pregnancy, running away, failure in school, drug and alcohol abuse, deteriorating health, and criminal activity.[22] Psychologists report difficulties with establishing an identity and maintaining self-esteem. Some teens may have been abused as younger children, and may be experiencing problems now that may not, at first, appear to be connected with their earlier trauma.

Here's what school counselors have reported about adolescent sexual abuse.

- physical complaints in the nurse's office
- self-destructive behaviors and constant comments
    about self-hate
- suicidal behavior
- a great deal of fear, some of which seems irrational
- intense guilt feelings
- problems with appetite
- substance abuse
- promiscuity
- depression
- attempts to run away

It is with no small amount of caution that I provide these markers. I'm always a little wary about such "definitive lists" because, though these symptoms may indicate abuse, they may also indicate the normal trauma of adolescence. Furthermore, we live in a hyper-vigilant culture, ready to jump at the slightest hint of impropriety.[23] An adolescent may exhibit some of the markers above, yet sexual abuse may have nothing to do with it.

It's a difficult call. Although a teenager's erratic behavior and wild fluctuations of mood can be caused by many factors, a qualified therapist needs to be enlisted and may, indeed, uncover sexual abuse. What the school can do is keep an eye out. Do not hide your fears from the school; this serves no one. If you have even the slightest intuition about your child's involvement with sexual abuse, do two things: (1) call a hotline, a counselor you trust, or the school and ask for professional help from a certified therapist, (2) follow through. Many families will take the initial steps, but avoid pursuing them because the issue has such enormity and emotional intensity. The earlier the intervention, the better.

AIDS

I want to put aside the role of shared use of dirty needles in the transmission of the AIDS virus and focus on sexuality. By the early 1990s, we have come to know that AIDS is not a disease limited to gay men and drug addicts; it has become a heterosexual disease, one that does not discriminate between race, nationality, or economic class. One must understand that it correlates more closely with a lifestyle and a set of behaviors than anything else. Most of all, we are all living with it.

Here are the numbers: Reports indicate that 78 percent of young people in the fifteen to nineteen age bracket are sexually active, and 20 percent have had four or more partners.[24] HIV has hit teenagers, and is growing every year, despite widespread education. It can't be pushed under the rug or moralized away.

Here are the facts: HIV can exist in a person's bloodstream for more than ten years before AIDS symptoms appear. If a twenty-five year old man or woman contracts AIDS, it is very likely that, due to the long incubation period, HIV was passed on during adolescence. Second, only an HIV test can indicate whether or not someone is HIV positive or negative, and so it essential that sexually-active teens get tested. Most people assume that they are not infected and do not get tested, so more teenagers than we think may be infected with HIV. Third, some kids start having sex around age 12; 16.2 is the national average age that people begin having sex (this age group is often the focus of AIDS education), yet some educators may not fully comprehend that their approach to AIDS education may have immediate, rather than future applicability. Fourth, the

Centers for Disease Control (CDC) estimates that AIDS is on the rise dramatically among adolescents.

We educators can work with parents to slow the growth, I believe, if we know how kids think. Here, I take a more comprehensive approach. There are three main objectives.

Once again, promote abstinence. This is one of the hardest tasks an educator faces—changing behavior. Often, schools will use teens in peer-counseling programs to promote the idea of waiting. However, when kids talk about a "stable relationship," statistics have revealed that these relationships don't last more than six months. So if they're doing it, they're doing it with more than one person. It is important to note, however, that abstinence may, in some cases, fall on deaf ears. One student comments: "Masturbation does not substitute for the real thing."[25]

Next, provide latex condoms. Although safer sex is not as preferable as abstinence, we have to work toward saving lives in the immediate sense while helping young people to defer gratification. It's time to let go of the notion that denying the idea of sex will make it go away. Furthermore, in adolescence, judgment is often impaired; sexual activity is also associated, among teenagers, with the use of alcohol. The more stoned they are, the more likely they are to get laid. The more we can provide possible protection, the better.

And finally, continue educating. But education cannot take the traditional forms of testing and regurgitation. In fact, forty-eight states require AIDS education, but the quality varies widely. Schools must take responsibility for discussing the issues, for creating a space for noncondescending, nonmoralizing conversation. Kids need to talk through various scenarios, any of which involve issues about peer pressure. Adolescents don't need a lecture about how they are a high-risk group; rather, they need an opportunity to think through problems. Teens overwhelmingly report a need for openness in the discussion of sexuality.

They also need the facts. Even the brightest kids engage in high-risk behaviors. Some communities have engaged in door-to-door campaigns, in which factual details are included in leaflets. Beyond discussions of abstinence and peer pressure, Joycelyn Elders, a former surgeon general, has noted the importance of educating teenagers about safety in the back, as well as the front, seat of the car. In fact, Dr. Elders believes that sex education should be part of a comprehensive health-education program.

As sensitively as possible, schools need to provide students and their families with opportunities to learn about AIDS, to test for it, and to discuss its implications for their lives. One of the most effective programs I have seen involves young people, infected with the HIV virus, who are willing to talk to peers. After all the descriptions and the discussions, nothing is as powerful as seeing a young man or woman, up close and personal, tell his or her story. Finally, teenagers also crave conversations about enhancing self-esteem, refusing peer pressure, and curbing physical urges. This form of education is as essential, though even more difficult, than the straight talk about facts or even an evocative narrative of a life in danger.

• • •

Although your children may be pushing you away, it is essential that you stay involved in your teenager's life. Just Do It. Don't abdicate this responsibility. The more you know, the more scared you may be, but you'll at least have a handle on it, and such concern provides your son or daughter with limits, safety, and a sense that you care. Yes, know where they are. Yes, try to get your child to date in groups. Yes, bring up the subject.

They're scared too. Think of it this way, when your children were very young, they may have experienced scary parts of books or movies or those incomprehensible instances of momentary terror. If you were paying attention, you could see that frozen, determined look of fear as they attempted to escape what perplexed and frightened them and sought the comfort of your arms. Part of that distance, silence, and resistance you may now feel in adolescence is a thin veneer, behind which lies that frightened child, looking for safety.

Again, partnership is essential. I cannot emphasize enough how unproductive it is for schools to abdicate their responsibility, declaring, "They need the five subjects—sex is the parents' job." It is also unproductive for parents to pronounce, "They won't listen to me, it's the schools' job. A recent questionnaire of junior- and senior-high school administrators shows that school administrators perceive parents as a major barrier to their efforts in formal sex education. Principals also noted that parents were "generally uncomfortable in talking to their children about human sexuality."[26]

Sex education is serious business. Neither kind of blame tossing does anyone any amount of good. No one can do it all. Schools have their part and you have yours.

5
Let's Get Moral—
Will My Kid Kill for a Pair of Nikes?

"I climbed the ladder of success wrong by wrong."
—Mae West

*"Children have never been good at listening to their elders,
but they have never failed to imitate them."*
—James Baldwin

The syndrome of adolescence includes temporary moral insanity (their manners ain't so hot, either). I'll start with the extreme examples, the worst-case scenarios, and build back your confidence. Promise. In Columbus, Georgia, "seven sixth-graders are accused of plotting for months against their teacher—dumping chemicals in her iced tea, trying to trip her on stairs and taking weapons to school—all because she tried to discipline them."[1] A sophisticated teacher-kidnapping plot is discovered in another town. Articles appear weekly on reports of the logarithmic increase in violent activity amongst teens. No longer the sole domain of the inner city, suburban youths, in increasing numbers, are turning from baseball bats and golf clubs as weapons in their arsenals, to guns, used in assaults and drive-by shootings.[2] Race hatred is on the rise amongst the youth; more and more fascist counter-culture groups—skinheads, militia groups, The Fourth Reich—are finding acceptance. New music groups stumble over one another to outdo each other's racial epithets and abusive lyrics—rape with a beat. Hard-core techno bands swagger and screech across the stage whipping up hysteria, like some well-calculated fascist pep rally. Political aspirants and pollsters extol the fact that negative campaigning works by at least 10%. Radio talk-show hosts are idolized for their maliciousness.

And, of course, there are the celebrated court cases of the 1990s—the Amy Fischer case, involving the shooting of her lover's wife, followed up quickly by the Menendez case, in which two sons are convicted in the killing of their parents. In American society, mean is in—even department store mannequins stare back odiously at the window shopper. Psychologists and social critics warn us about an increasing sense of dehumanization. People are objects rather than subjects and therefore can be treated with unfeeling cruelty.

Miss Manners claims that we are all born rude; we start out by disturbing others in the middle of the night. An eighth grade boy once responded to his parents: "What do they expect? All adolescent boys are slippery characters." As one New York City taxi driver put it: "Hey, yoot is yoot. They've always been a pain in the ass." To some extent, the taxi driver is right: the sad fact is that even Adam and Eve had a problem with impulse control. Here's a scary story: An anthropology instructor out of Rutgers University conducted a survey among his undergraduates that revealed how a sizable majority of students consider *cheating* an essential skill for survival.[3]

Taggers explain why they deface buildings; one tagger with confidence and a wry smile reports: "It's for the chase and the street fame." I'll finish up this depressing picture with a national study of seventeen hundred kids, 6th to 9th graders, that revealed "a majority of boys considered rape to be acceptable under certain conditions. Astoundingly, many of the girls agreed."[4]

Scratch anyone, and you'll find an opinion on why he or she thinks the world has gone to moral hell in a hand basket. Here are the top four: (1) the nuclear family has completely broken down, leaving no support structure for kids, and the extended family, including friends and neighbors, no longer functions as a safety net; (2) spirituality, along with it the values inherent in its beliefs, has been replaced by a sloppy moral relativism that justifies the worst sorts of behavior (in other words, "Hey, if it feels good, it's good; if it feels bad, it's, like, bad)"; (3) many schools, overwhelmed by demands to keep up with their role as the repository of all education, counseling, and parenting, do not see the teaching of morality as realistic; (4) parents have abdicated their responsibility to pass down the moral truths of the day and to perpetuate civilization, because they don't understand how to discuss moral issues or even understand their necessity, for they feel rootless themselves. The scaffolding of values has been torn down.

I'm sure you've heard this before. You may be overwhelmed or enraged. You may ask: why not just legislate manners? We've got too much liberalism, you exclaim. The Puritans prohibited nasty faces, flirting, swearing, gossiping, and finger sticking. Why not return to the good old days? The problem is this, a teacher noted: "Nothing guarantees civility, because nothing guarantees civilization." The world feels out of control. While we may wonder about how to develop a moral language and promote ethical deeds, thousands are being spent on bulletproof glass for classrooms and metal detectors at the front entrance of schools and government buildings.

The religious right has certainly taken up the challenge, running candidates in a guerrilla warfare campaign intended to "advance to the political arena their moral crusade against gay rights, abortion, cultural diversity and any other national inclination that they perceive as a secular evil."[5] They fear that atheism has taken over and that the schools are breeding grounds for lawlessness and promiscuity.

How to instill character, empathy, fairness and sacrifice? How can we help kids believe in and act out of trust, responsibility, an appreciation of rules, compassion, and conscience? If they walk an old woman across the street without being asked, have they arrived? (Well, yes, if no one else was looking.) And even if we get them to obey the rules, is this an indication that they have absorbed basic moral principles? We all want something tangible, yet morality is an intangible subject. And since this is an anti-intellectual culture with a deep suspicion toward complexity and nuance, we are inclined toward prepackaged programs in moral training to fix our moral ills.

Although programs to teach character and civility directly are honest and noble attempts to introduce vision into schools and neighborhoods to counteract those impulses toward greed and material success that dominate our lives, they're problematic when they assume that children have an undeveloped moral muscle that needs some serious exercise by burly instructors and a test on Friday. Kids can hear a stimulating lecture on morality, but still kill for a pair of Nikes.

Similar to the conflicts around issues of sexuality education, there's plenty of blame to go around. However, now that the problem has been identified, the dismal picture painted, what next?

Let's put aside the jail bait, the psycho nut-cases, and the ones with full-blown symptoms of malignant adolescence. For a moment, allow me to help you get underneath some of the issues of moral competence for those kids experiencing the normal symptoms of the adolescent syndrome, and what you and schools can do together about it. I do not, under any circumstances, think kids are a lost cause. In fact, the good things kids can do, the acts of selflessness and moral courage, are extraordinary.[6] Many can be downright inspiring.

• • •

It's time here for a little developmental theory, a necessary mini-lecture because these insights give parenting and teaching a necessary perspective and direction. (Take notes; there will be quiz on this later. And remember, cheating will involve dire consequences.)

Kids are supposed to grow into moral beings as they get older. The most notable theory of moral development, from Harvard's Lawrence Kohlberg, runs something like this: Babies start out acting purely out of self-gratification, then, as they grow, they obey rules to avoid being punished. Time marches on, and actions are motivated by the desire to get something—like a favor or a reward, then to avoid disapproval, then to avoid public censure, then to be seen by anyone as being good, then to avoid self-hate. Ultimately, they understand universal ethical principles. Kohlberg's notions assume that children climb a developmental ladder of moral reasoning. Although there is room for backsliding, the basic principle is this: the older children get, the more they are capable of understanding abstract moral notions and acting upon them. At a mature stage, they can enter freely into agreements and obligations and can act from a sense of conscience. (It is important to note how crucial schooling can be to assist the movement to higher and higher levels of commitment to ideas other than oneself.) At the top end of the scale, Kohlberg talks about those few great ones whose lives are based upon the sacredness of life. These are figures, historical and contemporary, who exemplify the greatest and noblest features of the human condition.

This pattern of moral development runs somewhat loosely

alongside the process of growth in one's thinking. Early on, the baby confuses life with objects, like reaching for a mother's breast. Then, as thinking advances, he looks to others as a means of satisfying basic needs, then as a source of affection. Life is valued in terms of being unique and valuable—whether in terms of religious training or a kind of understanding about rights and duties. As one continues to grow, life is then seen as meaningful because it plays a role in the community and because people have a right to exist and flourish. At this point, adolescents are capable of seeing life as a basic value, something worth valuing and preserving for its own right.

Theoretically, we all climb this ladder. In other words, we start out thinking and acting in very concrete terms, and then in more nuanced and complex and abstract terms. We are eventually capable of seeing beyond self-interest to the "higher good," to recognize and appreciate the golden rule, the ten commandments, and various other moral credos. Sometimes the stages of moral and cognitive development don't always jive, but there is a basic sense that they correspond. We start walking tricky ground, here, because logic isn't exactly applied to moral judgment; otherwise, rocket scientists or that genius down the block would have morality down cold. A quick look back at Nazi Germany will show a number of outstanding intellectuals who contributed to acts of the deepest and most profound moral depravity the human race has ever known. Nevertheless, Kohlberg understood this (after all, he was from a hot-shot university) and so made clear that brains do not a Jesus make. Nevertheless, Kohlberg's moral stage theory clarifies the complex relationship between growing up and becoming more responsible.

Here are the problems, as I see them. First, Kohlberg's stage theory is a bit too rigid. He left a little room for what he called "retrogression" (backsliding), but he still presents it as a ladder one has to climb, rung by rung. I believe that adolescence is fundamentally more fluid than all that, with moments of adult acumen and maturity, alternating with downright moral slovenliness and relapse. Sometimes they are climbing the ladder; sometimes they're dispensing with it and climbing up another structure of their own making, in camouflage.

That's why I have included a chapter early on about contradiction. How can it be that teenagers can ignore an apparent moral obligation and then turn around to work in a soup kitchen the next week? Why do some respond with self-sacrifice during a crisis and others of the same age do not? What is the rationale behind acts of selflessness committed by nine year olds, who are supposed to be concerned solely with their own rewards and punishments? Why was it that, amidst all the hoopla and concern by adults about Ryan White (the fifteen-year-old hemophiliac with AIDS), his new class-mates "went out of their way to greet him and made sure to invite him to a dance after the first home football game of the season?"[7]

Dr. Robert Coles, the Harvard psychiatrist, has written about a young African-American girl, Ruby Bridges, who was pelted with tomatoes as she crossed picket lines to enter her school after the desegregation laws were passed. Undaunted, Ruby trudged every day through the unholy terrors of degradation and bigotry. Coles asked her about her thoughts during that time. She ultimately responded by saying that she forgave the tomato throwers' rage because she believed that they did not know what they were doing. Ruby was not "ready" to think this way. She had not yet climbed the rung of the theoretical moral ladder. Nevertheless, out of the mouth of a child came a major tenet of western religious heritage.

In class and out, teenagers are driven by a set of impulses that only conversation and deep knowing can reveal. Those teenage acts of selfless love may be committed because they may receive recognition; or because they have seen a teacher whom they admire model that behavior; or because they feel a certain measure of shame or guilt about something that makes them want to "fix" it; or because they truly believe in its inherent principle. They are capable of all of it. Adolescence is simply one big moral roller-coaster ride. Rather than develop as stages, moral qualities emerge in context, within communities. Morality is part of a larger syndrome because it reflects a set of behaviors socially conditioned—by the home, by the media, by peers. In short, morality, like adolescence, is not only born; it's also made.

Second, though teens are quite capable of enormous sacrifice, the syndrome of adolescence is often identified with unbridled nar-cissism, a key stumbling block on the way to one's moral growth. For teens, the world revolves initially around their hair, their body, their clothes, their teeth, their peers. There are hundreds of people watching their every move, they fantasize, as they stand before the mirror rehearsing lines, changing clothes, walking back and forth. They may dig what they see or despise what they see, but what they see means everything. David Elkind, a distinguished psychologist, has reported: "The notion of an imaginary audience also helps to explain the observation that what concerns adolescents is not guilt but, rather, shame, for example, the reaction to an audience."[8] They feel like they're on TV at school and at home. What they do and what they say is subservient to how they will, in their own minds, be seen. And, by comparison, they often feel that they come up short.

Such self-absorption is naturally adolescent, yet it is also a deeply ingrained feature of our American insatiable self. American narcissism simply makes adolescence more pronounced because it celebrates the self so unabashedly and recklessly. Our work ethic has been obscured by a new American credo: "If it feels good, do it." Our culture is stuck on this low rung of Kohlberg's moral ladder. American adults have not necessarily transcended a narcissistic *stage* to live on higher rungs of the ladder, either. Many share some of the worst characteristics of adolescence with their kids. Kids and their parents may fight over the same brand of hair mousse.

This is not a particularly good message to send teenagers, who have uncontrollable waves of feeling good. The freedom to act on one's impulses is an extraordinary distortion of the declaration that we have "the right to life, liberty, and the pursuit of happiness." That permission is etched deeply within the national psyche.

Teenagers are therefore struck by the discrepancy between the indoctrination of morality in their early years and the *results* they see in the world around them. Adults are simply not setting the standard for exemplary behavior these days, for adults make the television shows and feature films filled with gratuitous violence justified by its producers as "realistic"; adults manufacture the guns or the drugs, adults publish the explicit magazines or Internet web sites. Teens witness middle-aged crime and corrupt politicians, prurient preachers, sleaze-bag financiers and deadbeat divorcees ignoring the obligation to provide child support. And then we blame the kids for being callous or insensitive?

"Growing up" is not necessarily the guaranteed answer. Teenagers are acutely aware, in a political sense, of adult hypocrisy.

They know about our contemporary debauchery. They read and re-read *Catcher in the Rye* and feel confirmed in their own belief that adults are "phonies." They study about "moral" societies that elevate high art and high ideas yet commit atrocities—the Holocaust of World War II, for one—and they watch the satellite coverage of countries currently engaged in ethnic cleansing. They listen to interviews of militia groups who justify their rage against authority by celebrating the bombing of a government building. And they're supposed to trust anyone over forty?

What's also a bit problematic with a moral scenario of this sort done with children who have names like Bob, Dan, Elliot, John, Jimmy, and Roger is that most of Kohlberg's studies were conducted with boys only. May I suggest that the girl who forgave the tomato throwers was not considered in the sample.

Studies have shown that, in many cases, boys concentrate on rules, rights, and responsibilities, while the girls focus on relationships and on a moral language all their own. Amy, a young woman interviewed in Carol Gilligan's *A Different Voice,* sees in young women "a world that coheres through human connection rather than through systems of rules."[9] Amy believes that people in conflict should try to work it out, to see each other's position, to hear each other's story, to examine the form of the problem, to show how people need each other for each other's sustenance.

If we looked at Amy's philosophy solely within the context of Kohlberg's model, she would be behind in her moral maturity, lower on the ladder, stuck in an inability to challenge assumptions or authority or to intervene, initially, to solve the dilemma. However, according to Gilligan, "Amy's judgments contain the insights central to an ethic of care."

It is wholly inappropriate to make automatic assumptions about how one particular gender will react to a moral dilemma. In fact, bipolar points of view, currently the rage in academic circles, may end up serving to reinforce stereotypes of boys and girls.

Perhaps you might think the attention on girls' and boys' approaches to moral development is all irrelevant, high-brow theory. However, these general observations and perceptions illuminate how teenagers think morally. Gilligan's contributions describe how *morality, relationship, and identity are intertwined.* How adolescents view themselves affects how one sees and acts upon the world.

Children who grow up with an inflated or exclusionary sense of self develop one kind of moral orientation; those who learn about themselves in connection to social obligations develop another.

The two moral voices—of justice and of care—matter in how we function effectively as parents and teachers and how we can both help develop character, a sense of self, and an independent, healthy identity.[10] The parent who serves as judge, jury, and prosecution without a demonstration of care may end up being dismissed as authoritarian and remote. The parent who campaigns mercilessly for the defense, in the name of justice or whose approach degenerates into sloppy and unclear sentimentality, can easily be betrayed. Moral role-modeling is imperative at all levels.

We have been around advertising enough to know that anything can be justified and extolled—bath soap and automobiles and tomato sauce and morality. Yet some critics have been skeptical of Carol Gilligan's work. They believe her approach to morality is ephemeral and vague. After all, boys and girls are equally capable of moral cruelties; according to Gilligan herself, girls may lie to preserve a relationship and boys may lie about their achievements. They both cheat and steal. Boys may taunt another who doesn't live up to the rules or the standard. Girls may suffocate each other in ugly, catty cliques, all in the name of relationship.

Critics also argue that those characteristics Gilligan associates with women are not internal and genetic as much as they are connected with socioeconomic, cultural, and historical movements and male dominance. Furthermore, they contend that Gilligan may be substituting a new form of moral relativism for the old. William Kilpatrick, author of *Why Johnny Can't Tell Right from Wrong: And What We Can Do about It* writes: "The problem is that Gilligan's ethic of care is not grounded in any solid concept of right and wrong; rather, the whole argument for it seems to be something along the lines of 'Trust us: we're women and we care.'"[11] The old moral relativism, "if it feels good, do it," is replaced; the *new* moral relativism, about justifying the unique quality of a woman's way of knowing, is another way of extolling the virtues of a *woman's intuition*. In this context, then, womanhood is idealized, a stereotype hardly distinguishable from the "perfect" Victorian woman, an image we now disdain as outdated and sexist.

Finally, some say that proponents have turned Gilligan's work into another political football, a set of politically-correct diatribes and gender wars that do not contribute in any concrete way to the development of character or care or moral literacy. Others claim that, to work, Gilligan's notions require a radical transformation of American society itself, a task so daunting that one is left exasperated and overwhelmed.

•   •   •

The Kohlberg-Gilligan debate helps us see adolescence as both a mirror of society and as a window into individuals. Despite their flaws, both contributions illuminate moral orientation and the fluctuations of adolescence. And when you live in classrooms, you end up engaged by those theorists as you grope to understand the differences between boys and girls.

Your kid is part child, part adult—attracted to, but simultaneously in fear of, what adulthood represents. Your kid is beginning to think about his or her thinking, balancing self-interest with moral maturity. Your kid is moving in and out of action that avoids guilt or shame, discovering a moral voice. Such are the contradictions and pressures of this syndrome.

Now that we've completed Educational Theory 101, we'll need to dive into a brief American Moral History 101.

Let's start with the founders. The Puritan "ethic" was a set of maxims intended for kids to obey—period. Religious codes were in, and kids had to submit to the higher authorities. When at home, there were three things kids must do: (1) "make a bow always when you come home, and be immediately uncovered (remove headgear)." (2) "grumble not nor be discontented at anything thy parents appoint, speak, or do." (3) "bear with meekness and patience, and without murmuring or sullenness, thy parents' reproofs or corrections."[12]

Strict, certainly; nevertheless, complaints continued to pour in to the local press about how wicked and obscene the kids were.

The nineteenth century was filled with a spirit of hurrying youth through the preliminaries to get them into the factories. Attempts were made in the early part of that century to teach certain moral virtues without a religious base behind it, so that those holding other points of view would not be excluded. Though the religious training in the nineteenth century appeared generic, thinkers of that day felt a sense of moral decline.

Later on, early in the twentieth century, morality training involved a different version of codes. These would hardly be objectionable. Memorize and follow this list, and you'll be just fine. Examples included "Good Americans Are Kind, Good Americans Are True," and my personal favorite, "Good Americans Try To Do the Right Thing in the Right Way." They stayed away from the plain-wrap religious scene, secularized the approach, and told students to get with the program. It fit perfectly with the melting-pot craze. Hey, we're all Americans—let's put distinctions aside.

It was not very successful. The 1920s were filled with their own moral code—"lewd" dancing and cigarettes, drinking and obscenities. The 1940s was a real scene, too—hep big bands and all night parties, sexy boogying to the jitterbug. Moral codes were not withstanding temptation, and by the 1950s and early 1960s, such programs were hard to find in the American school.

Educators began to conceive a more progressive approach. Students were asked to identify their own beliefs about moral issues and priorities. Those schools didn't buy into religious training or textbook moral credos. Teachers watched as children unfolded their systems of moral thought, and they took notes to see where the kids stood on Kohlberg's ladder. The students did climb the moral-reasoning ladder in the abstract, but were not necessarily stopped from stealing a Beatles album.

This nonjudgmental approach led to values clarification (V.C., the 1960s and 1970s version of P.C., political correctness). If young, impressionable souls find themselves in sensitive *spaces*—in a milieu that stresses understanding, the proponents said—they will be able relate to others more effectively and act accordingly. Teachers were not to play a role in determining right or wrong answers; they were to be morally neutral.

Alas, we have learned the hard way that students do not arrive at good moral decisions because they've had a chance to clarify their values. It doesn't go anywhere. Their values and their intelligence are not challenged. What's worse, values such as self-absorption, greed, and ruthless competitiveness at the expense of others, go unchallenged. In fact, students who have *clarified* their points of view—however incorrigible—feel more confirmed in the correctness of what they are saying. The pendulum swung too far in this direction. Those schools that celebrated the individual as their primary focus found themselves in a difficult spot, as their teachers became mute or obsequious and unable to teach moral thinking. Some schools began to slip imperceptibly and precariously into a whirlpool of heedless narcissism which, for kids, is as harmful a notion as second-hand cigarette smoke. Unfortunately, many schools are still there.

Critics argue that this open atmosphere in classrooms does not mirror the values that we want as a society. They are dismayed by words uttered in class that would not be permitted in a nice restaurant. Furthermore, they are not convinced that moral development is taking place. The Reverend William Sloane Coffin, arguing against a dogmatism of the left "permissiveness can be authoritarian" claims, "The only thing worse than banging your head against a closed door is banging it against an open one. You tend to lose your balance."[13]

There are interesting variations on this theme in the 1990s. Some schools present moral education as a course (for credit, of course). They use the "great" literary works for their lessons on character, and allow students to face and deal with moral issues discussed in music and literature, in myth, in politics and history and in science. When it works, I have seen fabulous discussions with kids in class about morality. Kids talk about moral choices and dilemmas they face. As an observer, I may die a hundred deaths as they express opinions to which I will never ascribe, but, in the hands of a competent teacher, one has to be inspired as they worm their way through the intricacies. The very fact that they are struggling means that they are listening and they are questioning. There's debate and a kind of intellectual discourse that makes for great classes. I have also seen student presentations at assemblies about peer conflict mediation or date-rape, in which the actors stop midscene and ask questions.

Moral scenarios are big these days, including role-playing, discussions of abstract moral issues, with room for discussions of teenagers' assumptions about morality. Students are asked to debate, to recognize, to elaborate upon a world view. They debate their intuitions about God, the moral nature of their intuition, why life matters, what responsibility is, why one acts morally. They start with personal ethics and move to larger issues and theories. They spend time on durable values. They hear their teacher struggle with ideas, react to smarminess, ask questions. Most of all, they are asked to challenge their own assumptions.

Proponents argue that one's convictions are changeable, that such flexibility is the hallmark of an engaged American mind, especially if it is open to the opinions of others. The teachers' role, here, is to respond and challenge, not necessarily to remain neutral. By necessity, teachers must then address the tension of issues dealing with personal issues, such as sexual morality.

Critics are not satisfied, however. They note that kids are still slipping compact discs into the sleeves of their jackets, that the various permutations in character education are pimples on an elephant's tush. If the sixties' free thought was liberating, and the period in between has been chaos, some may want to roll back history and slam the moral points and the high points of western civilization, down teens' throats.

At its most extreme are the textbook censors, who eliminate all pieces of literature that could mire the picture. *Catcher in the Rye* has been banned for its put-down of adults, and *Alice in Wonderland* for its approximation of a drug experience. *The Diary of Anne Frank* has been censored because, according to critics, the book was "a real downer." *The Wizard of Oz* has been seen as offensive because it advocates "the religion of secular humanism," in which the characteristics of courage, brains, and a heart do not come from God but from within.[14] In some towns, downtown administrators use felt-tip markers to delete passages from *Gorillas in the Mist* about apes' mating habits. No screwing around here. This is the immersion approach, including the inculcation of various texts of *correct* values, echoes the training from McGuffey's "Readers" (in which, earlier this century, grammar lessons used sentences about moral righteousness).[15] These practitioners hope to reclaim the object lessons in hero worship, in which great presidents, historical leaders, civil rights activists, and Nobel Prize winners are intended to serve as inspiration.

It is almost impossible to create a "good" student this way. Adolescents are not suddenly going to "get" that the Greek Gods' bravery and strength are an inspiration to them;[16] Teenagers are not going to act morally because they have been taught to do so and tested on Friday. Adolescents are simply not going to "receive" morality by absorbing or memorizing some set of universal maxims, such as Ben Franklin's list in his *Poor Richard's Almanac*, about being frugal or going to bed early and waking up wise.[17] Adolescents understand that life is far more complex than that. Sure, they'll spit back the answers about moral seriousness, about conscience, about the "big" ideas. In short, morality is not an advertising campaign drilled into our psyches with repetition; nor is it a program or a project; it is a set of discrete minute-by-minute actions and responses, based upon reflection and a consideration of another. It is a blend of appropriate experiences, psychosocial and intellectual readiness, and a sense of connection. *This* kids can understand.

The "hands-off" schools consider moral education too ambiguous and too heated a topic; it's just not worth the hassle. They spend their time blaming parents or society at large. Similar to their reactions to the gradations and intensity of the sex education movement, some educators claim that it's better not to be swayed by all the political pressures. Rather, they choose to focus on the business of teaching kids how to read and write. They fear attack from both the left and the right. Some are immobilized by the pressure; they worry that rocking the boat will only wreak havoc, so they back off. The problem, as I see it, is that not dealing with moral issues is, in and of itself, a moral stance. It is a sin of omission.

Finally, some schools are well aware of the daunting quality of this obligation, and so have chosen to focus their efforts on drug or sex education and the values implicit in them; they can concentrate in one area, measure the results, and leave the rest of generic moral education to others.

As an educator, whether schools adopt programs or not, I believe all must understand the following sensibilities.

1. Teaching is inherently a moral activity. One educator wrote: "Just as a physician who has no idea of why or to what end he or she practices medicine or a lawyer who lacks any sense of the rule of law in the just society, a teacher without moral purpose is aimless, as open to incivility and harm as to good."[18] The syndrome of adolescence needs good doctors; here, they take the form of teachers with a quality of moral presence in and out of a classroom that can make the difference.

Morality is engendered within a healthy set of relationships between students and their teachers and students with each other. As kids enter adolescence, their relationships with teachers may take on a special importance. They talk about how the worst thing to experience is humiliation or public shame, and the best thing to experience is some form of public acknowledgment. Such interactions and perceptions have an enormous amount of influence on a teenager's sense of self and his or her obligation to others.

The more truthful and human the relationship between students and teacher, the more teenagers feel like participatory members of the institutions they must inhabit, the less resistance they will erect to authority, to the material, and to the better parts of our culture. Acknowledged and needed, rather than accommodated and placated, they tend to treat people with greater respect. The more connected students are with adults who involve them in a moral life, the more they will think that issues of morality are important. The more they sense that each of us has a story to tell, the more morality has an arena in which human beings—adults and children—can flourish. The more boys' views and girls' views are given credence—both the voices of rules and the voices of relationship— the more capacity there is for hope. Classroom interaction can "provide a sense of community and fairness," of service, and of sacrifice.[19] Schools can emphasize the intangibles of connection, of relationship.

2. Students can also form a solid core of ethical beliefs when classrooms themselves become useful, human places. Schools can foster moral thinking by designing curriculum not as a subject removed both from their experience, but with kids in mind. The preponderance of attention on achievement, at the expense of thinking, is time-consuming, fruitless, and irresponsible. Education for competition with a foreign economic giant has replaced inquiry and intellectual discovery. In the headlong rush to exalt achievement, achievement actually suffers, for short-term memorization is ephemeral and disconnected. Imagine math classes with room for cooperation and discussion, rather than the regurgitation of numbers and facts in different order. Imagine the science class in which students solve real problems, where they sustain reflective inquiry to take intellectual risks as they sequence DNA for use to uncover a gene for a family in a foreign country,[20] rather than copy charts and fill in the blanks. Imagine the computer class, in which students use a data base to monitor a budget for a social service agency or a water management district. Imagine the history class that not only

examines world religions but also gives kids the opportunities to explore what is meant by the spirit. Imagine the biology class that integrates logic with imagination to transform excess space in the schoolyard into a viable plot to grow vegetables. Imagine a foreign-language class where students immerse themselves in another culture. Imagine a curriculum in which students gain facts to ask questions, rather than ask questions to gain facts.[21] It is precisely in the asking and in the reflecting that they grow intellectually and morally. Education must be connected to meaning.

3. Moral education works when it is inextricably bound to the world in which students live. When this happens, young people respond. They are willing to participate in school and society at large when they see its value, when they're given the opportunity to make a contribution. We must also reevaluate the artificial split between doing well and doing good. A good deed is not necessarily an extra; rather, it can be an academic enterprise. Conversely, a rich and rewarding curriculum naturally connects the subject in class to the subjects out of class. When kids are experiencing the symptoms of adolescence, they need to get out once in a while, to get some air, to see the world in worthwhile terms. Morality is not necessarily engendered by automatic development alone; kids need challenges, experiences of hardship, opportunities to feel pity and sacrifice and compassion, and the triumph of will over adversity. It's an integrated process.

Moral education works when kids are given opportunities to serve and to talk about their experience. Morality is a behavior as well as a state of mind. In an essay entitled, "What It Takes to Be Good," a philosopher writes: "When morality is executive as well as legislative, when it is robust as well as righteous, it requires the capacities and abilities necessary to realize moral principles, to actualize their purport in the right way on the right objects at the right time."[22] I have witnessed this in my own experience, as a sixteen year old, when I joined a program with other kids my age to create a park in the mountains by digging up a tarred-over baseball diamond and planting trees that would then resist destruction by smog. We lived and ate together and shared our experiences. Nothing did more for my sense of human connection than digging a ditch with a stranger, who subsequently became a friend. Something equalizing and stirring happens when one works according to one's abilities and is fed according to one's needs (sounds like a little Marxism creeping back in?). Service is tangible and concrete and meaningful. Service engenders a feeling of love for the sanctity of human life. This theological concept, even in its secularized form, is often forgotten in schools.

I remember talking casually with a group of students about a homeless man on the street corner near our school. I asked the students what they thought of him. Some characterized him as a leech, others as a crazy man and hopeless alcoholic, others as a victim of circumstance. We decided to serve meals to the homeless at a local shelter and afterwards share our experiences. It was an extraordinary experience, because they saw results; they bonded with each other in the act of giving. At another time, we had organized a rally for our SADD chapter (Students Against Drunk Driving) at a local mall, complete with celebrity coverage, a crashed car for effect, and news coverage. The students wanted to make a difference, to show the public that they were capable of organizing an event of this magnitude. The event itself was an enormous success, but the crowd size and enthusiasm was not, for me, its measure. Of greater significance was that, knowing I had forgotten to "assign" them clean-up duty, they had long in advance organized a massive clean-up campaign, far more extensive than any I had imagined. They did not need a lecture. They were simply lifted *out* of themselves to see something more important.

When kids find themselves in a position that requires sacrifices—handing a brick to someone else in the process of building low-cost housing, planting trees for an urban forest, working in an AIDS hospice, stacking cans for a food distribution program, tutoring a peer, cleaning up after a natural disaster, organizing a community watch—they grow. They forget to look into the mirror. They respect the work. They get a rush from responsibility. They come to think of others not just in utilitarian ways, but as true partners. At those crucial moments when teenagers wonder what they're all about, they can say to themselves, "I did this, I helped that."

By freeing themselves from the obsession on themselves, they sense community. It is nothing short of a spiritual experience, from which—I strongly believe—they are transformed. Real work, real responsibility, real conversation leads to the highest quality of relationship, of empathic connections, and to thinking that takes on the qualities of moral discourse. They say that morality is a social construct, like a set of Christmas lights; when one goes out, the entire chain is disrupted. They see themselves as part of that chain. With enough of these experiences, young people begin to exhibit an ability to understand and walk our moral tightropes and develop a kind of ethical backbone that can last a lifetime. They have accessed the world and their own innate goodness.

The role of an educator is to sustain the momentum so that the students can answer these questions. It is one obligation as adults to provide those opportunities so that the heart-swelling features of this syndrome are given expression. As John Dewey pointed out: individuals do not learn from experience; they learn from reflecting upon experience.[23] A contemporary educator, William Damon, author of *Greater Expectations: Overcoming the Culture of Indulgence in America's Homes and Schools,* sees morality as a function of both habit and reflection.[24] Combined with evocative personal experiences, this combination of repeated action and reflection constitutes the profile of those people who have been transformed into moral human beings.

4. Moral education arises from meaningful experiences of diversity. When young people find themselves in schools that personalize education and acknowledge different kinds of people, when the teaching and setting is such that kids of different cultures and backgrounds and orientations can listen to and need each other, kids enter into another's realm. They are less isolated. Controversy and growth are woven tightly under a rubric of appreciation. Experiencing another's culture in a setting that values diversity and makes it safe is liberating. Very often, moral growth is the inevitable by-product.[25]

5. The school itself, as an institution, sends its own set of moral messages. Something is being said in the architecture both of the buildings (many are modeled after prisons) and of time (for the most part, variations on a theme of forty or fifty-minute periods, one after another, with two breaks), in the rows of desks and the role students play in decision making. A moral credo is inherent in those schools whose primary mode of operation is a perfunctory and mechanical delivery of education to its students, much of which eerily simulates a manufacturing process in which empty vessels (students' heads) are "filled" with the "product." In fact,

schools can often be so alienating or dangerous or competitive a germ field that they serve as breeding grounds for immoral behavior, places where cheating for survival or the avoidance of work is raised to an art form.

It is all the more imperative that students feel some sort of ownership over their lives at school, for they can be places of enormous benefit to the moral development of teenagers. Teenagers need opportunities to express opinions in writing, without a fear of censure; they even need to argue with the school administration in a setting of mutual respect. Here, moral development is not necessarily reduced to following the rules; in fact, kids are willing to follow rules if they are given the time of day to discuss the reasons for them. But the issues are larger. Moral development is evoked, rather than invoked; it emerges from the feeling that one's voice has been put to good use.

Kids will falter along the way, and it is all the more imperative that schools combine clarity with sensitivity, justice with mercy. When the moral guidelines out there are not clear, the least that the school can do is articulate and enforce them. Consequences play a serious and significant role in helping to deter kids from crossing the line. Although they hope to be heard, they also want to be responsible. If they have erred, they need to talk about it, but they also need to repair the problem. All too often, students get the lecture, but feel as though their reputation is somehow sullied; they want to fix the problem, feel clean again, and be judged on par with others.

John Dewey spoke of how character is built from social-mindedness and farsightedness. Schools can be a crucial link in that process. Though high-schools, like many institutions, may not be able to claim enormous successes turning immoral kids (those with a malignant form of adolescence) into moral ones, they can play an essential role in helping unconscious kids develop a set of ethical beliefs that would make a stone-hearted cynic gush at graduation. They can achieve significant progress within the context of moral communities, where, in Aristotle's words: "persons of good character can visualize their lives."

That's the School's Part—What about Yours?

1. Model It. I'll never forget a parent conference that took place during tax season. Father, mother, and son entered the room. As the son began to settle sheepishly in his seat, his father—to engage me in conversation—asked me about whether or not I had done my taxes. Without really giving me a moment to answer, he launched into a fairly detailed array of the spurious ways in which he had circumvented the process and lied about entertainment expenses. I had called the conference to discuss an issue concerning his fourteen-year-old son—stealing. A white student once reported that he is lectured about the importance of racial tolerance and has tried to understand it all, even though he smelled the smoke from the Los Angeles disturbances following the Rodney King acquittal. "I try not to draw conclusions; I try to say to myself that the people who did all this violence do not represent an entire race. I mean, they're my friends. But then I listen to my parents talk in whispers about declining property values and a fear of anyone different. Dang! What's a kid to think?" If you are unethical, the apple will fall close to the tree.

2. Actions speak louder than words. If you want your children to appreciate the sanctity of human life, you must look at the ways in which you are demonstrating it. How do you react when you see people suffering? More important, how do you act? Are homeless people, for example, just annoyances? Or is the complexity of the issue something you can talk about with your child? Most of all, does your family conduct any moral activity as a unit, such as volunteering to cook for a shelter or participate in a neighborhood antilitter campaign? By actively participating in social responsibility, you are sending a message to your teenager that he or she is worthy and capable and needed. It does wonders.

3. Look at your modus operandi for clues to the way in which your family operates—morally. How your home is organized suggests its own system of values. Are people a priority? Is conversation? If you asked your child what he or she most values about the family, what would it be? If you could describe your family politically, who has the power? The voice? The representation? How is change dealt with? Who is heard the most? What are the forms of

punishment? What emphasis does success play? What are the biggest sins? How much chaos is there in the house such that any behavior might prevail? What is tolerable? What is intolerable? (I remember a meeting in which a father said to his son, after a difficult baseball practice: "You're not allowed to lose here. A loser is a loser.")

4. Talk with your teenager about moral issues. Discuss the implications of actions you see, statements you hear, TV programs you watch into occasions for conversation. They need to question what they experience, to hear the voice of their own conscience, like a bee buzzing in a glass jar. Such little voices may very well be heard in the middle of the din at a raucous teenage party.

A Note about Religion

Kids try on different hats—heavy metal, grunge, jock, rebel, wizard, clown, fashion mogul. Kids look into that mirror and ask who is the fairest one of them all. When they don't hear anything back, they start to worry. And then they experiment. Because they are coming to an age where they can think about their thinking, where their mind begins to send them abstractions, they start to wonder. They want some help. They are looking for an answer to their impotent rage. They want to believe in something, to belong somewhere. They may be attracted to ritual or fasting or prayer. They want to explore their subjective experiences.

In walks religion, most likely the one to which you don't ascribe. Crosses, stars, crescents start to appear. They pump up the volume for satanic lyrics. Teenagers want to see what the Zen Buddhists, the Bahais, the Hindus, and the Muslims have to say. For the most part, this is normal; they're attracted to the inklings they get, in waves, of the spirit. They simply want to try religion on, like all the other masks they wear at this time in their lives. They ask themselves: Is this religion the right one for me? Am I right for this religion? In some ways, the awakening can be enormously positive—a chance to talk about questions in an open-ended way, to explore life as a mystery, to gain a spiritual dimension. And in other ways, kids can fall victim to it.

Because adolescence is a syndrome, the quest for a spiritual identity in adolescence is an attempt to feel better; it comes at the same time as one's mid-life crisis, when many adults are trying to feel better as well. And so, nothing flips out parents more than the conversion to a new self. Many articulate some concern about their child's newfound religious experience; at just about the same time, these same parents talk about the need to find meaning in their own lives. They want to change jobs, to travel, to find new ways of being, to explore the life of the spirit.

My advice is this: allow your children to explore their spirituality, for the more you resist them, the more attracted to the extremes they will be. Adolescents operate out of a "do the opposite" framework, especially if the authority figures in their lives are vehemently espousing a particular view. However, if they start to rant and rave and bring home scary literature, read it and start doing some homework. Enter into a conversation about the spirit by talking around the subject. Choose a back way in, and do not enter into a power struggle over your child's beliefs—you'll both lose. If your child is easily swayed by ideas and speaks with an "unholy" holiness about certain religious tenets, find out if your child is being attracted to a cult. And if so, get professional advice. Explore the scenario with a counselor or a cult hot line. Your kid does not need to roll his or her eyes backward and spit green gunk for you to get a sense that there's trouble. And if you are sure, reach for the red telephone.[26]

Most important, allow your religious heritage and tradition and ancestry to guide the soul of belief. If you cannot do it all, do what you can. Whatever the form it takes, there must be some measure of spirit in your home in the thousand subtle ways a teenager may come to absorb it. It could come in silence or prayer, in a weekly acknowledgment of appreciation, in a dabbling of ritual, consistently. Homes that seem to function well during crisis have an appreciation for and practice of spiritual belief.

• • •

My words on morality may ring as unusually idealistic. When teens are climbing the walls, lessons with a moral component may have to give way to basic police work. However, a much higher success rate occurs when we adults pay attention. Adolescents are teaching us to question more and tell less; to allow them opportunities to recognize, elaborate, and act on the real moral dilemmas they face rather than to lecture them on abstract and hypothetical situations or ask them to respond with phraseology they expect their teachers want to hear; to provide opportunities for girls to be heard and respected, to focus on both boys' and girls' unique perspectives rather than force them to assimilate ours; to work on behalf of others.

Moral growth and development reflect a complex pastiche of intellectual, physical, spiritual, environmental, developmental, psychological, temperamental factors. Although we are all adept at articulating psychological jargon, popularized in the talk-show circuit and the steady stream of self-help books, we have not developed a vocabulary for discussing wider issues, some of which have to do with the development of character. An addiction to stealing or promiscuity or violence may indicate a psychological need for control or to be loved or to vent anger, certainly. However, these issues may also indicate a hole in one's moral integrity or even a genetic disposition. We have to be careful as we observe our children and, as parents and educators, open ourselves to the possibility that some behaviors can be considered naturally "developmental," and others characterological.

Certainly, the psychological and developmental intersect with the characterological. There certainly are connections between *who* and *how* one is. These epistemological discussions of causality, though interesting, may only go so far in helping you determine whether or not your son or daughter is going to be like Charlie Manson. We educators and parents must be prepared to do is recognize when they're slipping into the chasm. Usually, it comes when we get the willies, when our visceral responses are telling us that we are consistently frightened of the behavior and/or the person, when huge "lessons" go unheeded, when we feel an intense darkness or coldness in the room.

But I'll tell you this: for the most part, the odds are that negative behaviors you see will probably pass. As a principal, I have seen it time and time again (although we must not be complacent, or we risk damage to the teen and society). Schools and parents can help build a moral intelligence. There is a conscience there; we need to give that conscience the space to prove itself. Those millions of times they were told to share, to wait their turn, to help others is deeply embedded. It's just buried under thick make-up or cheap cologne. They will surprise and inspire you.

A student once wrote for the school newspaper, "When I do

something good, I feel like I'm worth something. It's sort of like in *The Wizard of Oz;* you finally notice that you've got brains and a heart." When young people find themselves in meaningful classrooms, when they are in a position to make a difference and to feel heard, to talk about their experiences, to see the vulnerability and frailty of human life, something entirely new, utterly transformative, happens. There is room for reconciliation and hope. And arising, like a phoenix from the ashes, is the capacity for reverence.

6
Lying, Cheating, and Stealing
A Short Guide to the "Ethically Challenged"

How's a kid supposed to make it without doing this kind of stuff?
My parents laugh and say, 'Do as I say, not what I do.'
What do you expect?
—a teenager, after having been caught stealing compact discs.

Surveys are often conducted to determine the degree of adolescent delinquent behavior. Teens are asked about vandalism, about shoplifting, arson, breaking windows in empty office buildings, buying stolen property, taking drugs, playing hookey. Although boys generally exceed girls in these behaviors, all are participants in one form or another. The syndrome of adolescence involves an occasional brief foray into mischief.

Here's a great example: A study analyzed character education in school, Boy Scouts, temple and church training or other character-building programs for young people to determine the nature and extent of the connection between moral training and honesty. The disappointing news was this: it doesn't matter if you're Catholic or Jewish, black or white, boy or girl. You're going to lie, cheat, and steal just the same. I'd like to avoid the political theorizing about the fundamental reasons why such behavior is rampant.[1] Rather, let's take a look at the big three, one by one.

Lying

When your kids were young, they may have lied just to get the world to jive with the reality of their thinking. They may even have believed the stories they created. But adolescent lying is often done with intent, and that is particularly exasperating for parents, for many believe that they have a trusting relationship and cannot conceive that their child would lie to them. They may also have lied as teenagers, have consciously established a parenting style accordingly, and can't stand the fact that they are now being betrayed.

Lying is another form of asserting oneself, a necessary feature of adolescence. Terrific, you say—my kid needs to lie in order to grow up? In some ways, yes; lying is one of many coping techniques at a teenager's disposal. Some lie to get ahead or get out of doing or confronting something; some lie just to piss you off. Kids lie about their grades, mostly to get you off their case. "Yep, the homework is in." They lie about where they've been. "We were at the movies, and it broke and we like had to sit there for an hour and a half until they fixed it." They lie about their relationships: "We talk, that's it." They lie to protect a friend or they lie about themselves and tell a story about a friend. "I have this friend, see, and he's, like, been taking drinks from his parents' bar, like Vodka, and filling up the part he drank with water." They lie about accomplishments because they may not have the skills to establish themselves. They lie to be in charge or to win friends and influence people or to save face.

When a child deviates from the straight and narrow, telling the truth might be so painful that a lie might save a great deal of heartache. In authoritarian families, kids lie to get out from under the heat, for they can predict the fierceness of consequences if the bubble of the perfect, compliant child, is burst. I remember speaking with a seventeen-year-old whose family's reins were suffocating. They believed that he deserved only one night out every third weekend. In the early morning, the father would check the odometer against the figure he jotted down the night before, just to ensure that his son hadn't traveled anywhere. The boy went out and lied about it. Infuriated, the father grounded the boy for two months. As a form of retaliation and as a means of maintaining his social life, the boy spent a great deal of time figuring out how to tamper with his odometer. Needless to say, when the car was traded into a dealership, the discovery was made there, and the boy and his father hit bottom. The father was inconsolable, even abusive. As a result, this young man concluded that his lies needed to be much more sophisticated.

In permissive families, the "open" atmosphere assumes that there need never be a reason to lie, yet this same atmosphere is deceptive. Kids tell me that they watch their parents pretend to be concerned about their welfare on an intermittent basis, and so they lie just to keep the good, loose thing going. I have noticed, too, that some kids lie, sadly enough, to please their parents. They collude with their parents' own specious way of approaching the world. Here's an example: After a few weeks' separation in their marriage, permissive parents began to invite their own girlfriends and boyfriends over to spend the night. Their fifteen-year old son was the confidant of each, caught up in a web of each parent's lies to maintain the intrigue each of his parents had constructed. He, in turn, lied to the other parent to protect the one staying home that night. And he lied to the school and to friends, feeling a pressure to maintain the semblance of family.

Here are some suggestions to deal with this aspect of the adolescent syndrome.

1. Try to take the authoritative (not authoritarian or permissive) approach. Set limits and rules clearly and in advance, and provide the reasons for them. Do not give your children a tokenistic sense that they are being consulted, for they are enraged if they feel played with. Let your children participate, at least initially, in the formation of the rules, as long as you have ultimate veto power. For instance, swearing at your mother-in-law might, on your scale, rate at something near a beheading. A verbal threat at a sibling might receive a somewhat lesser sentence. It's best to leave room for some measure of negotiation. Stress the importance of trust. (After all, they've been lording it over you for quite some time, now; it's about time you used it to your advantage.) Talk about your nonnegotiables for which lying can have severe consequences.

2. Go for the three-strikes theory. The first serious lie requires a conversation about trust. Lie number two requires a more in-depth conversation that involves an examination of motives and more direct consequences. These conversations are a bit tricky, because they may often degenerate into blame or excessive psychological analysis. The third lie constitutes trouble, and although it may take enormous restraint not to take things personally, you're going to need, as rationally as possible, to require proof of purchase. Your kid has broken trust and must earn it back. If, after you are con-

vinced—really convinced—that trust has been restored and the damage repaired, then your son or daughter can start with a clean slate.

3. Examine your home atmosphere. Is lying an M.O.? Are your contradictions apparent? Does your child live in a do-as-I-say-not-as-I-do culture? You may lie on the phone to get out of going to a boring relative's house. You may lie to the policeman when you get stopped for cruising through a stop sign. You may lie to your business associate in a conversation over dinner, while your dutiful son or daughter is clearing the dishes. When the phone rings, you may ask your child to answer it: "If it's my lawyer (or boss or mother—you fill in the blanks), I'm not home." In short, though teenagers may not be particularly adept at lying, they are great lie detectors, and so can spot your own hypocrisy. Lying needs to be a subject worthy of discussion and a crisis needn't be the justification. There are hundreds of moral dilemmas from which to choose. Pick up the newspaper or watch the news together. Talk about integrity and the need to trust another person as a measure of character.

Cheating

Among teenagers, cheating can be viewed as a skill. Given a risk-free situation, a large majority of students claim they would cheat or help someone to cheat. Kids may use their intelligence more at the service of creative types of cheating than by actually doing the studying itself. Here are some examples: some insert narratives into programmable calculators or slip cheat sheets into Bic pens or the sleeves of calculator jackets. Kids plagiarize their papers, even from the textbook issued to them. They may alter an older sibling's paper. They copy homework from peers, prepare elaborate and often irrelevant crib sheets or suddenly become sick on test days. Books lie open under desks; the desks themselves may be cleared of temptation, but the notes may be scribbled on the arm of a letterman's jacket slung over the back of the chair or in the folds of their extraordinarily baggy pants. Some get excessive help on essays from college friends or tutors, download sophisticated reports from an anonymous web site, or contact a term-paper mail-order catalogue advertised in newspapers at the local colleges. Many do not really know what cheating is and need help understanding when and where it takes place. And here comes a real problem. A *US News and World Report* inquiry revealed "widespread cheating *[by teachers]* on standardized tests in order to make their schools and their particular classrooms look good."[2]

The same features of the adolescent syndrome apply here. Cheating can be contagious—the peer pressure in school or the amount of competition in a classroom that skews the grading curve may indeed cause an infectious spirit. Cheating may be induced by environment (in which outside entanglements may play a role) or from the host organism (a way of life passed down from generation to generation and observed in obsessive doses in early childhood). Cheating can be acute (just a one-shot, desperate attempt to pass the final exam) or chronic (an inveterate condition, a kind of modus operandi for getting through school).

Cheating is often accompanied by other symptoms, too, characteristic of adolescence, namely depression ("I'm dumb") or anxiety ("What if I fail?"). And if cheating continues, an adolescent's tenure in school can be terminal. Some kids even cheat to get caught; they may be sending a message that they need some attention.

Some cheat and justify their actions with the "me-first" approach. As one student admitted, "Hey, I'm not like hurting anyone. It's just getting ahead. What's the big deal?" Getting ahead, or looking out for number one, can easily be justified. This point of view is not dissimilar to cheating on one's taxes ("Uncle Sam won't miss it" or "Why pay for the MX missile?"), to driving at ninety miles per hour or through stop signs once the radar detector has been checked.

Some cheat to defy authority or assert rights. "It's the teacher's fault—he's too hard. How is anyone supposed to survive in here?" "He's an asshole. This class is his way of hating kids. Why doesn't the son of a bitch retire?" Loyalty to a friend's struggles or to an unwritten adolescent code of ethics comes into play here. If a friend is going down the tubes, other friends may find ways of seeing him or her through the crisis. The code may be a reaction to an unfair or unfeeling teacher.

Students may feel enormous pressure to get into college or to avoid what they perceive as unyielding and excessive parental expectations.[3] Parents may have set up a series of expectations that kids cannot possibly meet. These teens feel under the gun. Kids' papers are checked obsessively; parents conduct incessant phone conversations with teachers at school; children feel as though they are slaving away in six classes to ensure that their parents feel good about themselves. Thus, they turn their attention to elaborate schemes for survival. A colleague once reported a story in which her friend cheated throughout high school to get into an excellent law school. He was living a treadmill existence, satisfying his family's desire to have at least one success story. Everyone knew about the young man's cheating habits, but all kept quiet. The ending is anything but success, however, for this young man was not allowed to complete the bar exam because he was caught cheating within the first half hour.

Still other students cheat because they may have a learning problem; cheating becomes a kind of coping mechanism by which they can get through it all. The attraction of certain portions of text they see somewhere else is just too tempting. Without the confidence to write the paper, they rely on their judgment to pick and choose those passages that will surely impress the teacher. However, teachers soon note the discrepancy between work turned in from home and work that must be delivered to the teacher in class. The house of cards collapses.

Some schools have established both honor and discipline codes, as well as contracts that students sign—a vow not to cheat. Student discipline committees, which may discuss the possible consequences for cheating, have been established in the hope of serving as powerful deterrents. (It is important to note, here, that such committees may help to establish, in students' minds, the fear of public peer humiliation; for other students, such a notorious reputation may be just what they are looking for.) Teachers have created more assignments that help young people establish and augment their own voices, rather than appropriating the voices of others. Such assignments may center around group or independent inquiry projects, portfolios, demonstrations, or exhibitions, rather than the competitive regurgitation of facts.

Parents can help, in partnership with schools, to minimize cheating. Here are my suggestions:

1. Model integrity. The value system you want your children to adopt should be evident in your home. The theme of "getting away

with it" is a potent one in the United States. Kids need to observe your struggles, along with your honest attempts to do your daily business without cutting corners illegally.

2. Familiarize yourself, as much as possible, with your child's schoolwork. The more you know about the assignments, the more you can reinforce good models of academic integrity. Since cheating may often come from panic, try to help your child budget time and thereby reduce the temptation to copy.

3. Reinforce your child's school's expectations. Whether or not the teachers have explained the principles, parents need to fortify them. You can help your kid understand that taking someone else's ideas without accurately citing the source or paraphrasing work from others is plagiarism; copying someone else's answers on a test or homework assignment is cheating.[4] These are commonly-held notions worthy of repeating. Kids need reminders about the overt crimes, as well as the subtleties.

4. Make sure that your child understands the issues associated with cheating. Talk about the circumstances in which cheating has backfired and allow your child to ask questions, brainstorm scenarios. Do not assume that he or she fully understands the complexities of the issue. Such a discussion of the reasons why cheating is unethical and its connection both to the deterioration of self-respect, personal integrity, and community standing may not be sufficient. They need to know that the school and you take the issue of cheating seriously. For more literal thinkers, the moral issues may only sink in only once the consequences are perceived as serious. After all, grades are tantamount to money; they get you what you want. And if they're stealing money, they have to pay. Depending upon the school, they can get a zero, be removed from the course; be suspended; be placed on academic or behavioral probation; be expelled. One of the most powerful deterrents I have seen, comes when kids are aware, at the high-school level, that their teachers have to write recommendation letters for them for college. On most applications I have seen, teachers must decide whether to check a box: "Do you have any reason to doubt this child's academic integrity?"

5. Strengthen your child's faith in his or her own work. Certainly this process is not limited to questions of academic integrity, but also—and even more important—to self-reliance and

self-esteem. Schoolwork is a good place to start. Although excessive praise for a child's work is often disregarded as hollow or saccharin, kids need their efforts and achievements acknowledged. Teens crave clear and straightforward feedback in a way that respects their intelligence.

Stealing

Some kids steal simply because they don't have enough. During the Los Angeles disturbances following the verdicts of the Rodney King trial, when viewers saw youth streaming in and out of openings in broken window store-fronts to steal official sports jackets, many critics drew immediate conclusions about moral depravity. But although these actions were wrong and illegal, many teenagers were stealing bread, toilet paper, and other staples. In one inner-city classroom discussion, kids admitted to thievery, but their teacher learned later that kids sold the merchandise and gave the money to their families.

Some steal because they have too much. Some live so much in a world of possessions that more is never enough. They want it all and they want it now. They may be addicted to the idea of "stuff" as a means of justifying their existence or making friends. Some steal just to do something illegal or exciting or to get back at parents. They test the limits of society itself. If your kid starts wearing excessive gold jewelry or a fancy Walkman he didn't earn, a little internal burglar alarm should sound.

The reinforcement for stealing is quite high. After all, teenagers who crave something can use their wits to get it. They also feel a sense of omnipotence; powerless under normal conditions, they've figured out how to feel power. They become masters of their own materialistic fate.

Here are some suggestions for dealing with stealing:

1. Don't make possessions a primary part of your family: I have seen the connection between families who adore things and kids who like to steal them. Parents have said, "Fred, we've provided everything the kid could possibly need. Why does he want to steal?" We live in a society where the credo "Life, liberty, and the pursuit of happiness" is increasingly translated into "the pursuit of

stuff." Try to de-emphasize the exaltation of things. Try to highlight notions of giving. The teenagers I see sincerely involved with projects involving food distribution to the homeless or clothing drives for the Good Will or the Salvation Army are not, generally, the ones who steal. Try to get your family involved in such service.

2. The "high" that kids get from ripping things off needs to be accompanied by a serious "low." I believe in logical consequences connected to the crime. If your son has stolen something from a mall, for instance, the punishment needs to be reasonable, but clear and substantial. You might restrict him from going back to the mall for a very long period of time and return the item or earn the money to pay for it, requiring him to apologize to and compensate the vendor for the damages. If stealing recurs, it is time to consider serious consequences that will make a lasting impression. There needs to be absolute clarity here; a pattern of behavior that may approximate an addiction must be stopped.

3. Avoid temptation. Kids often steal from you. Some kids take their first chance at the easiest opportunity—your purse or wallet. One other primary source of theft is car keys; they're stealing a joyride. Don't make your keys easily available. If stealing occurs, kids need to earn your trust back, and if they get an allowance, they must relinquish it until they've paid back the debt.

4. Teach teenagers a connection to something larger than themselves: Stealing can indicate that something is missing; there may be a little hole inside that a young person is trying to fill with things. Although therapy may assist teenagers in discovering the features and dynamics of that hole, kids also need opportunities to transcend the temptations by feeling a sense of belonging that substitutes a narcissistic high with a magnanimous spirit.

American life makes teaching these lessons quite difficult. The focus on getting ahead at all costs seems to prevail. Very few models of exemplary behavior exist, nor is there a particularly heavy emphasis on those qualities of character that would validate the resistance to stealing as an exemplary and commendable quality. Until and unless we redefine success in more productive and ethical ways, young people are going to look around them, take note, and act accordingly.

7
Crossing the Line
When Behaviors Go Too Far and Your Child Is at Risk

"It was so quiet, one of the killers would later say,
you could almost hear the sound of ice rattling in cocktail shakers
in the homes way down the canyon."
—Vincent Bugliosi, Helter Skelter

When your children were young, you knew them. When they become adolescents, you only know *about* them. Perhaps they won't let you know them; perhaps you are unable to know them. They may withdraw from you and lie in the fetal position in the living room or they may act out and scream at the slightest provocation; you, alas, are left guessing the reasons why. It makes seeing difficult, yet seeing is half the battle.

Adolescence is confusing because teenagers stretch the bounds of normalcy. Their experimentations, those masks they try on, the veracity of what they say—they all change. We may hear their rage, but we may not hear other, more important voices. They may often feel out of control or depressed or unsure of their own identity. They live a life of transitions, many of which they experience as traumatic. They cannot tie a particular mood to a precipitating event; they're bummed and they can't figure out why, other than to spew forth a set of global notions that their lives are going to hell or that their friends are stuck up. They may want to deaden their cluttered feelings, or they may want to feel something else, desperately—even greater depression and apocalypse, just for the drama and intrigue of it. Or perhaps they want to feel it all—manic largesse, sexual ecstasy, total coolness.

They are influenced profoundly by the world around them. No less intelligent than generations before them, teenagers are forced to absorb a daily barrage of images and experiences from which most of us, as teens, were protected. A political science professor writes: "The young, with their keen noses for hypocrisy, are in fact adept readers—but not of books. They are society-smart rather than school-smart, and what they read so acutely are the social signals emanating from the world in which they will have to make a living."[1] We must reevaluate the assumption that being "at risk" applies to a small group of wayward youth who come from deprived or wayward families. Inflammatory as it sounds, the syndrome of adolescence can make any child susceptible to risk.

Depression

Many principals have observed an increasing number of depressed teens who seem to cross the line into territory that requires additional professional assistance. Although teachers and parents may *expect* adolescents to be depressed (after all, adolescence is often identified with storm and stress), some teens succumb to their dark side. One indication may be the difficulty a child may have in bouncing back from a disappointment. If, for instance, a poor grade continues to erode self-respect long after its effects should have worn off, and if little shocks and injustices and disappointments continue to turn your child into a doormat, you may want to take a closer look.[2]

I am certain, however, that whether an incident begins depression or depression begins an incident, adolescent depression leads to other symptoms. It's a matter of degree. Kids get depressed when their image of themselves does not live up to the standard—when they fail socially or physically or academically. They get depressed when they feel out of control. They get depressed if they live in a depressed family. They get depressed if they live with excessively authoritarian or permissive parents. They are unable to eat or they eat too much; they are tired because they are unable to sleep or they sleep too much; they are unable to cry or they cry too much; they are unusually silent and blank or they can be hostile; they lose interest in those activities they once enjoyed; they cannot get the energy to consider schoolwork of any value. They spend a great deal of time berating themselves and convincing themselves that they are worthless; they do not think the future holds any promise; they may want to run away and hide or even take their own lives.

At moments of crisis or serious depression, it may be impossible to gain a sense of self, for they may not have the necessary tools to cope; the contradictions between the clarity of childhood—now unwelcome—and the uncertainty of adulthood loom large. Some may go too far because they are simply unsure where the limits are. The syndrome of adolescence may feel like a full-blown disease. You may have long ago given up on curing it; it may feel impossible to manage. It may also be difficult to determine when the elastic of adolescence is merely stretching those bounds of normalcy, or when it is truly frayed at the edges. It is a time when one must make a decision by answering the question: Has my child just crossed the line? And if you think the answer is yes, the moment then comes to fine-tune intuition, to put aside self-interest, to notice certain cries for help. Now is the time to move past bitterness and past memory, to assert adulthood and inner courage. Professional (and even psychiatric) intervention must be put in place; safety is everything, all bets are off, and nothing else matters.[3]

Drugs

Experimentation with drugs and alcohol is almost an inevitability among teenagers.[4] However true, such a statement is disconcerting because it is your obligation, as parents, to pay attention, even when you feel that the odds are against you, to note the onset of certain behaviors and to try to recognize patterns. Ultimately, here, you're the one who will have to gauge whether or not what you are sensing is experimental or exponential. It's not easy. I'll try to help.

A great deal is written about the famous sex talk, yet conversations between parents and their teenagers about drugs and alcohol are less evident. Perhaps this is the case because the hypocrisy quotient may be so high. After all, our generation made drug use popular. We justified it in the name of love. Remember "Lucy in the Sky with Diamonds"? Drug and alcohol abuse never seemed anywhere near as pressing a problem as nuclear power or the War in Vietnam.

But times have changed. Back then we didn't know about crack or crystal meth or ecstasy. We didn't have to worry about peddlers selling tattoos, laced with acid, to little kids enamored of the cute pictures of Disney characters or Bart Simpson or butterflies and clowns. Unregulated drugs can be found in abundance at "raves," unchaperoned parties held in isolated downtown warehouses.[5] Ritalin has become a street drug. (I sat in a meeting of drug-treatment counselors who claim that some teens call a peer with A.D.D. "Another Drug Dealer.") Although drugs may once have been associated with love and mind-expansion, they are now more often associated with violence, self-destruction, and abuse.

The same motivation to "escape" pressures are there, too, but teenage life is more complex. And teens are looking for bigger and bigger highs. Drinking to get tipsy has always been a part of teenage life; binge drinking has skyrocketed. Some adolescents these days say it is impossible to enjoy a party without getting loaded. Although they think drugs and alcohol can serve as an expanding experience, the last thing that kids need is an expansion of the traumas and pressures they experience and the need to "best" their last experience. Furthermore, designer drugs, like ecstasy, are becoming increasingly popular, but no one knows their long-term effects. Young people are self-medicating the symptoms of the adolescent syndrome, yet, by doing so, make their condition more intense. The stronger the case of adolescence, the greater the need for the "relief." Unfortunately, this is when adolescence can be terminal.

All this takes place, of course, in a user society. The consumer culture in which teenagers live gives them tacit permission to take, to consume, to exploit, to horde. It's our way of coping with depression and anxiety, loneliness and fear, jealousy and emptiness. Drug fashions are a booming business. Beavis and Butthead sniff paint thinner and grunt. Beer commercials are most often associated with sports or sexual prowess or slick cars, a destructive connection we've all known for years. All this complete with public service announcements with images of brains, like eggs, that can get fried through dope use.

Most disconcerting of all is the thin white line between use and abuse. In short, American society serves as an incessant and ubiquitous outside pathogen for the syndrome of adolescence. And it can be addictive.

Here are the numbers:

- 42.9 percent of high school seniors report having used an illicit drug at least once in their lives.[6]
- The leading cause of death among teens is alcohol-related traffic accidents.[7]
- 35 percent of high school seniors have had five or more drinks in a row in the past two weeks.[8]
- In 1993, 50 percent of senior high-school students witnessed classmates drunk during school.[9]
- There is a geometric rise in statistics of young people who have sniffed dangerous inhalants, such as gasoline, nail-polish remover, and Lysol.[10]
- LSD has been called "the fastest growing drug of abuse among people under age 20."[11]
- Since 1992, although teens' level of resistance to hard drugs has remained steady, marijuana use (which is now much more potent than a generation ago) is on the rise.[12]
- An extensive study has revealed that only one-third of high-school students surveyed have acknowledged having had conversations with their parents about drugs.[13]

Clearly, no one's immune. (But you knew that already.)

Let's take a closer look at some of the symptoms of drug use that may signal that your child has crossed the line.

Warning Signs

- problems in school: absenteeism, grades taking a dramatic drop or a slide
- sudden changes in friendships
- deteriorating relationships all around, especially with family members
- stealing and lying (or evasiveness)
- red or inflamed eyes, sore throat, dry cough, rash around mouth: excessive use of mouthwash, dark sunglasses, eye drops
- intense nervousness
- slurred or dramatically loud and/or fast speech
- wild mood swings, hostility, or abusive behavior

- major changes in eating or sleeping patterns
- loss of interest in favorite activities, hobbies, sports
- unusually hard to arouse in the morning
- parental use of drugs
- antisocial behavior
- alienation, rebelliousness
- concerns registered by your friends or your child's friends
- peers who use drugs.[14]

Teens using drugs are great at avoiding the consequences of their actions. They may say, "What's the problem? My grades are up and I'm just partying on the weekend. So what? Give it a rest!" Let's put aside the business about lost brain cells but rather report more intangible factors. Kids who smoke dope consistently think they sound insightful, but they're just free-associating words and images, extemporizing little riffs of nothingness; they're also boring. They exhibit a weird (and in some cases, delayed) sense of timing, though they think their timing is superb. Smoking dope is like any other addiction in society—sex, drugs, shopping, running. When you get stoned, you're liberated by the feeling, although you end up trapped by the craving.

They think they are connecting with the world, but because stimulus is being registered differently, they are actually disconnecting themselves from meaningful relationships and from each other. For the most part, they end up getting drunk or stoned to be out of it, to *lose* connection. A young woman in one school reported to her health counselor: "When my boyfriend and I start to fight, we just smoke a joint, then the fight just goes away." Fighting can be problematic, but this couple has lost its ability to confront their problems without a crutch. In fact, kids who use drugs in this way are simply copping out on life's project to grow up naturally, however much pain may be involved. This disconnection is particularly harmful, because kids need social interaction to learn about themselves and how to function effectively in the world. Their emotional development is retarded. They cannot achieve their developmental tasks if they're grooving on Pluto.

They become less and less ambitious and forward looking. I am particularly concerned about this last factor, because the pressures on adolescence are greater than they were in earlier generations.

Nothing's worse than exacerbating a self-defeating spirit with an illegal substance.

They can get hurt—emotionally and physically. And because kids don't even know when they've lost their judgment, they cannot explain their actions. Research has revealed correlations between drug abuse and sexually transmitted diseases. Women counselors have repeatedly reported connections between getting drunk or stoned and having sex. Unprotected or not, young women always regret it later; connections are made between drug abuse and psychiatric disorders, ranging from deficits in attention to dependency to psychosis; connections are made between drug abuse and violence. The child who may be experiencing "a little problem" with drugs may also find himself acting desperately. In short, kids who are stoned can consistently and easily lose touch with reality, get laid in the back seat, and cause car accidents.

The jury is still out on marijuana's long-term effects, but we do know that THC (tetrahydrocannabinol, the psychoactive ingredient of marijuana), is up to twenty times more potent now than it was twenty years ago and stays in the system for a while. We know that pot intrudes upon short-term memory; scientists are exploring its effects on hormonal changes. No longer reduced to a few hits, some teens now "roll giant joints by slicing open cigars—Blunts, White Owls, or Dutch Masters—replacing the tobacco with pot."[15]

Furthermore, a teenager is much more susceptible to alcohol addiction than an adult. Occasional marijuana toking or drinking does not a drug addict make, but after an episode is over, the residual effects are there. The residual effects are there emotionally, too, if parents and schools don't treat the subject and the students with respect.

Smoking

For the teens on the street corner, lung cancer is an abstraction, regardless of the alarming facts on which they were tested in health class. The Centers for Disease Control have noted a steady rise in teen smoking, especially among young women, despite antismoking campaigns. "3,000 young people become regular smokers every day. More shocking is the fact that 70 percent of high school seniors who smoked one to five cigarettes a day were still smoking five years later. Young people who have smoked as few as 100 cigarettes report they would like to quit, but can't, and 70 percent regret the decision to start."[16]

For many, a cigarette is a rite of passage, a way into social acceptance, an initiation into adulthood, a powerful incentive. To hide it, they tamper with smoke detectors, leave the windows open, go out for evening walks, consume mints. Vendors don't ask for identification; the movies associate smoking with supreme coolness; teens love the idea of a cigarette break; they react in ways opposite to antismoking campaigns, yet are attracted to the aggressive advertising for cigarettes targeting youth. In short, the adolescent syndrome defies reason.

And reasons there are. Kids need to know that, besides the black lungs and yellow teeth caused by cigarette smoking, the recipe for a cigarette includes ammonia, arsenic butane, carbon monoxide, DDT, lead, formaldehyde, methoprene (an insecticide), methyl isocyanate (the cause of deaths in Bhopal), napthalene (the ingredient in mothballs), and polonium (a cancer-causing radioactive element).[17]

Along with the facts, teenagers need to create settings where not smoking is the social norm; they need role models who do not condescend to them, but who take their smoking problem seriously. Research suggests that peer-resistance training may help some teens find the strength to withstand or avoid the social pressure to smoke. For others, the facts may speak powerfully for themselves. Some may quit when their friends do or when they alienate the very peers with whom they smoked to bond. As a parent, you need to determine where you stand on the issue. Because cigarettes are often gateway drugs, I believe you should take a strong stand and stay consistent with your consequences. If you catch your child smoking, try to work out a reasonable and responsible system—perhaps using incentives—in which he or she can stop. Keep brochures of smoking facts lying around. Check with your school about their antismoking program.

Parenting and Drugs

Let me demystify the idea that kids who take drugs look the part: Fashion, hair-length, and affect—though clues—should not be relied upon as accurate or consistent correlaries to drug use. Seemingly "perfect" families are nonetheless vulnerable to the influence of drugs, because peer culture is so dominant. Counselors in schools everywhere report the shock on parents' faces when they inform the family of a drug problem. The parents talk about how their son or daughter is a model student—good grades and extracurricular activities and nice manners. Those "perfect" kids may, in fact, lead a dual life. In one particularly troubling development, top, clean-cut students in one high school were discovered to have taken large doses of drugs from their grandparents' medicine cabinets—treatment of memory loss from Alzheimer's. These students simply wanted to do well on their final exams. And then there are the ones who may look like "druggies" but who may, in fact, just be trying on the masks of adolescence and may eschew drug use entirely.

In my experience, the biggest indicators related to drug abuse occur when young people exhibit a series of other high-risk behaviors, like the serious depression I described earlier. The family itself may be undergoing stress: financial hardship, divorce or parent absenteeism, or the death of a parent or a close relative. As a result, a teenager may be unusually morose or distant, evasive or hostile. Although there is no one-to-one correlation between stress and drug use, the conditions are ripe.

Children who live with a parent who is, or who has been, drug or alcohol dependent may take the plunge into a pool of vodka, despite all their best efforts to stay away from the diving board. A parent once told me that her own sobriety was a serious issue in the family, and so she took her son, at eight years old, to Alcoholics Anonymous meetings. Although her intentions were good, it backfired. He listened there to the pain that accompanies alcohol dependency; he learned that some people drink to forget their problems. When he became thirteen, that is exactly what he did. The parents were appalled, because they exclaimed, "Alcohol? Impossible! We worked too hard for this to happen!"

A number of factors are revealed in this story. First, families need to be aware of the special vulnerabilities with which children of alcoholics need to contend. Research has yet to establish conclusive evidence correlating parent alcoholism with child alcoholism, but the propensity is apparent to many of us in the helping professions that see whole families. Second, their child's choices may, in fact, reflect a reaction against the intensity of his parents' insistent efforts at drug education. If they're so against it, their son might have thought, let me see what made it so attractive in the first place. If the tension in the family was high, he may even have been attracted to drug use as a form of punishment for his parents or as a confirmation of his sense of worthlessness. The reasons are manifold.

Although it may be close to impossible to prevent drug and alcohol use, the least you can do is set limits, be involved, and work toward maximizing the odds.

1. Be prepared to deal with the inevitable question: "Did you smoke dope when you were a kid?" The answer depends upon the degree to which being explicit is going to help. If you think your child is looking for permission to get blasted, then I would not go into the graphic details. Rather, I'd respond with: "I experimented." You may be required to fess up. If your child wants a conversation, you might want to tread lightly and try to ask those open-ended questions that might reveal to you the degree and intensity of interest, without becoming too suspiciously circumspect. You might ask: "What's making you ask this now?" The key is to blend authenticity and the truth in such a way that both the child's and your integrity is intact.

2. Take a stand, but be reasonable and clear. This is truly an authoritative position. Fuzziness can confuse kids at a time when they need clarity the most. The authoritative parent listens carefully but also sets the limits. It is essential that you understand the pressures your teenager feels. In the end, you must be clear about drug use as wrong not only because it is illegal, but also because it can be harmful emotionally and physically, and because drug users don't know when they become drug abusers. It is important to validate your teenager's sense of judgment, but also to step in, if need be, to make sure that good judgment prevails.

The authoritarian parent may not allow a teenager to go out at all, or may punish without knowing the facts. Such a position leaves no room to breathe and may, in fact, backfire, for kids are just as likely to punish their parents for their "insensitivity." When teenagers feel as though they are living in the same house as a parent's vigilante drug war, the troops invariably will go underground.

The permissive parent may see drug use as a natural part of growing up. Some may even condone its use, provided that it is in a controlled setting. They tell the child, "If you're going to experiment, do it in my house." Such a "sensitive" approach presupposes a kind of parental omnipotence that implies that your son or daughter will limit experimentation to your home. Most likely, however, your son or daughter will partake of the offerings at your house *and also* indulge in the forbidden fruit at some back alley or at another friend's house. Although they won't admit it, these same teens crave rules. They claim: "My parents are never around; they don't really care." These words may sound great to other teenagers, who may think that their friend's parents trust their child implicitly, but it doesn't last long.

3. Note your own inconsistencies. Do you share prescriptions with friends? When friends come over, do you offer them a drink as they're slipping off their coat? Do you joke about drugs or about drunkenness? Are there lots of "mother's little helpers" around? Do you start off your diets with pills? Is drinking or a little pill a way you comfort yourself?

4. Try to keep them off the streets. This rule still applies to the current generation. Numerous correlations have been made between lack of supervision and a marked increase in drug abuse and adolescent depression.[18] Many youth groups, sports programs, and clubs extend supervision to hours beyond the school day.

5. Talk about the facts. The *Just Say No* program may work for elementary school kids, who are quick to say that drugs are "dumb." But teenagers generally see such catch-phrases as patronizing and ineffective. In responding to such programs at the high-school level, students sarcastically tell me, "Oh yes, gee, I forgot. I'm just supposed to say 'no.' The *Scared Straight* program has immediate results; students avoid drugs *that day*. However, like speeding tickets, such programs do not reside in memory. They focus on the legal issues and on basket-cases. The invulnerability syndrome kicks in here; adolescents do not think something of that nature can happen to them.

6. Teenagers need information about drugs in practical terms. You, too, need the same information. It is better to speak intelligently and specifically—rather than categorically—about drugs. The truth is that things really *don't* go better with coke. You should know about uppers and downers and about the current names for drugs and their effects. Local agencies and the library have excellent pamphlets. The national drug help line is excellent as well: (800) 662-HELP.

7. Do what you can to support motivation. Certainly idleness can lead to trouble. Kids need to be admired for their accomplishments. If they're interested in something reasonable, support it. Don't do backflips; just ask them to elaborate on their new passions, and show an interest. I have found that, in school, a noncritical attitude toward a teenager's avocation can go a long way.[19]

8. Pay attention to school work. They may not show it to you, but you can, at the very least, ask about it. If you're worried, talk to the school. Your child may tell you that the homework was completed at school, and they may be right. However true this may be, it is not so all the time; there's plenty of homework in most schools to keep kids occupied. Searching through their book bag will only get you into trouble. A more realistic approach is to ask about the studies, to offer help, to attend open houses, to find out about the curriculum, and to check in occasionally with teachers. Show interest and support for school activities as well.

9. Pay attention to the peer group. The friends may look like they're doing it, but don't jump to any conclusions—yet. Their dress may only be a style. Particularly problematic is the sensitivity issue. If you infringe too much on your child's privacy, and with incessant regularity, you may end up engendering a great deal of passive resistance. However, there may be times when Just Say No should serve as your maxim. "No, you can't go to that party. There's no one there to supervise it." It may feel like war: "But all the kids will be there; I'm the only one staying home. You are single-handedly destroying my social life!" Your child may secretly thank you for your clarity, by relieving him/herself of the responsibility and tension for having to make the decision. Your teenager can then say to his or her friends, "My mom (or dad) is an asshole, and they won't let me go." Inside, your child may be relieved because he or she may be worried about the risk involved, and now has an excuse to

resist peer pressure. They want limits, even when they're stretching and bashing them.

10. If you know a party is going on someplace other than your home this Saturday night, call the parents. Find out if it is being supervised, and if it is, find out the specifics. By an older brother? Will the parents be there in the house or near by? Some parents are at home, but stay in another room or upstairs and never check out the action, on occasion, to see what is going on. Parents must network with each other. Legal cases have been brought forth that place liability squarely on the shoulders of parents, should there be an accident resulting from an unsupervised party where alcohol or drugs had been present. If you are not satisfied with the degree of responsible adult presence where your child wants to go, you need to make an unpopular decision. Your kid may say, "Why the @!*?*&!," and blame you and tell you that you are the only one who has been so mean, but your priority is safety, first and foremost. It is true that, though you can place your child in a plastic bubble with purified air, she'll still find a way to sneak a cigarette. It is also true that you can take the necessary steps to avoid trouble before it starts. If a party is planned for your place, be there and around. Don't serve alcohol—it's illegal under the age of 21. Notify the parents of a child you see who arrives at the party under the influence.

11. Set up a designated driver arrangement. At the risk of appearing contradictory ("Don't you dare drink; if you do, don't drive."), do whatever you can to help your child get home safely. Local chapters of organizations like SADD and MADD and Friday Night Live can provide the literature you need and often include contracts kids sign, as well as shuttle services.

12. Treat your child as a separate and unique individual. Don't compare him/her with a sibling or a friend. If you wish to set a standard this way, it will haunt you. Teenagers become enraged or sullen when they hear that their older brother or sister or a friend didn't get into the same kind of trouble, or dressed more appropriately, or treats his or her parents with greater respect. They end up feeling put down and not good enough. This sense of comparison tends to weave its way into conversations about drug use.

13. Talk with your child about feelings and about peer pressure. Such conversations can easily degenerate into lectures or shouting

matches, but kids do want to know what you think. They want to tell you about their experiences, to make mention of their risks. They crave a setting in which they can discuss life outside of the home—at school, at their hang-outs, on the street. Many are not forthcoming at all, but if the setting is right, they may drop a few hints which, if delicately handled, can result in a meaningful conversation. An open door can mean a way out of solitary confinement. Assertion is not an inborn trait, but a characteristic learned and nurtured. Teenagers often tell me that, for a variety of reasons, they would like noncondescending tutoring on refusal skills.

14. If you suspect drug use, it's time to break rules you may have established about privacy. I'm not suggesting that you rally a paranoid search party, but I would take note. Are there drinking straws cut up into small pieces in the trash? Little spoons? Parts of screens you have been missing? Paper bags or zip-lock bags with spray paint, Scotch Guard, Pam, Liquid Paper? Are you bowled over by an intense smell of room freshener as you push open the door to your child's room? Bongs can be made out of crushed Coke cans with holes poked in them, toilet-paper rolls with tin foil, even out of tampons or tire gauges. If you suspect inhalants, run—don't walk—to get medical help. We are talking about the potential for nerve and or brain damage here. There is no time for "strategizing."[20]

15. If you sense real trouble, find a neutral party and talk about your kid. Don't hide your intuition behind a cloak of appropriateness. Talk with other parents to get some kind of reality check. Check in with the pediatrician or the school counselor or the clergy. Tell the truth and ask for honest feedback. When your teenager is exhibiting multiple symptoms of adolescence, you may need a reality check. Parent support groups provide concrete information and emotional reinforcements.

16. When your intuition is strong enough, confront your child. I don't care how much flak you get; your conscience may be clear. Many years ago, a young man, Eric, walked in my office to inform me, a few years after he had graduated, that his life had fallen apart, that he had come close to being arrested, and had spent many weeks in a residential drug-treatment program. I was humbled and squirmed as he described, in detail, the ways in which his parents and his teachers never acted on their suspicions. His grades were

great; he had a wonderful and engaging sense of humor and great intelligence. He was the star of the school play and always participated in class discussions, but his decline into drug use became increasingly apparent. He was absent a great deal and he always had a runny nose. He began to wear sunglasses to school even on cloudy days. But he was *successful,* and the stereotypes of the drug addict—as one who froths at the mouth—occluded our vision. Our window onto Eric was foggy. And so was he. He had begun to lose his ability to make and sustain connections with friends. When he spoke with me that day in the office, he looked me in the eye and said, "Why didn't you guys nail me? What were you afraid of? I could have died!" Although we may make unjust accusations from time to time, my advice is this: better safe than sorry.

17. Never confront your child when he/she is high. The conversation can turn inflammatory or be easily misinterpreted. Go for safety. "Let's talk in the morning" is more helpful than the third degree once he or she stumbles in the front door.

18. Fight your own natural impulse to deny the truth. It may be true that your child's experimentation rests there and does not take on the qualities of a chronic condition. However, information may come your way via your child's peers or their parents. Investigate their claims. Do not let your own vulnerabilities, past experience, or biases about your child prevent you from facing a possible medical or psychological emergency. Treat possible alcoholism as an illness; however, in so doing, do not protect your child from the harsh consequences of inappropriate behavior and its effect on others. To do so is to enable destructive behaviors.

19. Involve your family. Even if you think the problem rests solely with your child, the family becomes an integral part of the solution. If drug use is obvious, I strongly suggest entering a counseling program that will help determine the degree of adolescence in the home, help set up parameters to let each member of the family be heard, and set forth a course of action.

• • •

It is particularly frustrating to witness an intelligent young man's or woman's descent into drugs. He or she may know both the effects and the consequences of drug use and ignore them completely because the moment and the opportunity looks appealing. In conversations with the young people I have caught, I have asked: "Why did you do it?" The answer is often: "I don't know, I wasn't thinking."

All the more reason that drug education must reflect a partnership between school and home, coupled with enough vigilance to help block that descent. Though it may, for both of us, feel like the information we provide has gone in one ear and emerges as smoke out of the other, our voices are, for the most part, still there. We may very well have implanted a kind of script that, indeed, they may need to rely upon when we're not around.

One father told me, "before my son goes out the door on a Saturday night, I always say, 'Remember, I trust you.'" But it is not solely a matter of mere hope on late nights. You must rely on your own powers of observation and intuition. And talk with your child.

Suicide

First, some more numbers:

- Over one-hundred thousand suicide attempts are reported among youth, each year. Approximately six thousand attempts are successful.
- Girls are three to four times more likely to attempt suicide than boys. The boys are four times more likely to succeed.[21]
- Approximately seventy percent of successful suicides are from white males, although rates for black males are rising.[22]
- The suicide rate among adolescents has nearly tripled in the past thirty years.[23]
- The death rate from suicide among teens has surpassed that of cancer. It is the only age group in the country in which the death rate is rising.[24]

Some psychologists call thoughts of ending it all "terminal thinking." It's in teenage music and in teen magazines. English teachers stay up nights rereading and obsessing over their students' dark poetry in English. Suicide knows no bounds in terms of race, creed, color, or economic status. It's downtown in the projects, and its in the "burbs." It hits the dropouts who feel as though they have no future, and it hits the valedictorians, whose future seems bright. It affects the ones who don't seem to have a will, and those who fall apart at the slightest blemish to a perfect record.

Many kids think about it, and not just in flippant and silly conversations on the phone: "the way he looked at me, I thought I was going to kill myself." It's much more serious than that, more like: "Everybody would be better off if I were dead." Depression is a fact of life in teenagers, and it requires close attention. Some slip imperceptibly into a dark mental chasm, without a flashlight to help them find the exit signs. They fantasize about who will come to the funeral, as if they would then be in a position to watch it on closed-circuit television. In fact, some psychologists report that the attraction to suicide may not even include the notion that it is final. They may not be able to see that this is a permanent solution to a temporary feeling. And, because it only takes one successful attempt, suicide, like drugs, is an issue that must force parents to get past their own self-absorption.

"We once thought that 'anxious perfectionistic kids' were at particular risk. Now, however, the most vulnerable group appears to be marginal kids with impulse, mood, or conduct problems—problems significant and long-standing enough to be considered psychiatric in nature."[25] These may be kids with either an acute and/or malignant case of adolescence. Although many suicidal kids suffer from social or emotional difficulties, mental illness is not the only necessary precondition. A very depressed kid, for example, who may have just experienced a great loss (of a friend, of self-esteem, of a loved one or lover, for example) may turn around and surprise us all.

The correlations continue. The more violent the means chosen, the better the chances for success. A bullet is forever. Connections are also made between alcohol and successful attempts; drinking can so skew one's thinking that suicide seems a reasonable alternative to rid themselves of their immediate and harrowing pain. Statistical connections have been made between a teenager's suicide attempt and attempts made by other family members; here, suicide may be contagious. A family history might reveal a genetic link, for the suicide of a biological family member increases the odds for those who follow. A suicidal teen may live in a family unraveling at the seams. Some teens are suicidal because they must face problems in their own families that range from depression, to alcoholism, to domestic violence or sexual abuse.

Gay youth are two to three times more likely to attempt suicide than other young people. An estimated twenty-five percent of young gay males are forced to leave home because of conflicts over their sexual identity.[26] Gay teens have a dual task—to develop as individuals and also to establish a sexual identity, yet the culture does not leave room for this growth. Homosexuality in itself does not lend itself to suicide; however, more likely, homosexual teens experience enormous feelings of abandonment and hate that has driven some to seek desperate solutions. The pain is extraordinary. An estimated thirty percent of all successful suicide attempts come from gay youth, mostly from boys. For gay teenagers, it's not AIDS but suicide that is the leading cause of death.

Warning Signs

- depression (number one)
- a traumatic response to a recent loss
- unreasonable anger and self-hate
- disturbed sleeping patterns—too much or not enough
- jokes or statements about death and/or suicide sustained over time
- changed eating and grooming habits
- drug and alcohol abuse
- giving away of prized possessions
- impaired concentration
- frequent complaints of illness
- marked downturn in academic performance and school attendance
- frequent panic about, and inability to bounce back from, life's natural setbacks

Parenting and Suicide

I have seen and read about too many emergency-room stomach-pumping procedures to be able to take suicide attempts lightly. Book after book and article after article indicate the importance of looking for the warning signs. Many authors suggest that, in conversations with panicked teenagers, we ask for more and more specific information, without revealing our own panic. "What happened that made you feel that you had to end your life?" "Have you thought about how you would kill yourself?" It is important, in this regard, to be able to describe these conversations in detail to a professional, and decide when to break confidentiality. The rule of thumb is this: it is better to inform authorities and get professional advice (first in private) than to keep a secret that, though your intentions were good, may result in a fatality.

Suicidal teens are crying out for help. Most want to be stopped, but are feeling out of control. Some leave clues so that they can be discovered, instead of facing the embarrassment of an open confession. Smart teachers have noticed the Tylenol bottle sticking out of the backpack of a particularly depressed teenager. It is a primary adult responsibility to coach them away from the precipice and to arrange for a large cushion below.

If your child is crying out for this degree of help, come to his or her aid. Make the appointment, because teenagers may be too lethargic and incapacitated to make any moves on their own. Communicate with your child's school to describe or learn about any precipitating events. Your child's school also has a right to know what is going on at home. Direct intervention may be critical. Therapy will be necessary—for the individual and—most likely—for the entire family. Perhaps psychotropic drugs may need to be prescribed or hospitalization required.

If the situation requires more immediate attention, there are three direct forms of action: (1) call a suicide or crisis hot line (every major city has one); (2) go to a hospital nearby and make sure your family doctor is notified; (3) call 911.

What shall we do in the long run? As a principal, I will invariably land on the side of education. Students need to talk about suicide. They need to know the facts. They also need to be enlisted in a campaign to save each other's lives. They need to be engaged in activities and conversations that test some beliefs they hold strongly, the strongest of which is adolescent loyalty. Ask any group of teenagers if they know of someone who is thinking seriously about killing him/herself, and an alarming number of hands will go up. If adolescents are feeling alienated from their parents and other adults, they're going to talk with each other. Many of them will tell each other secrets that can become fatally permanent. They don't want that on their conscience, but neither do they want to betray a friend. Young people need to hear that there is a time and a place to betray confidences, for the sake of health.

Young people need to be trained in crisis intervention, and they need to be aware of the resources out there. Peer counseling programs have been effective in using teenagers to talk with teenagers. Although there is no substitute for professional intervention by doctors and psychologists, teenagers who take on the responsibility can help other teens through the rough periods and encourage their peers to reach out for help.

Eating Disorders

The body is everything. Teenagers think that some of their parts were sold to them separately from a bin of mix and match items at the ninety-nine cent store. They are immersed in an elaborate system of self-examination. It's vanity, vanity, vanity. Supported by the advertising world, thin is in. And for the most part, the obsession with thinness begins in the seventh grade, or earlier.

Some teenagers don't eat to stay thin; others don't eat enough to eat a lot later. They diet without a doctor's permission. Some fast or induce vomiting or use diet pills or diuretics. Statistics indicate that boys are engaged in this behavior, but girls take the cake (of course, I mean this sarcastically) on this one. In short, there is a correlation between fat and self-esteem, and girls are the greatest victims, tenfold over boys. Anorexia nervosa is a disease that operates alongside of the syndrome of adolescence.

Here are the ugly details. The symptoms of anorexia are similar to those of starvation, plain and simple. Doctors report that anorexia complicates the normal functioning of the pituitary and the thyroid glands, such that growth is slowed. Menstrual functioning is disturbed. A child who loses 25 percent of his or her body weight may experience diminished thinking abilities. Pulse rate and blood pressure drops. A third of anorexics are deficient in iron. Skin can yellow and hair can turn brittle, even fall out. Some cannot get goose bumps. Difficulties arise with cardiac arrhythmia and anemia. Some may need hospitalization to ensure weight gain; others may have a medical emergency requiring immediate attention. Between ten and fifteen percent of anorexics die.

Heart disease can develop as a result of using vomit-inducers, such as Ipecac. Bulimics become constipated. The enamel of their teeth wears away; they're subject to gastric rupture, esophagitis, and osteoporosis. Vomiting can create a hormone imbalance that produces muscle cramps and an irregular heartbeat.

For a while, researchers thought that eating disorders of this sort were concentrated mostly among white, middle-class teenage girls; however, recent evidence challenges those assumptions, finding the problem to transcend race and class.[27] At school, anorexics avoid the vending machines and drink Diet Cokes all day. The teen magazines they leave behind at lunch on the bench include feature articles on the devastating features and consequences of the disease, but, alas, the kids aren't reading that article; they're looking at the ads of anorexic-look-alikes modeling cool clothes. Many are high achievers. "Ballet dancers, gymnasts, figure skaters, runners, swimmers, and divers are most at risk."[28]

It's a psychological problem that becomes a physical problem. Anorexics lack an accurate perception of their bodies. The one picture they form is way out of whack; they always think they're fat, and they always think they're losing the battle to stay thin.

They often feel out of control. Anorexics work obsessively to gain control over their lives by being in charge of something no one can take away from them—the distance between hand and mouth. They may therefore also engage in obsessive-compulsive rituals that keep them from thinking.

They want to be independent, but they are slavishly dependent upon external acknowledgment. A boyfriend, a parent, a doctor, a friend may mention to a young girl that she is getting a bit round. Mix that with something emotionally stressful, like separating from parents or the sense that a possible love connection may be slipping away, and you've got the recipe for an extremely diet dinner.

They constantly feel imperfect, but may be consumed with perfectionism. They work toward the elation they believe will come from looking like Miss American Teen, but they often feel depressed because they're convinced they're far from this ideal.

They may be good at school, achieving well to keep parents satisfied and at a distance. They do their work, yet may seem unapproachable. At home, though they won't eat, they'd rather do the cooking. I have listened to anorexics explain how they can cut up a carrot into tiny, even slices to create the impression that they're preparing a big meal.

Not all anorexics exhibit these behaviors. Again, it is all a matter of degree and intensity. Nevertheless, these are some of the features worth noting. Psychological research on the families of anorexics reveals a number of complicated dynamics. Some families of anorexics include another family member who is under stress, making consistent care unwieldy. Some families have significant secrets, but the truth is always broiling under the surface.[29] For example, a family may have a home environment that is so controlling that the only thing the child can control is eating. Many anorexics are the youngest, who may be not be allowed to develop an independent personality, or who have to be a person they are not. Some are not allowed to grow up. Others are subtly turned into surrogate wives or companions for the father, or a best friend or a confidant for the mother, a child who is privy to mom's inner thoughts. Some families turn the anorexic into the primary caregiver, in which the roles of nurturer are reversed.[30]

That's a thumbnail sketch of research—medical and psychological—on thin. Let's talk fat. Obesity can certainly have immediate consequences, like anorexia nervosa, yet its biggest effects are seen later, when heart disease, diabetes, and hypertension take hold. The mortality rates for obese adults who were fat as adolescents is twice as high as those with average weights. In some psychological literature, obesity is not considered an eating disorder. I think it is. As a principal, I see an anorexic at one end of the lunch benches picking at a stalk of celery; at the other end, a very heavy kid may be inserting another Twinkie down the gullet. And while anorexic teens may get compliments in the early stages of their weight loss, the obese kids are ridiculed at their weight gain.

Experts have maintained, "the childhoods of many obese and anorexic adolescents are characterized by intense parental involvement marked by enmeshment, overprotectiveness, and rigidity."[31] They claim that many of these kids come from unhappy homes with unfulfilled parents who may not have had a particularly satisfying teenage life and may be trying to deal with earlier, unresolved issues. They may be trying to fix the past through their own children. Although some professional caregivers have seen this pattern, I have no crystal ball into the complicated and nuanced dynamics of each family whose child has an eating disorder. However, I do have the opportunity—at school—to witness the extraordinary pressures on all teenagers, especially young women, and am convinced that, though many of these research findings are worthy of note, teens with eating disorders do not reflect any particularly discernible family pattern.

I know one thing for sure: overly heavy and overly thin teenagers often feel ineffective. Some tell me that they cannot possibly live up to their parents' expectations. Others, particularly the obese ones, may report feeling dependent and unmotivated. Here, a food-for-feelings cycle begins: I feel sad and lost; I often embarrass and disappoint my parents; I want to hide in a closet because it's too intense; there happens to be pound cake on the top shelf. Eating disorders are a red flag and signal the need to involve the medical and psychological professionals who can confirm or deny these intuitions.

There's a way to understand and address these issues. First, describe what you observe. Eating disorders do not require an emergency for you to talk to an internist and a nutritionist.

Second, be prepared for some straight talk. Issues may flood forth for which it is best to look into counseling. In some forms of therapy on eating disorders, families are asked to look at their structure—how they do business, how they react to each other, so be prepared. These therapists work toward establishing healthy forms of independence and limits, and toward a reliable sense of confidence and competence. These professionals may identify other affective or addictive disorders, some of which—like the pulling out of one's hair (trichotillomania)—translate as self punishment. They explore ways the family can resolve its conflicts and hear, with respect, all the voices and opinions. Many therapists look at ways of helping all the family members feel respected as a part of the solution.

Third, follow through with advice and don't let your own denial get in the way. In consultation with a pediatrician, a child with an eating disorder may help to design an eating program, to feel more in control. Some psychologists are using direct confrontation; others use behavior modification, in which positive movement forward is reinforced. Still other approaches include stress-reduction techniques, body-awareness exercises, visualization, and yoga. Fourth, if doctors feel that the situation is critical, your child may need to be hospitalized. Get a series of opinions, and if they all concur, do it.

On the Fringe

Not every teenager who joins a fringe group is a basket case looking for a basket. In fact, fringe-group membership may be a temporary form of normal adolescent experimentation. Recent research indicates that those teenagers who take "radical departures" are not necessarily predisposed to sickness.[32] Teenagers may not be pushed away from alienating and dysfunctional homes, but may actually be pulled to notions that they feel are more reasonable than that of their parents and the society they experience. They are largely white and middle class.

Much of the attraction is tied up with the natural desire of an adolescent to separate. Adolescence involves parting, which is painful. For some young people, separating is extraordinarily difficult. And, in the process, they're going to look for answers. It becomes their religion, their politics, their therapy.[33] Though such "solutions" eventually wear off, they are extraordinarily attractive and alluring.

However, there is a dark creepy side, when features of modern life make it worse, when teens seek images in the media of how they are *supposed* to feel. It's the *cult* in culture. And the most frightening notion of all is the panic parents feel that this little foray is not temporary, but permanent, when their teenager's healthy skepticism about the world around them fades into a clammy subservience, when they seem possessed. Parents describe how they are at a loss as to how to exorcise those demons. What's worse, they may feel guilty as well, because teenage membership in a fringe group can often be an extreme extension of their parents' beliefs.

When it is severe, teenagers have given themselves over to the yellow-brick road to la-la land. Some may stare at you with that glassy-eyed-subservient-look, those same kids who so vehemently resisted authority. Others look beautiful—stress-free and enraptured—because they have fallen in love. The skin is clear and the hair is clean. Upon seeing her beautiful daughter at the cult site, one mother said: "Give me a hug, Julie! You look wonderful!" As her daughter approached, she reported, she felt an intense coldness. Later, she learned, her daughter had complained that her mother staged the whole intimate scene.

Cults target teenagers because kids are vulnerable, because they feel out of control. Such groups are attractive because they offer an immediate and close community. And just at the moment when kids are thinking in abstract and global terms, they offer a kind of connection to an antiintellectual, yet spiritual, experience. They provide an identity just at the moment when kids are looking for one. Experts discuss how young fringe-group members develop both a real and cult self; in short, unhappy with the self they had but cannot fully shed, they try on another self. One is not sure how to interact with such youth, for it may be almost impossible to access them.

This new self provides a clarity of thought about the meaning of life—answers—when kids only have questions. They are armed with a vocabulary and a belief system that transcends their own lives, and provides the glorious opportunity to escape the self and to escape the constraints of their own families.

Call it a church; call it a sect; call it a religious order; call it dangerous. They're irrational and they require total allegiance. They may talk about saving the world, but they work toward saving themselves; they discuss themselves as alternatives, but once in, there's no alternative. And though an adolescent may have a fine mind, intelligence has nothing to do with it. In fact, much of the time is spent in a kind of education that simply puts brains to work to support the cult, a mind-clearing reconnaissance mission. It's time to dust off your old thick paperback of *Helter Skelter,* the one that didn't sell at the garage sale, and take another look.

But, again, those are the extreme cases, the ones that get the press. For the majority of teenagers, the connection is short-lived, a kind of one-stop diversion on the way to adulthood.[34] In fact, most kids who join fringe groups leave. They may just be trying on a mask which, after a while, they'll take off. And many kids turn their skepticism onto the group itself.

When kids eventually move away from such groups, there are unhealthy and healthy forms of reentry. Federal law now prohibits kidnapping or any other kind of forcible removal of young people from cults. Unhealthy forms include an equally doctrinaire form of deprogramming, which takes into consideration the same tactics used to help prisoners of war. Kids feel marched through another set of drills; they are suddenly confronted with their parents again.

It is all too sudden and too intense. All the growing is done for them. They are not given the opportunities to think for themselves nor build back their relationships.

Successful forms of deprogramming include meetings with non-threatening exit counselors on cult turf. The most successful transitions involve an internal, voluntary change, a gradual disgust with the leader and with a more positive sense of self. In retrospect, some young adults report that their involvement helped them form a healthy skepticism, either in spite of them, or because of them. Some report that they'll never again fall for any ideology that purports to have all the answers. In my own adolescence, my involvement in the communist party, albeit short-lived, provided me with an ongoing sense of moral outrage at injustice. Although their tactics became offensive, if not cult-like (I now recoil when political groups make such hyperbolic, dense, and dogmatic statements.), I am grateful for the opportunity to help others and make sacrifices for "the cause." I may have simply left my mind for a while to come to my senses later.[35]

Gangs

Gangs mix a cultlike and slavish loyalty with a vigilante zeal for survival, with a desperate plea to be someone. A July 1993 *Newsweek* article on gang life, entitled "Life Means Nothing," describes a "youthquake" of dysfunctional families, drug-addiction, and guns. A gang member claims: "You started out for need, and now you stuck in it because of greed."[36] Violence has become a spectator sport. The eleven-o'clock news reports "wilding" expeditions, in which teenage gang members kill to feel that special sort of high. Beyond the disturbing stories of senseless killings, experts are expressing alarm about sociopathic behavior. Kids, many of whom come from fragmented homes, can commit acts of violence, even kill, with no remorse.

Many, however, are victims themselves of an intense and abject racism that erodes self-esteem and hope. While some psychologists talk about adolescent invulnerability and their own mistaken sense of immortality, kids in gangs don't think that they'll live very long. While some kids in safer neighborhoods may fall asleep to the sound of a *Beauty and the Beast* tape, others are kept awake by the sound of gunfire, their little brothers or sisters forced to sleep in bathtubs for safety. You need only watch an urban drama group comprised of former gang kids talk about their lives to feel the extent to which these kids have experienced a lifetime of unprocessed, overwhelming trauma in their fifteen years. In fact, interviews with gang members who are teenage parents in the inner city reveal that they are having children because they want to see junior *now*; they simply may not live to get that opportunity later.

Anthropologists often make a distinction between the poverty of culture and the culture of poverty. The former notion has overtones of condescension, classism, even racism, as if those who live in ghettos have no culture, no tradition, no history, no sense of art—in short, ghettos lack culture. The other notion seems much more accurate in the modern world. In the ghetto, an additional culture arises. Many young people join for basic survival because there simply are no jobs. They may pack lead not so much because they're sociopathic thieves, but because they'd rather be in jail than be six feet under. They may be aware that juvenile offenders of this sort are often tried with the same force of the law applied to adults, but it may not matter; it's more a matter of life or death.

Sometimes the gang leaders themselves act as parents, providing clothes and structure and a kind of livelihood. Unfortunately, although the gang initially serves this nurturing function, it gets out of hand. "A human being gives less of a damn what he is accepted into. At that age—eleven to seventeen—all kids want to belong. They are unpeople."[37] They may want to be loved.

Such a statement can, alas, characterize many teenagers today, regardless of race or class. It's also an issue about being accepted, being called a homeboy or homie, being a part of something. One gets free training and structured activities. It's the satisfaction of kickin' it, or hanging out, of being in the set. It comes with hand signals and a dress code. In some neighborhoods, crack dealing is the best inner-city job program they can imagine; the hours are cool, the pay is high, and you get to dress in silk. Gang life gives new meaning to the definition of syndrome—*running with*. Luis Rodriguez, in his book on Los Angeles gangs, *Always Running: La Vida Loca— Gang Days in L.A.,* writes: "Gangs are not alien powers. They begin as unstructured groupings, our children, who desire the same as any young person. Respect. A sense of belonging. Protection. The same thing that the YMCA, Little League, or the Boy Scouts want."[38] It takes commitment, intense peer pressure, and often an initiation with a misdemeanor or a close encounter. Kids are attracted to the creation of this small society which, in its crude way, has come, in Hamlet's terms, to "arm itself against a sea of troubles." They become soldiers of misfortune.

Gangs have become the subject of serious research. We have learned that, in the 1990s, they are not limited to rag-tag sharks and jets. Many are loosely knit, but the new breed is "better organized, remains active longer, has access to sophisticated weaponry, and are much more mobile."[39] Gang membership does not rest with the ghetto. It's in the 'burbs and in the countryside as well. No longer the domain of the poor, gang membership has involved students from every geographic and economic strata. Neither are gangs limited to males. Young women are joining gangs in increasing numbers.

To make things worse, gang colors and clothing have become part of the mainstream, a fashion statement, especially among suburban youth who do not think in terms of such affect as anything other than style. They're called "poseurs," because they want to look and act the part. Certainly, if your child wears a cap backward, a flannel shirt, and baggy pants you can fit your friends in, he or she may be doing nothing more than emulating a Macy's advertisement. However, such choices need to be made carefully. Kids have been killed for status clothes or for wearing gang colors. You should take note if your child comes home "wearing new types of clothing, or if they insist on wearing the same style or color of clothing each day. New, unexplained amounts of money also should raise questions from parents."[40]

What to do if your child is about to or has already signed on the dotted line? There are no magic antigang measures, for the impulse to join may be inspired by both psychological and financial reasons beyond our control. The top-down, authoritarian approach has not been effective. If gang leaders are arrested, others tend to take their place. Police raids work for a short while, but soon afterwards, resentment brews. Big cities have been approaching the situation with techniques relating much more closely to adolescent development and to good parenting. Some are developing gang diversion programs and youth outreach programs that target youth at risk.

Well-supervised gyms are staying lit late. Special sporting events, even with rival gangs, are being sponsored in neighborhoods. Job-placement organizations are being formed. Parents' unions and family counseling are made available. In Milwaukee, plans are under-way for two schools for young black men, whose leading cause of death between the ages of fifteen and twenty-four is homicide. Though hard-hitting in its approach (some say the "school for crime" notion is dangerous and segregationist, even inherently racist), attempts are being made to address the problem directly, yet sensitively, along with clear limits.

Such limits include still curfews in cities plagued by gangs. Schools are insisting on strict dress codes, many have installed metal detectors, have eliminated lockers and therefore diminished the capacity for storing contraband, and have adopted policies of suspending or even expelling students who engage in gang activity. Antigraffiti teams are painting over scrawl as soon as it appears. Ex-gang members "have patrolled the streets with walkie-talkies to monitor gang activity."[41] One of the most moving programs I have seen involve mentors, who serve as teaching assistants in schools, on whom young people at risk can rely. Other successful programs involve community policing with real responsibilities and outlets for artistic expression—visual or performing arts programs that give room to vent about violence or parents or school or neighborhood issues. In short, teens involved in gangs or violent associations need to become involved in social work projects through which they can be seen as valuable, needed, contributing human beings.[42]

Extremist Groups

From a city near you, a young man exhorts: "Why is racism such an ugly word? What's wrong with being proud of my race?"[43] Let's look at the underlying issues.

Extremist kids deface synagogues with swastikas; they talk about white revolutions; they call themselves Reich Skins or Bashboys, the Gestapo, or Youth of Hitler.[44] They're into "unity" and "pride," "patriotism" and "heroism." They find the rhetoric necessary to pour gasoline on smoldering emotions. Inside, they're pissed and hurt. They grow rabid.[45]

Your child may have a swastika hanging in his or her room. However repugnant this is, it does not make him an active fascist. He may be acting out, trying to say something. He needs education, discipline, and attention; parents need to be vigilant, too, and make a determination if this is a passing, disgusting fascination or an indication of a serious problem.

If such symbols are combined with noticeable antisocial behavior, it is time for a much more substantial intervention before they end up in jail, for this kind of extremism is often bound up in a entanglement of anger, order, and control. If at all possible, the family needs to get some help immediately, either from a social worker or therapist. In lesser cases, the family may be asked to examine its own beliefs, for some of these teens may take on ideologies that are the exact opposite of their parents; others may extend their parents' beliefs into new, unimaginable arenas. At its worst, if your child is a threat to himself or to others, he may have to be placed in a twenty-four hour hold, whereupon a psychiatric evaluation will be conducted.

Running Away

A night of tension that drives a teenager away to stay at a friend's house does not constitute running away. Sometimes, in fact, a time out is just what a family needs. If this happens a few times—for a day or so—and your child returns, the temperature is rising, and so attention must be paid. But if your child escapes for a while under some misguided romantic notion that the streets offer solace, it's time to act. Don't let your righteous indignation prevent you from calling a local youth agency for counsel, a help line, a counselor, a family friend—for help.

We've all seen homeless and lost youth on the streets. Even if they choose to camp in a shelter, they're required to be out by 7:00 A.M., left to wander the streets for at least twelve hours before the doors open again. They do *not* view their state as romantic; the streets are cold and hard and tear at them. They have few advocates; many distrust the police or any local agency of social service.

And it's usually borne in the family. Kids on the street have escaped alcoholism at home, parental neglect, abuse, an excessively punitive or hostile atmosphere, neglect or disinterest, disorganization, and little emotional warmth. However, kids on the street, who have been disowned for significant periods of time, find themselves involved in substance abuse, prostitution, and the justice system.

Sometimes, when runaways or throwaways return, their condition worsens, for control becomes a dominant issue. The parents want to take the bull by the horns, and the original reason for running away becomes suddenly attractive again—a vicious cycle. Many of these kids were drinking before, during, and—if nothing changes—after the runaway experience. Some become pregnant and hope to provide the kind of love they feel they have never received. In short, these teens may take on all the most dangerous symptoms of adolescence. They and their families are at risk, and so a social service intervention must take place, in which individuals and the family constellation itself must be evaluated.

Homeless youth feel distant and disenfranchised. They avoid interactions, yet desperately crave living skills, social skills, decent medical treatment. Some go to school, yet are humiliated by other teens who point out body odor or the condition of the same clothes homeless youth wear every day. Your child may have met homeless youth or be on the verge of running away. As for the former, it is essential that you have conversations about what your child experiences and feels. As for the latter, run—don't walk—to counseling and to other accessible professional help. Although a psychiatric condition may be emerging within your child, prepare yourself to take a plunge into a deep, reflective look at your family—how it uses authority, how it solves problems, how it treats all its members.

•   •   •

When the syndrome of adolescence appears, the basically healthy body is ready to fight it off, to protect itself, to bear the brunt, and so the disease runs its course. The internal workings put up their dukes and the best man (and woman) wins. The whole system may suffer for a while, but the damaged part makes some adjustments, and the human system finds its balance again. Problems occur when the resistance has broken down, when one's homeostasis is thrown off balance. The body's internal order becomes disordered, and the defense systems cannot rally the strength necessary to fight the invader. After a while, Hamlet's voice rises again: the thousand natural shocks that flesh is heir to have eroded away the self.

Someone is bound to identify the problem. It may come from

your most basic intuition, from your son's or daughter's teacher, from a friend who betrays a confidence to ensure safety, from an adult who has the objectivity and distance to notice a pattern reeling out of control. A teenager may mention casually to a teacher that he or she has something important to talk about. "I have this friend, see, and she, like, is having major trouble." Teachers are often placed in a situation in which they must override confidentiality to clarify and perhaps expose the problem, especially if they can safely assume that someone is in danger. Given the option to reveal the truth, teenagers talk anyway—nine times out of ten—because although they express a bravado about independence or an initial romantic attachment to the adventurous life, they're scared, they need adults, and they're seeking advice. My experience has taught me that, though they may act bad, most kids want to be good. Teachers are therefore charged with the task of keeping attentive, or working through the problems, teaching young people to be responsible, and reporting danger to authorities. It is nothing short of their moral duty to the child and a moral obligation to society.

Certainly, adolescence includes a wide range of normal behaviors; the syndrome takes many forms. And though many kids lock themselves in their rooms, experience wide mood swings, and act out in behaviors both surprising and appalling, there comes a moment when a decision needs to take place whether or not to see a therapist.

As a principal who observes adolescents alone and in groups, I can honestly say that not all adolescents need counseling, but I have rarely seen a child damaged by the experience. You might be told that your child is doing just fine, that you may want to work on your own form of adolescence. It is better to be told such facts directly than to spend your time in blame or guilt or confusion. You might be told that a third party, unconnected daily with school or with home, might serve as a way of facilitating understanding and insight. You might be told that your child is suffering from a series of unresolved and oppressive problems for which intensive therapy, even hospitalization, may be required. You might be told that you and your child have recurring issues—levels of adolescence you may both share. In therapy, your child and you might have homework.

Some may even recommend intense treatment or further psychiatric work. Depending upon a thorough professional assessment (please demand one), they may recommend a pull-out intervention for in-patient care or a wilderness-oriented therapeutic environment, in which—removed from peers and temptations—they must face themselves. This is the adolescent syndrome at its most acute. The immunities are shot and the antibiotic of a tearful and heartfelt conversation may be ineffective. You might have to send your child away to get him or her back.

Before any of such action takes place, make sure that you have engaged in a thorough set of conversations. When I trace back interventions, I am most comfortable when parents have taken cues from teachers and school counselors (or any other source, for that matter—neighbors, clergy, bystanders), and then have sought professional advice first from psychologists and medical doctors, then psychiatrics. In this way, anecdotes and observations are discussed by those who have frequent contact with your child and then by those who are in a position to synthesize information. This is where a partnership between home and school are essential: the educators and counselors can be descriptive and the doctors, psychologists, and psychiatrists can be prescriptive. If any of these connections and conversations do not occur, the job has not been thorough enough.

If you see trouble, teenage-proof your house. Thirteen years earlier, you may have covered up the electrical sockets, after crawling on all fours to see the world from the perspective of a toddler. Look up, now, at the shelf with the booze. If you have a gun, lock it up and never tell your child where it is. Store the pills someplace else.

Finally, a piece of advice. Keep a journal. Note the time and place for your observations. Be brief, specific, anecdotal, and descriptive. Avoid judgment. When a health-care professional reviews your notes, he or she can see patterns where you may not.

A teacher once passed along a cartoon in which two adults at a cocktail party are talking about their teenage children. The woman turns to the man and says: "I know what you mean, my daughter doesn't know whether to get married or live alone or just move in with somebody or to quit smoking, except for marijuana, or to become totally drug free or to quit drinking altogether or to have a child or to adopt or just to ignore sex or become celibate and take more sedatives or . . ."[46]

Indeed these are complex times. Again, nothing cures adolescence, but there are means by which suffering can be abated. We are dealing here with nothing short of human life, messy and altogether exasperating at times. As fallible human beings, the least we can do is join the company of others who are willing to extend a hand to ensure that, if a young man or woman has crossed—or is about to cross—the line, we can do what we can to pull him/her back into safety.

8
Young Women
Finding Voice and Heart

How come if you're not close to everyone,
you're a bitch?
—fourteen-year-old woman

I wish I could be treated less as an object to be studied
than a subject to be known.
—fifteen-year-old woman

Something stops me right as I feel that I can go for it,
do something great and try something amazing and great.
It's like a little voice "you're not worth it; don't try it."
So I just stop myself from giving it a shot.
—sixteen-year-old woman

The syndrome of adolescence is accompanied by an additional set of complications for young women. Much scholarly work has been done about how the adolescent girl covers up her identity. Her "I," her sense of self, can become muddied, if not completely submerged, and it may take many years for such an identity to return, if at all. The adolescent girl also covers up her "eye," for ego, to live in the world of predetermined expectations. Smothered in make-up, she may not be able to see. In fact,

149

much of a young woman's adolescence has to do with a struggle to see and be seen, to hear one's own voice and to be heard. A Harvard psychologist notes that Freud "highlighted a particular problem in female adolescence by noting that girls at this age appear to undergo what he called a 'fresh wave of repression.'"[2]

Such is my broad characterization of girls' experience in junior and senior-high school. If, during the teenage years, finding an identity is a struggle, what must such a struggle be like for the young woman, whose identity may be prepackaged? The same girl who acted like a pistol, brassy and confident at five or seven or nine, may transform into the more taciturn young woman at fourteen or fifteen who comes alive only in the company of close friends, or who finds herself a paltry comparison to the glossy identity of *Cover Girl*. Of *Vogue*. Of *Cosmopolitan*. Of *Seventeen*. She notes, with unusual scrutiny and displeasure, the discrepancies between her body and theirs. All too often, when she looks in the mirror, she doesn't like what she sees.

But you know that already, and though this notion is frightening and depressing, it may feel impossible to tackle. Certainly while you're living with a teenager, it is a fruitless battle to combat America's obsession with its narrow range of beauty. I would rather examine those features of life with which girls and boys must contend and provide parents with some coping tools by which both boys and girls can benefit.

Some psychoanalysts have postulated that, for girls, intimacy precedes identity. Current experts claim that girls need to feel connected in their relationships before they are able to establish an independent self. Boys, on the other hand, are viewed and reinforced in the opposite way; they must establish identity before establishing intimacy. They are encouraged, first and foremost, to find the self; intimacy comes later. Girls want to get to know you first, before branching out. Boys will get to know you later. Some analysts say that their points of view are guided by their anatomy. After all, girls have one that goes in; boys have one that goes out.

One can take issue with the enormous generalities of it all. But bear with me a while. I can't help but report a similar set of perceptions about young women from conversations with teachers: "When I look around my classroom, I see boys answering the questions, and I find myself asking more from them. Little did I know, until I asked, that the girls were intimidated. It's almost as if the boys have some kind of permission to speak up, even if only to express a half-baked idea, but the girls have to be forced to talk. Is it because they are in the presence of boys? Is it because they don't have the same permission? How come the girls suddenly talk when class is over?" Another: "When young women start to talk, boys just shut them down. After a while, some just give up. It's disheartening."

Still another: "When I teach my poetry class, it seems to go like this: the girls find their heart first, then they find their voice. The boys find their voice first, and then they find their heart. The girls look for the connections, the relationships, the emotional center in a character. Only then can they develop a sense of an individual's integrity and uniqueness. The boys take the individual's uniqueness for granted. Rather than talk about what the character said, they talk about what the character did. Only then are they willing to go back and find out what drove the character in certain directions."[3]

Professional educators and doctors and anthropologists spend a great deal of time and energy understanding human behavior, but no one really is certain about gender-specific behaviors. At this point, we have only relied on observation, anecdote, and some speculation. As Buffalo Springfield sang, "Something's happening here, what it is ain't exactly clear." The nurture-nature relationship applies here: society, family dynamics and structure, history, and genetics constitute an ecology of personality and character and presence.

The confusion over gender roles within the syndrome of adolescence is intense. If adolescence is contradiction, such dissonance is pronounced in girls—between looking good and being smart; between behaving the way girls are "supposed" to behave and having permission to be inappropriate; between feelings and thoughts; between maintaining a sense of self amidst friends and competing for boys' attention; between falling for a boy and falling from oneself; between taking advantage of opportunities and allowing oneself to be taken advantage of; between being cared for and being left alone; between the urge to talk and the suppression of one's point of view. A young woman may be torn between her attraction to a career she would like to make and the one expected of her. She may feel wonderful about her successes, but then pose a threat to her mother, who may be jealous of her vitality and looks, or a threat to her father, who may be intimidated by her intelligence and assertiveness.

As parents, you may just experience unadulterated emotion. It's normal. However, our society tends to dismiss young women's emotive quality as "hysterical." From what I see, it is a myth that girls are more emotional than boys. The forms change, but the content remains the same. When the internal struggles get to their most intense peak, boys explode. Boys act out; they don't talk; they may often turn their depression into anger. They revel in risky business. They'll put their fists through their bedroom doors. They're allowed to be aggressive, and sensitivity is seen as a sign of weakness. Girls tend to implode; they turn anger inward, into depression and self hate; they'll share their pain with a few close friends. They'll often cry at unpredictable times. Rather than put a fist through a bedroom door, they'll put a finger down their throat. Aggression is seen as pushy and inappropriate; sensitivity is expected.

There is an enormous price for both boys and girls. Boys often feel caught in a vice. They cannot emote in traditional ways and therefore find themselves acting out, powerless and angry. Girls can only emote in traditional ways, also powerless and angry. A group of eleventh grade girls once described how, independent of each other, they ripped the arms and legs off their Barbies in the privacy of their rooms.

If depression is characteristically a reaction to loss, perhaps depression in some young adolescent women may reflect the loss of voice. Much of contemporary feminist scholarship does, in fact, pay close attention to the qualities and development of women's voices. Writers and psychologists have collected evocative stories of young women; a girl who fits in because her culture expects her to do well in elementary school, but slowly loses her nerve in high school; the eleven-year old girls at the school play, their voices booming out from the stage, and their transformation into more docile beings as they enter junior high; the mother who talks about how, during rain storms, her child would run out onto a hill, her arms outstretched, her mouth open to catch the rain, and yet, as an adolescent, this same girl becomes taciturn and internal.

Excellent books have been published, in recent years, on how something happens to young women entering adolescence. The syndrome may tax their will; they often lose their courage.[4]

I have watched countless faces of young women who recognize themselves in those passages of literature that address the depth of this feeling. If only I could invite you into a classroom to hear a discussion around the following passage of Zora Neale Hurston's extraordinary book, *Their Eyes Were Watching God.*

> The years took all the fight out of Jamie's face. For a while she thought it was gone from her soul . . . she said nothing. She had learned how to talk some and leave some. She was a rut in the road. Plenty of life beneath the surface but it was kept beaten down by the wheels. Sometimes she struck out into the future, imagining her life different from what it was. But mostly she lived between her hat and her heels, with her emotional disturbances like shade patterns in the woods . . . come and gone with the sun.[5]

They read passages from their journal that corroborate this character's experience. They make contemporary parallels with their own classmates. They tell stories and speak from the heart.

It starts early. The seventh grade has often been characterized as a period of slump. The transitions to junior high are great; the campuses increase in physical size population; the social setting becomes more complex; an adolescent must readjust to another adult every forty-five minutes. Some kids dim their own intellectual wattage to fit in the social scene. Though much has been said about how such a phenomenon affects all adolescents, I have noticed, as a principal, the changes that take place within young women.[6] Educational research often affirms that male students tend to get more attention than female students. In specific studies having to do with "talk time" in classrooms, even through college, young women are often interrupted; men "compete for the floor by 'overtalking' the current speaker."[7] Girls then tend to compromise and to feel compromised.

Research even suggests that, in Western societies, as boys' physical voices develop, girls' physical voices do, too, but they learn to modulate them. Their voices become breathy, "a diminishment of clarity and power."[8] At lunch I have noticed a range and a pattern of young women's voices, some high and others low, some boisterous and others soft, some grating or undulated or carefree. Yet, in class those same voices take on a narrow band on the air waves. In classrooms the acoustics and the decibel range for girls undergoes a change.

In schools, teachers are often firm with boys and more sympathetic with girls. In terms of discipline, there may be a different standard for girls than for boys. Boys may get harsher treatment, even strenuous work detail. Girls "tend to be let off lightly" and are more likely to receive detention.[9] Boys are seen as unreliable and girls as reliable, therefore girls are seen as capable of handling the chores necessary in classrooms.

Boys are often reinforced for being smart; girls are often reinforced when work or their appearance looks good. Teachers often wait longer for boys to answer a question, or ask them to elaborate on an answer; girls do not get the same amount of time or opportunity.[10] Boys are often forgiven for being active, even though they may be exasperating; girls are often understood for being passive. Boys who assert themselves in class may be valued; girls who do the same may be seen as aggressive. Prior to middle school, girls are as strong as boys in mathematics and science; when girls start to go underground in adolescence, their scores decline. According to the American Association of University Women, boys and girls respond to having difficulty in math and science in different ways. They maintain that girls internalize, saying problems are the result of personal failures. Boys externalize, saying that math and science are unimportant.[11]

The problem worsens when one observes academic placement and counseling. In many schools, girls are often steered into courses that are ideologically "suited" for them; they may be steered away from science or math or may not be counseled for college acceptance with the same amount of attention paid to boys. Whereas boys may be forced to compete in academics, despite low ability, girls with high ability may not even be given the chance.

Listen, for a moment, to the voices themselves.[12]

"Sometimes I get up the nerve to talk, but it's like there's a feeling in the room and I get so uptight. I mean, I could probably be saying something great, but I forget it."

"I'm trying to become my own person. Sure, I end up screaming a lot, but it's like—these last few months—my mom's not there. She's checked out. What gives? Is she jealous or something?"

"I am fourteen years old. I have always been a good girl. Maybe you can give me a sign letting me know what is happening to me."[13]

"I feel like because maybe she had to stay home and didn't get all the chances, my mom's really laying it on thick with me."

"How come if you're not close to everyone, you're a bitch?"

"I wish I could be treated less as an object to be studied than a subject to be known."

"There are these days when I just forget. And then suddenly I'm reminded. There's a cute guy right in front of me and I'm dying because what I'm wearing isn't right or I just said something totally stupid, or I'm too loud."

"Sometimes being a leader is hard. I mean, you have to make serious decisions, but you have to keep your relationships intact. You've got to be in charge, but you've also got to listen to the people. And it takes so much time, because you have to talk about things if they get out of hand so that people feel okay afterwards."[14]

"Guys tease a lot. At first, I find it really bothers me, but then I end up teasing them back. It's a kind of game so I play it. But after a while, it really hurts inside, because that's what they do whenever they see me. I guess some of it is my fault, but guys never know when to stop."

"It's hard to be your own person in school, because to really be one, you have to kind of separate yourself from the others. And I don't really want to do it. I guess the trick is to be a part of the group but to keep your head together."

"Something stops me right as I feel that I can go for it, do something great and try something amazing and great. It's like a little voice 'you're not worth it; don't try it.' So I just stop myself from giving it a shot."

"It is like two people standing on a boat that they both know is sinking. I don't want to say anything to you because it will upset you and you don't want to say anything to me because it will upset me. And we are both standing here in water up to our ankles watching it rise. I tried to get into his needs, doing what he wanted, and to be the person that he wanted to be with. But I am not that person. I can't be that person. Then I tried. Can I give him what that person would give? I couldn't even do that. And at that point I was making myself so miserable."[15]

"I feel torn apart. As soon as I graduate, I want to get on the first plane out of town. But I have the hardest time leaving my life behind and all those connections I made."

At School

Young women are playing on their high-school football teams, but if you were a radical back in the 1960s at about the time the women's movement began to take its modern shape, you would be surprised by the lack of progress today. Despite our best efforts, and through a thousand subtle and overt ways, young women often still feel oppressed and depressed in schools. The beat goes on.

Schools need to be aware of the necessity for a working balance between voice and heart. A particular focus should be the transition to the seventh grade, where the transformation begins to take place. In the counseling process, girls should be encouraged to pursue areas of interest. If, in fact, girls show a propensity for math and science, they should be encouraged to pursue these interests and to be given the opportunities to succeed. They need to see role models—women mathematicians and scientists—who demonstrate this success. In leadership opportunities, girls should be on par with boys. In class and out, students need to be given opportunities for participation as equal partners. Self-reflection must be considered a paramount educational value, such that a young woman's own voice is given room. In the daily interactions with young girls, teachers should also examine the degree to which they may be either perpetuating the problems that contribute to lower self-esteem or assisting young girls in the development of a strong and viable self-image.

Such a focus may involve an examination of curriculum. Are girls and women represented? Are the accomplishments of women seen as secondary? Are there consistent, rather than patronizing or peripheral places in the curriculum for young women to see themselves as highly capable? Special units dropped into syllabi "for the sake of the girls"—family life in Elizabethan England, for example—may perpetuate the same types of stereotypes one may be trying to avoid. Peggy McIntosh, the director of the Center for Research on Women at Wellesley College, provides an excellent example. In designing lessons around the civil war, many curricula focus on the greatest hits, the highlights: free and slave states, Lincoln, and the Emancipation Proclamation. Although the classroom work may touch upon African-American women heroes of the time, or even on the extent to which racism or sexism may have led to such momentous historical movements and events, the focus largely rests on the list of facts to be memorized for the test.[16]

Such an approach is more inclusive, but the lessons still drift above kids' experience, still in the clouds. "In any case, high summits do not support most forms of life. They are deoxygenated, and it is well known that people on too little oxygen do not make very wise decisions about the welfare of themselves or others."[17] McIntosh suggests that the teacher start with where kids are—with girls' and boys' lives. She suggests that teachers find means of requiring kids to find out what life was like for a slave girl in the valleys. McIntosh contends that both the mountain tops and the valleys need attention—not one at the expense of the other. If one starts with a slave girl, one will eventually get to Lincoln, but if one starts with Lincoln, one will most likely not get to a slave girl. Certainly, McIntosh's approach strengthens scholarship for young women, for their voice is heard. Her notions of inclusion also make for effective, engaging, interactive teaching for a wide range of human experience. It is sound pedagogical practice.

Young men have a great deal of difficulty with the climate of heightened sensitivity to the issue of a young woman's growth and development. They feel teased and berated as well and shout for equity and fairness when the issue is brought up. Schools need to give voice to these concerns; however, they need to be engaged in a climate of conversation that allows them to see how the odds are stacked in their favor, how a young woman's private self ebbs away by the force of psychological erosion, and how young men may contribute to such a debilitating process. A good school can bring these issues out in the open.

At Home

Fathers are surprised by the intensity of their daughter's voices. They're struck by how much time is spent on the phone in conversation that seemingly doesn't get anywhere. They're often immobilized by the range of emotion they witness. Many want to silence their daughters or force them into an immediate and compliant "appropriateness." A young woman may therefore bemoan her father's rational distance, his inability to engage in a conversation of give and take. They complain that, instead of trying to connect with what is said, their fathers tend to place it immediately into some kind of perspective or framework.

Fathers also need to understand not to take it personally when girls are mean. Fathers have to keep their antennae up and determine when to allow their daughters a chance to get it all out, to be emotionally sloppy, to be alone and have the space to let it pass. They have to second-guess, to determine when to listen and when to ask questions, when to make a decision and when to allow a young woman to make her own decisions, when to be protective to provide safety and limits, and when to allow their daughters to experience life independently.

They may focus on appearance as an indication that their little girl is happy. If they are incapable of tolerating the painful parts of their daughter's human drama, they may resort to media images or other supplicants—they'll take their daughter shopping because they sense that such an activity will pacify their daughters. However, if a teenage girl reduces her self-esteem to a one-to-one relationship between appearance and identity, she may believe her only source of power is in her packaged attractiveness. This can be a dangerous and destructive connection, for she is developing a *sexuality,* and one day will be ready to meet a lover. She should do so on equal terms, not as a princess or an object of desire, but as the primary subject of her own life. Rather than focus on sexuality as a means of turning another on, that sexuality (and we have to remember its eventuality) can be a source of power and inner strength. Ideally, the only "preparation" a young woman should need for a date is to take a few minutes to feel comfortable in her own skin, for nothing is so attractive as that, and perhaps to remind herself that she is the co-author of the date about to happen. Fathers can help make an immeasurable contribution if they can reinforce this point.

Mothers have complex relationships with their daughters. Many are at each other's throats; others sustain close relationships. Though some theorists have said that this connectedness can suffocate a child's growth and natural urge to separate, mothers and daughters often comment on how such a closeness, however volatile at times, gives them both strength and perspective.

However, other mothers impose an impossible set of contradictory expectations on their daughters. They may express the need for girls to achieve in school and yet send less ambitious messages about their future. For some mothers, their daughters often serve as empty canvases on which to paint the picture they never got a chance to express in their own lives. Some mothers may not be able to let go. These are destructive patterns, exploited in talk shows. At their most extreme, they may feel like something out of *Mommie Dearest*.

Many mothers are also concerned about protecting their daughters, but also want them to be a significant and contributing part of society. "Mothers grapple with the harrowing task of reconciling their overriding desire to keep their daughters safe with their desire to keep them strong and free in a world that insists on women's inferiority and subordination."[18] A psychologist has talked about the importance of vigilant trust, in which mothers are "keenly watchful to detect danger or trouble," but are not excessively intrusive.[19] Vigilant trust is time-consuming, because it involves the extra efforts necessary to stay in touch, to know your daughter's friends. It requires conversation about a wide range of subjects—schoolwork, friends, relationships, politics—topics beyond rules and regulations. However, it also takes clearly spelled-out consequences if trust is broken, and the ability to renegotiate and build trust again.

What Can Parents Do?

1. Notice the difference between and the emphasis of the "I" identity and the "Eye" ego. A young woman growing up must find a balance between the two. Either extreme may throw her off base. To

focus on identity alone, out of some strong ideological notion that girls need to compensate for years of oppression, may do little to help a teenage daughter get ready for her first date. To obsess over appearance, either of homework or clothes or body size, is to limit one's opportunities.

2. Try not to reduce everything regarding daughters to heart and with boys to voice. To do so undermines a young woman's intelligence and a young man's ability to take the time to notice and to process emotion. Young women report being trapped in school and at home by a set of expectations that preclude the voice from expressing itself fully. Balance occurs when both males and females are given the opportunity to allow one form of knowing to inform the other. One's voice should give sound to one's heart; one's heart should provide strength for one's voice.

3. Watch the double standard. Do we really believe she wants to do the dishes while her brother is splayed on the couch, channel surfing, thumbing through comic books and sipping a warm Coke? If there is both a son and daughter in your home, is your son allowed to suffer and become victorious and your daughter given a way out? What about curfews? The responsibility for birth control? Driving? Certainly, we live in a society that requires parents to teach girls to take extra precaution; in other matters, however, what one does for the goose one must do for the gander.

When a young woman struggles in school, fathers (and mothers, too, for that matter) tend to work toward fixing them. They may blame the teacher for being too hard or the material for being too abstruse or the world for being too harsh. They mollify the struggle; they want to smooth out the path; they can't stand the notion that their daughter must suffer. There is often a double standard in the home if there is a son, who is encouraged to overcome the hurdles of work, to study harder to understand the material and to conquer it, and to steel himself for the struggles that lie ahead. More often than not in parent conferences, a daughter's pain associated with her math class will be so intense that the family may capitulate. Though parents may talk about finding a tutor for both a boy and a girl, they are more likely to talk about dropping the daughter from the Honors section or from the class entirely at a rate much higher than that for the son. As a result, they may develop self-reliance in the son, but not necessarily the daughter.

4. Look at your own relationship. This is a complicated one. Kids are keen observers of family life since infancy. I'm sure you can recall those moments when your toddler mirrored back a behavior or dropped an insight that blew your mind. Kids know who the important decision maker is long before you articulated anything explicitly, and so they will establish their strategy accordingly. If "wait until your father comes home" prevails, young women may come to understand that the truth—the bottom line—does not come from collaboration but from the man.

Is there room for both voice and heart in your relationship with your spouse? Is dinner-time conversation one in which the wife focuses exclusively on relationships and appearance and the husband exclusively on his position in the pecking order, the wins and losses column? Are your arguments based upon equality? Do they end only when the wife submits? Is your daughter's voice limited to screeching or topics of sexuality and appearance? How are issues of dependence and independence handled?

5. Listen. When we parents or teachers talk, we communicate power. When we listen, we communicate fairness. More often than not, kids crave an ear. Kids will say, "I don't want you to do anything; I just want you to hear this. That's all." The act of listening is tantamount to a validation of another's voice.

• • •

One of the primary tasks of adolescence is to form an independent identity, to experiment, to discover one's personal views and a working value system, and to determine one's future. Girls and boys go about this process differently. For the most part, boys are encouraged to find their identity as separate beings; girls are encouraged to find their identity in connection and in communion. Henry David Thoreau, the great transcendentalist, left the city to find himself in Walden Pond—alone. After two years, he returned with new insights. I observed an American literature class in which the teacher asked the young women in the class what they thought of such a search. One girl exclaimed: "How can I learn about myself if I have no one to analyze my findings with?"

At its most extreme, when identity arises solely in the context of independent isolation, boys may end up lonely men. In one group of fathers of adolescents I facilitated, many admitted to abandoning the notion of the best friend. As one father admitted: "I just don't call someone up and chat. It doesn't happen. It would be nice; I think about it, but I just stop myself." Girls may "more readily become foreclosed, defining themselves in ways that significant others would approve, or become diffuse, maintaining no self identity—rather being attached to someone else's identity."[20] A boy may end up a man who defines himself as a doctor first, even though he is a father and a husband. A woman may end up a mother and wife first, even though she may be a doctor. And when asked about whether or not boys and girls could anticipate conflicts between family and career, "males, for the most part . . . declared it not to be their problem. Females were far more likely to recognize the problem and perceive of it as their own issue."[21]

We live in a complex world and in a tumultuous economy. The role of breadwinner is no longer limited to men. Women are breaking free of adolescent oppression, entering graduate schools in high numbers. Older ways of knowing, which have defined women in a psychosexual context ("Your mission in life is to be attractive to and catch a man.") have given way to a vision of identity that allows young women greater possibilities for self-definition.

Yet the woman of the future will face an increasingly complex life. The chances are fifty-fifty that she will live alone or be divorced. If she is divorced, she will most likely be the custodial parent and be financially responsible. She will compete alongside men as equals in professions that are no longer gender-specific, yet, if present trends continue, she will receive less pay. And, at the water cooler, she may get pinched.

Young men will face the same fifty-fifty chance that they will be divorced and share custody, thereby experiencing conflicts between family and career. A man may not be able to rely on his gender for the promotion.[22] He will have to watch what he says and how he acts when he is attracted to a woman at the water cooler.

• • •

Although I have focused on the experience of young women as an underrepresented *majority*, parents and teachers must pay attention to the development of young men as well—how they, too, may not be served by our attitudes and our schools. Academics and policy lobbyists have been clamoring for our urgent attention to nurturing young women's self-esteem, yet the discrepancies of attention to and judgments of particular kinds of boys should cause equal alarm. American schoolboys are also seriously at risk. For example, African-American girls vastly outnumber African-American boys in higher education.

In short, although we may be struck by the differences between boys and girls, stereotypes pigeonhole them both. We need balance rather than a struggle for gender hegemony and political advantage. Women should not be marginalized nor men canonized.

Mary Pipher, Ph.D, author of *Reviving Ophelia: Saving the Selves of Adolescent Girls*, writes in terms similar to the concept of the adolescent syndrome: "Unlike Ophelia, most girls recover from early adolescence. It's not a fatal disease, but an acute condition that disappears with time."[23] I wish this were always the case. Parents and teachers have an obligation to help young women transcend what poet Lucille Clifton calls "the feathered hum of silence," for positive growth and strength in adulthood may very well be scarred by the trials experienced in adolescence. We must give our daughters and students all the opportunities for expression of both voice and heart. Most of all, we must hope and believe that each young woman's voice will be free to soar and sing and shout and swear like every other adolescent.

9
Difference in the 1990s

Lift ev'ry voice and sing
Till earth and heaven ring
Ring with the harmonies of Liberty . . .
—James Weldon Johnson

To be an adolescent is to feel different, most of the time. You can imagine what a "different" adolescent must feel like: The gay or lesbian kid, a minority in a school primarily of one ethnicity, the disabled kid. For some kids, the notion of their difference makes the loneliness, separation, or despair of adolescence more intense; they have to deal with their normal adolescence *and* the features of modern life that conspire to impede their growth. Many teenagers feel as if they live in a whirlpool of declining expectations. Features of the adolescent syndrome are held in common, but a true understanding requires us to defy stereotypes, to notice and to acknowledge difference.

Our kids live in a complicated and diverse world, and the menu for offending someone is extensive. Discrimination continues to tear apart families and relationships and neighborhoods. A virulent strain of intolerance is out there, an antiintellectual, anti-human virus for which antibodies have not yet been developed. Hate crimes are on the rise, and they embody a venomous and capricious nature. Gay bashing, racist attacks, and discrimination have reached epidemic proportions. We live in a world that stigmatizes that difference, and young people are particularly susceptible. Kids can be gloriously open-minded and contemptuous of such bigotry, transcending all barriers to become friends. Yet, again, they are walking contradictions, capable of enormous acts of cruelty against anyone who strays from the ideal they have been taught to emulate and idolize.[1]

They have effective role models. Whether or not they live in an isolated community, teenagers have ready access to the media, which delivers to their cable station or computer an unprecedented barrage of stereotypical images capable of establishing a mindset in the space of a sound bite. Although a few more faces of color or wheelchairs have cropped up in advertising, an impressionable pre-teen can form an appalling image of the "other" in a single evening in front of the tube.

We're entering sticky territory, here, for lumping all kinds of difference together can be considered another form of discrimination. Indeed, gay teens may simply wish to be validated as human beings, unexposed and unconnected to special interests. Families of color may resent being associated with the "disabled." Disabled children may not want to consider themselves different, or associated with the diversity movement. In fact, many in the deaf community do not consider deafness a disability, but rather "a linguistic minority," (speaking American Sign Language)."[2]

Here are my reasons for focusing on gayness, race, and disability, specifically. Each of the three groups I discuss here faces extraordinary discrimination in schools and in neighborhoods, exacerbating the pain of adolescence and the task of forming a distinct identity independent of stigma.[3] Gay and lesbian teens may try to hide (at an enormous price) within the mainstream of daily life, yet they are often rudely "discovered" and join minorities and disabled kids in a daily exposure from which they cannot escape or experience relief. And each group is associated with a civil-rights movement that can make dramatic changes to American thinking about diversity.

On Being Gay or Lesbian

Studies show that approximately eleven percent of American teenagers are unsure of their sexual orientation; approximately ten percent are homosexual or bisexual.[4] This still remains an area—within the school and the home—that has not yet found acceptance. It had better. Students are coming out of the closet, where they have found it musty and claustrophobic, and they are leaving the skeletons inside. They are more and more articulate about their sexuality as an *orientation*, rather than as a *preference*. Armed with research on genetic factors, they are ready to take issue with those who discriminate against, or negatively moralize about, one's homo-sexuality. And their teachers are coming out of the closet, too.[5]

Some school districts are approaching the subject with caution, if not all-out war. The Salt Lake City school board voted to eliminate all clubs at the school rather than allow a gay group to function in the open. Other schools embrace and encourage conversations about gayness. Either way, educators and parents are uneasy, perhaps because the very subject of sexuality of teens is so uncomfortable. Whatever the approach, in the same setting where students may discuss same-sex relationships exists an enormous amount of homophobia, the same sexual hazing that has always been a traditional American form of an adolescent's "coming of age." Boys call each other *fags* and *homos* and call girls *lezes* with the same amount of regularity as they did when we were in school. And, if they're identified as genuinely gay, they are the subject of overt discrimination. In society at large, gays are one of the most frequent victims of hate crimes, nationally.[6]

Imagine the gay teenager, whose feelings of natural uncertainty and low self-esteem are exacerbated by hostile messages aimed at them. They may feel invisible one day and become the object of scorn the next. They may be prevented from engaging in the kinds of social interactions that help them, like all adolescents, get a picture of who they are. They are often alienated from their peers, lose motivation and give up easily, fade from class activities or discussions in class, and express negativity. Some even become sexually aggressive.[7] School counselors face young gays immobilized by anxiety and conflict, increasingly alienated, and sinking deeper and deeper into despair. They are, like all teenagers, prone to the dark side of adolescence. "Gay and lesbian youth are two to three times more likely than their straight peers to attempt suicide."[8]

Some parents will talk about their own guilt or their own failures as parents. (The domineering mother, the detached father used to be the parenting "model" that experts used to attribute to the predisposition for gayness.) Some will cite religious injunctions against such behavior. Some will talk about the importance of finding a "cure" for the malady, often through therapy. (Just a note, here: although therapy may be a useful tool for the gay son or daughter or for the family to process feelings, research shows that therapy is ineffective as a means for "reversing" a gay orientation.)

Here are some voices of gay and lesbian teens:

"When I came out to my parents, they said, 'pack your bags. You don't belong here anymore.'"

"When I came out, I heard nothing about me, only about them. 'What did I do to make you gay? Was I a failure as a parent?'"

"I am attracted to another guy. It's just in me. Why do I feel like I'm a Martian?"

"I don't want to have sex with her in front of the whole school, for Chrissake. All I want to do is be a couple like everyone else and hold hands and maybe kiss or just be together."

"My voice is small and unheard—damned."[9]

I can say one thing with absolute certainty: No amount of lecturing or moralizing is going to transform a child from one sexual orientation to another. Even if your child is gay, he or she is gay. Acknowledge and accept it. If your son, for instance, has become convinced, as a young gay man, that God hates him for his transgression, he will remain gay; he will also, however, carry with him a deep and abiding guilt from which he may have a great deal of difficulty extricating himself. He is not going to change. If you withdraw your love for him, eject him from your home, or treat him like some strange third, mutated gender, you will accomplish nothing. Instead, he may find unprotected sex in "the baths, bars, or bushes."[10] The chances are one in three that the man with whom that son is having sex is HIV positive.[11] If a young gay man or woman is experiencing inner turmoil, he or she needs information, guidance, support, and conversation—not rejection.

Increasingly, old ways of dealing with sexual orientation will be viewed—along with other boy-to-girl sexisms—as forms of sexual harassment.[12] Gay students are holding their districts accountable, and may even press abuse charges. Schools are responding to the protests over discrimination by instituting programs that teach tolerance and respect. Curriculum has been developed to address homophobia, and counseling programs have been created that provide opportunities for gay teens to express themselves and feel safe at school.

When students feel comfortable enough to speak about such issues at school, teachers and counselors should not be obligated to inform the parents, nor should schools pressure students into coming out to their parents. Educational institutions must see their role as educators—of choices. Some students, armed with information, a considerable amount of deliberation, and support, may choose to come out. Some may stay inside and wait until college, at which time there may be a great deal more acceptance.[13]

It is extraordinarily tough being a gay teen. Most spend a great deal of energy hiding or playing politics or hating themselves. Most are deathly worried about rejection. Paul Monette's extraordinary book, *Becoming a Man: Half a Life Story,* addresses the loneliness of gay youth, and the need to push through the obstacles to forge and nourish a sense of self. At the end of the book, he looks back, with the perspective of an adult.

> It's hard to keep the memory at full dazzle, with so much loss to mock it. Roger gone, Craig gone, Cesar gone, Stevie gone. And this feeling that I'm the last one left in a world where only the ghosts still laugh. But at least they're the ghosts of full-grown men, proof that all of us got that far, free of the traps and the lies. And from that moment on the brink of summer's end, no one would ever tell me again that men like me couldn't love.[14]

On Physical Disability

From my perch as a principal, I watch physically disabled teenagers traverse their way emotionally, socially, physically around schools and their own adolescence. If the body is everything to teenagers, a body that does not work in traditional ways can be quite disconcerting. Adolescence is a time when fitting in takes on monumental proportions, when dating is of paramount importance. Yet disabled teens have difficulty making it in the peer group of choice, and though able-bodied kids will have friends who are disabled, neither they, nor their families, necessarily see that friend in a wheelchair as a possible date Saturday night.

Disabled teens often feel that they must outperform nondisabled teens. They feel impelled to be "super-crips," who achieve despite their disability. One teen said, "If I can't see, then I guess I'll have to be smarter than they are." These adolescents often work accordingly to prove themselves—to themselves—and to others. Yet such a motivation can erode their morale and self-esteem.

Here are some voices of disabled teens.

"My brain wasn't damaged when I was born. I've just got different hands and feet. Why do you talk to me so slowly? Why do I feel so awkward around you?"

"I've always wanted to be an actress. But how many parts are there for teenagers in wheelchairs? I guess I'm not going to be an actress. I'm just a distraction."

"I'm not sick; I'm just disabled. I'm not a gimp, goddamn it. I'm a person!"

"As people with disabilities, we are deprived even of women's traditional double-edged status of sex object on the pedestal."[15]

"Why can't they see me sexy?"

"The problems are different, but the answers are all the same."

Able-bodied teenagers often have a difficult time in their daily interactions with their peers who have disabilities. Some may patronize them in such a way as to make the disability clearly the most prominent part of every interaction. They may have a "blind" friend, rather than a friend. They may become friends with someone with muscular dystrophy because it is cool or kind to do so, or because they pity the condition.

Mostly at the junior-high level, others may ignore teens with physical disabilities, avert their eyes, stare, or jump in front of them at the lunch line. Some disabled teenagers have talked about how such ignorance tears away at their self-esteem. One young woman, paralyzed from the waist down after having been rear-ended, felt as though she had to defend herself from blame, from a constant barrage of questions that made it seem that her condition was somehow her fault. "Were you drunk?" "Did you wear your seat belt?"

There is hope here, though, for this same woman recalled a conversation at a party that left her inspired. A young man walked over to her, as she sat alone in her wheelchair, and asked her about her condition. She said that she was in a car accident. "I'll never forget how he looked at me at that moment. He said, 'Whoa, that's a drag. So what kind of music do you like?'" The young man acknowledged the disability but looked, immediately, for the person behind it. He noticed difference and then searched for common ground. That young woman felt nothing more than her own basic humanity, and she felt released from the responsibility of having to protect the feelings of others or to protect herself from others' feelings.

Adolescence is challenging enough without extra obstacles and extra pressures. Teens with disabilities undergo both the syndrome of adolescence and the special conditions of their own disability that make growing up difficult. When they were younger, these kids were often viewed publicly with certain measures of affection and sympathy.[16] Yet such pity feels like a form of oppression as they grow older. An advocate writes: "Rejected is society's deeply held thinking of tin cups and Tiny Tim—the idea that disabled people are childlike, dependent, and in need of charity or pity."[17] As they grow and become more independent, cute fades, and they may be seen as a burden and a question mark. As able-bodied teens plan their future with the adults around them, disabled teens may suddenly become a "special" problem. They may not be given the opportunity to engage in conversations about achieving one's dreams because no one wants to broach the subject.

The recent passage of the Americans with Disabilities Act has signified the necessity for civil rights legislation to address the years of inequity. "People with disabilities are demanding rights, not medical cures."[18] Other laws legitimize the importance of the mainstreaming movement, so that disabled and able-bodied students can interact as equal partners and learn from each other.[19] Though the issues of rights is finding wide acceptance, an additional set of educational responsibilities exists for parents and teachers to breathe life into law.

• **For Parents of Able-Bodied Teens** (1) Don't ignore disabilities, but do not obsess on them, either. If your kids ask you about disabilities, tell them what you know and try to find out what you don't. Like the young man flirting with the young woman in the wheelchair, acknowledge the disability but do not make it that person's essence. (2) Encourage your kids to ask honest questions. (3) examine the messages you may send your children about disabilities: Do you park in a handicapped zone? Do you avert your eyes? Do you consider people with disabilities a burden?

• **For Parents of Disabled Teens** You may feel a great deal of stress as your child experiences the various symptoms of adolescence. You may wonder about his or her readiness for the developmental, intellectual, physical tasks and challenges that lie ahead.

You may hold deep concerns about your child's rejection, depression, or state of mental and emotional well being. You may worry about how much to hold on and how much to let go, about your child's own need for dependence and independence. And, like all other parents of teenagers, you may fear that your son or daughter will be victimized when alone."[20] Families of disabled teens may find it difficult to allow their disabled teenagers to go out without their supervision or experience the opportunities—and the risks— that other adolescents face. Yet there are also many families who have found their own smooth way, and when times are tough, these families serve as bastions of strength and conviction.

Families of disabled teens, or of teens with a chronic illness, need to move beyond feelings of social isolation. Disabled teens need to participate in activities that require social interaction. At school, the more familiarity students have with difference, the better. It is essential, then, that teachers be enlisted in assessing the social dynamics in and out of the classroom. And so it is all the more reason that disabled teens get themselves out there. Teachers must also be encouraged to value, yet not patronize, your child; they must acknowledge achievement, success, special talent. They must see the child for who she is, not what makes her a special "case." It is important for parents to understand that schools may move slowly—perhaps too slowly—for the change you want to take place. Intimidated, schools may perceive parents as intimidating or impatient. Once again, a partnership between school and home can create a consistent, familiar support network to see through stereotypes and create an individual plan that serves the best interest of your child.

One student of mine once confided: "Disability is not a burden, not a handicap, not a tragedy. I am what I am; I do what I do; I feel what I feel. I am here at this school because kids know this, too. They treat me with respect. They know me."

Parenting and Difference

Life is no longer a 1950s suburban sit-com. In the 1990s, your kids are going to school with kids with a wide variety of complexions and cultures and circumstances. Marion Wright Edelman, the

Director of the Children's Defense Fund, has written: "Too many people—of all colors and all walks of life—are growing up today unable to handle life in hard places, without hope, without adequate attention, and without steady internal compasses."[21] Most adolescents of today will enter a workplace in which they will experience their own arc of the Rainbow Coalition. They'll meet all sorts of people in different shapes and sizes and colors and attributes and cultures. They had better function in these situations. It's a wonderful opportunity to grow. Ignorance will be no excuse.

Though a great deal of research has discussed the early and lasting inculcation of prejudice, it's not too late to make an impact on your teenager. It starts at home. Kids often report at school about their parents' own discriminatory remarks about the neighborhood, about the personalities on TV, and in the stories they tell about work. They listen to their parents' jokes and stereotypes. They learn to mimic what they experience in their home and in the media. They learn not to look at anyone askance. Kids cannot affirm a positive sense of self in a family that may denigrate the rights of others; they can, however, move forward in a family that welcomes difference, that is open to flexibility. Such an environment does wonders for acceptance and for positive intellectual, social, and moral growth. Here a number of ways you can help:

1. Explore your family's heritage. Most kids don't know that they have a culture, much less one that is rich and rewarding and affirming. The formation of a healthy identity for adolescents can be fulfilled, in part, when they know where they come from. Though kids want to be invisible, there is a price—a certain evident loss of direction, of home base, and of heritage. As they develop the power of abstraction, they need a sense of place, of ethnicity, and of heritage.

2. Understand that fear feeds upon itself. A white parent told me that, upon picking her kids up from school, she watches the kids "bused" in, who scare her. 'They look mean; it's just the way they gather, with their hats backward and the bass booming. But then I tell myself, They're just kids. How come I've judged them guilty before they've proven themselves innocent?' " Young people have reported that their parents have kept them away from the disabled for fear that the disability may be contagious. They report the discrepancies between their parents' liberal statements about differ-

ence and their parents palpable discomfort when they bring home someone their parents did not expect.

3. Ask yourself, "How does our home environment address diversity?" Is your culture represented in your home? Are other cultures represented? Do you read about other cultures? Are your friends all of the same "kind?" Are there books for your kids written from authors outside of your nationality or orientation? Is the artwork in your home of a singular type? Do you attend cultural events and talk about them in your home? If your son or daughter asks, "Guess who's coming to dinner?" how do you think you'll react?

4. How do you react to racism and discrimination? When you see stereotypes that denigrate ethnic groups or cultures or types of people, do you bring up the subject, or let it go to avoid embarrassment or discomfort? Does the subject of stereotypes ever arise in your home? Is there an air of superiority in your family? In homes that are "politically correct," is there room to breathe, to ask questions, to make mistakes?

Schooling for Difference

This is, and will continue to be, a world of difference, and schools of the 1990s need to see diversity as a fundamental part of their existence. This is not a plea for harmony but an intellectually viable concept. The more students respect difference and come to know about it, the more successful they will be in life.

The heat and tension of diversity in schools is intense. There is enormous paranoia about criticizing someone of another ethnicity, for fear of reprisal and being labeled "racist." Private schools may suffer from a lack of diversity and the perpetuation of stereotypes; it may be quite difficult for a young man or woman of color, or anyone visibly different, to feel comfortable. They are often forced to interpret a look, a nuance, a gesture, and feel worn out by the process. Public schools can be diverse in population, but segregated and hostile as different groups struggle for hegemony and turf. And while the some public and private schools are making extra efforts to diversify, other public and private schools are making extra efforts to develop separate-but-equal schools that allow minorities to be the dominant majority and enjoy a sense of safety in numbers, for families of color have argued that racial balance and busing have not produced appreciable gains.[22] For them, integration has been frustrating and, ultimately, discriminatory.[23]

It is my belief that creative educators, inspired and supported by families and communities, can create active, cooperative, multiethnic, multireligious, multicultural schools. I believe that desegregation works against an ability for an adolescent to grow and function in a diverse world. We must work toward unity in diversity, comfort in numbers, a sense that different groups may exist as entities in school and coexist with others. As a flexible, living organism, our society and—of course—our schools, must value and welcome the synthesis of ideas, of people, of culture. *In The Quantum Society: Mind, Physics, and a New Social Vision,* Danah Zohar and Ian Marshall have written: "In society, the larger and richer the range of diversity the greater the opportunity for that society to express its own underlying potential. The greater and richer the range of my experience the closer I am to realizing my inexpressible true self."[24]

We must begin by listening to the painful, the insightful, and the hopeful adolescent voices.

"Okay, if it takes acting white to succeed, I will. But it sure is tiring. The white kids think I'm artificial. The brothers in my neighborhood sometimes pressure me to stop playing the white game. Sometimes I ask myself some really basic, scary questions, like: Who the hell am I? What am I doing here?"

Another: "When the subject of my race comes up, everyone looks at me. What do they expect me to be, the black Encyclopedia Brittanica?"

"I don't want to be tolerated. I want to be appreciated."

"Sure I hang with my other black friends. Why don't people get uptight when the computer nerds hang out together?"

"I'm Asian but I'm not good in math. Yes, you heard it right here. Why does everybody think I'm supposed to be? And when I'm at a new white friend's house, how come their parents want to order Chinese take-out?"

"Sometimes I feel guilty that I'm white. Sometimes I feel that minorities are blaming me for most of the shit that's happened in history."

"How come, whenever we start talking about issues of race, the teacher always want the class to be nice and polite? It's not a nice subject."

"We Latinos don't all come from over the border to have babies. Remember the Mayas and the Incas? We're not all gang-bangers and flower and orange sellers or fruit pickers.

"My mom always told me this: When you forget you're a Jew, someone will always remind you, and it won't be pretty."

"We American Indians don't always wear beads and drink. Our parents wear suits, too, and have respectable jobs and don't drink."

"Kids say to me, because I'm East Indian, 'Does your dad work in a 7-11?' And I just burn up when they imitate me in that sing-song way. I hate when people make fun of how I dress. I believe in *ahimsa,* which means that we do not injure. I wish other people would not injure, either."

"There is so much tension between kids of different backgrounds in school, I just don't know what to say or how to act, or what's offensive. I wish we could just talk together."

"Do I have a culture? If so, I wouldn't recognize it if I saw it. And I feel hated because I don't have one."

"Don't overlook color—confront it. You've got to see it and hear it. Face it—everything you say will offend someone. But if you avoid it, it will catch up to you."

"I never thought I could learn so much from someone I was always so scared of."

The key is to find a common denominator, a sense of oneself as being an important part of a community of learners. Successful schools are using the following measures.

1. Put faces together and create a setting for significant conversation. With adolescents, familiarity does not breed contempt. Different kinds of students get used to and accept each other when they consistently sit together, eat together, study and play and struggle together.

Awareness groups, which represent the cultures and backgrounds of the students who attend, can help, too, by providing information and discussion. Such groups are not focused on "sensitivity," but rather on providing recurring opportunities for kids to talk to each other about difference and responsibility. Here, diversity is not a "theme" to be explored or appreciated on occasion, but a way of life. I have watched eyes open when kids go in groups to different neighborhoods to witness cultural events or to witness their own sense of deference to and honor of spirit as they sit in different churches. Such groups, part of the fabric of a school and its curriculum, avoid hollow and tokenistic gestures like "good neighbor weeks." In fact, they acknowledge the pain that emerges when the truth is told. And though the can of worms may be opened, participants in such programs come away with an appreciation of each other.

2. Familiarize students with difference, but do not dwell on history alone. Education for diversity must acknowledge the painful side of discrimination, but it must not rest there. Persons of color or persons of different abilities or sexual orientations should not be categorized as objects of study. One African-American student said: "I'm not just a descendent of slaves. I'm not just the daughter of civil-rights protesters. I want to know about this, but I also want to know about me, now."

3. Counsel everyone equally. All too often, young people are categorized and labeled. They live in schools with ruthless hierarchies of "better" or "worse" students in the form of the current tracking system. Much research has emerged about its pernicious effect on students, who are grouped by ability and set off on various tracks, the end result of which may be college or other vocational outcomes. The most vocal of critics acknowledge that such a system may, from appearance only, allow for a more homogeneous grouping of students such that educational objectives can be facilitated. However, they claim, tracking also segregates students; students of color have often been placed in a lower, vocational track. School becomes a temporary way station until they are ready to enter the labor force. Students of color end up deeming academic accomplishment useless, while many of their Anglo counterparts are pushed into college tracks. These critics also claim that tracking is unethical. Less vocal critics see tracking as pedagogically unsound, claiming that advanced kids and slower kids can benefit from each other. For them, homogeneity of skill levels does not make for a rich and diverse classroom. In fact, they say, such classrooms are impoverished.

4. Create mediation seminars for crisis and retreats for interaction. Tensions inevitably arise. Schools that have taken the risk of gathering groups together for conversation and council tend to

diminish such tension that otherwise ends up erupting out of control. Furthermore, opportunities exist in which kids from different backgrounds gather together in a camp or a work setting, where challenges and a common purpose allow them to recognize difference but witness the transcendent quality of commonality.

5. If you are a teacher, do not let your political agenda prevent you from being a good educator that challenges all children. All too often, intransigent points of view filter down to the classroom. Extremists on the right may find attention on culture or background or ethnicity a nuisance; extremists on the left might bore us with political jeremiads about how culture or background or ethnicity are preventing quality work. In a letter to the *Harvard Educational Review*, educator Lisa Delpit addresses the issues surrounding an experiment in which she decided to cover up the name on a poorly-written paper by a Native Alaskan Woman at the University of Alaska and circulate it among her colleagues. The traditionalists told her that the student should not have been admitted, for she can't compete; the progressives blamed Delpit, claiming that she had internalized 'the repressive and disempowering forces of the power elite to suggest that something was wrong with a student just because she had another style of writing.' "[25] All children need to be heard and understood, challenged and held accountable.

Multicultural Curriculum

Almost every educational journal I read has articles and arguments about what we teach, and a great deal about books—which ones to choose, which ones are to be included or excluded from the curriculum, which ones have inherent assumptions that can be construed as discriminatory. Books are in or out with a speed that approximates the fads in breakfast cereal. *Huckleberry Finn* is trashed because whites disapprove of the closeness of a black slave and a white free teenager; some are offended by Huck's and Jim's relationship, intimating that they are gay ("After all, Jim calls Huck "honey."). The African-American community is offended because Jim is called "nigger." *The Diary of Anne Frank* is too depressing, *The Color Purple* is considered too racy, the *Koran* too inflammatory.

Political correctness, on either side of the spectrum, has become a flashpoint in curriculum and a household word. And it's not getting better; already looming are struggles in cyberspace, so far an unregulated sphere of words swirling about, accessible through a modem and the deft hands of a teenager. A book may be banned in school, but can easily be downloaded via the Internet. According to an article in the *New York Times*, "Most anti-censorship organizations are still studying the issue. 'It's incredibly complex,' said Candice Morgan, chairwoman of the American Library Association's Intellectual Freedom Committee. 'The most difficult situations are those faced by school libraries.'"[26]

Multiculturalism is too serious, too academically-rich, too fundamental to intellectual development, too essential a part of maintaining a democracy, to be reduced to political football. A curriculum is not rich or full or meaningful unless it encompasses a global view that incorporates difference. It is not a question of guilt or appetite, but of necessity.

Some faculty want to ignore the subject altogether and teach the curriculum in its most classic forms, allowing students to "experiment" later. Others have made discrete choices of inclusion, but worry about being patronizing. The vast array of possibilities can be incapacitating at times, yet these teachers worry that minorities or women are reduced to footnotes or addenda. Others have denigrated the importance of this movement entirely by manipulating it to serve their own narcissistic ends. In fact, the multicultural orthodoxy end up promoting exclusion.

Instead of serving as a pervasive part of the curriculum so that it is a seamless part of a good education, the multicultural movement has often plunged into political factionalism. Such infighting is frightening, for instead of reading western *and* non-western books, books written by gay and straight authors, books where people of all kinds can contribute to civilization, ideologues dominate the landscape with an overwhelming presence and obsequious obstinance to the party line. Books are chosen not for their literary or historical merit, but to satisfy partisan lists of the left or the right.

We have a long way to go. If students do get a chance to read the *Koran* in one of their classes, they may experience a school in which a Muslim kid's Middle Eastern accent is mocked, or a scene in which that child is beaten up in the stairwell after class. They may attend an integrated school, yet without significant and meaningful contact with others, they may live in fear. They may come into their own sexuality on an unsure footing, but may be ostracized if their orientation is not within the mainstream. They may require the assistance of a wheelchair as they enter class and may achieve as well as any of their peers, but may face the humiliation of being talked to in slow and measured tones.

Joe Hicks, Executive Director of the Southern Christian Leadership Council (founded by Martin Luther King Jr.), emphasizes how Americans have not held any significant, mature conversations about race. He believes that we simply do not have the vocabulary or the courage. I believe this statement applies to all notions of difference. Americans neither make it their business to enjoy the diversity of our country nor to ask the questions. Such ignorance is a chronic condition, an affliction that destroys the fabric of the American quilt.

• • •

Robert Pirsig, in *Zen and the Art of Motorcycle Maintenance,* describes an old South Indian monkey trap, which depends on value rigidity for its effectiveness. The trap consists of a hollowed-out coconut chained to a stake. The coconut has some rice inside that can be grabbed through a small hole. The hole is big enough so that the monkey's hand can go in, but too small for his fist with rice in it to come out. The monkey reaches in and is suddenly trapped— by nothing more than the rigidity of his own values. He can't revalue the rice. He cannot see that freedom without rice is more valuable than capture with it.[27] That monkey is prejudice, and the rice— limited in supply—represents the protection of one's individual world.

Kids need to be educated—at home and at school—about the world around them. They need to learn how not to be trapped into the rigidity of stereotype. They must learn to stop yanking at media-fed notions about ethnicity or orientation or class or condition that ignore individual differences.[28] Perhaps a turning point is around the bend, where various civil rights movements have given voice to diversity. Young people need to see true diversity as an unwritten covenant and a celebration. We, like the monkey, should open our hands and let go of our rigid patterns of behavior. Once we learn to revalue our freedom above our perception of reality—we will be free.

The choices of curriculum, of what one reads and experiences in school, must take into consideration the intellectual, social, and cultural development of the adolescent. Kids long to know about difference. Just as a primary feature of adolescence is fitting in, they feel the need to know about that person sitting at the next desk over and they must be prepared. They crave the intellectual stimulation and literacy that multiculturalism can provide.

I once observed a diverse class of junior-high and high-school students in which the teacher asked each student to reach into a bag blindly and pick out a potato. They were asked to examine it and return it to the bag. The bag was shaken and the students were asked to find their potato, which they did quickly and readily. "What was it about your potato that distinguished it from the others?" she asked. Students talked about size and shape, pock-marks and skin color. Very quickly, an astute student answered, "I get it. We're all a bunch of potatoes." The class laughed along with this young man, who acknowledged the realization that the potatoes were more similar inside than different outside. This statement came from a young man with cerebral palsy.

There's hope, I believe. And it comes from the mouth of babes: An 8-year old writes:

I dream of meeting our Hopi ancestors, and we sit together and talk about the time when all of us are together, and the waters of the rivers are full, and the sun has warmed the cold part of the world, and it has given the really hot part a break, and all the people are sitting in a huge circle, and they are brothers and sisters, everyone! . . . When the day comes that we're all holding hands in the big circle—no, not just us Hopis, everyone—then that's what the word "good" means.[29]

10
Let's Get Educated—
Schools and the Adolescent Syndrome

"Ninth grade drowns in a hormonal swamp . . . twelfth grade is a wash. In any grade at any time, attention spans snap when atmospheric conditions are too exciting, as when it rains or snows, or does neither and is perfect, including all of spring. All Mondays are lost to laments at another week's beginning, and all Fridays are treated as early weekends. During first period, students are too bleary to think; during the period before lunch, they're too hungry to think; and during last period, they're exhausted. Days and sometimes weeks are spent preparing for and recovering from vacations, and in those few slivers of time when there is no other excuse for goofing off, kids get sick."
—Jillian Roberts, I'd Rather Be in Philadelphia[1]

"By spring of the school year, one-third (35 percent) of eighth-grade students said they had not talked with their teacher about coursework during the school year."
—U.S. Department of Education Office of Educational Research and Improvement

Schools can either remediate or exacerbate the symptoms of the adolescent syndrome. There are bastions of health throughout the country, schools that challenge, acknowledge, and nurture young people's intellect and social responsibility. Nationally-circulated newspapers, news magazines and documentaries exalt compelling, inspired classrooms, highlighting them as exceptional. Unfortunately, these classrooms are more the exceptions than the rule. Many other schools are submerged in standing water, breeding the germs of discontent and disaffection.

At present, the national profile of American schools does not look promising. The complaints run something like this: school buildings have not been adequately maintained, casting a pall of disregard over the physical spaces. A principal may boast that seventy percent of the senior class is college bound, but may fail to acknowledge that, year after year, the senior class is an eighth the size it once was four years earlier, when they were freshmen. The students themselves report a rise in attendance at "skip" parties, which take place during the day at unsupervised homes or corners of public parks. The amount of television watching in class competes with the amount of time students are transfixed in front of sets after school. Although a great deal of controversy surrounds the value of S.A.T. scores, student achievement by conventional means has declined for more than twenty years, curriculum has been watered down or eliminated, and abstract feel-good programs have replaced substantial, engaging, respectful work.

Theodore Sizer, former dean of the School of Education at Harvard University, and author of *Horace's Compromise,* has described a fictional teacher named Horace, who has "made peace" by compromising himself, the students, and the school itself: He requires the minimum and does whatever necessary to avoid hassle; "I won't bother you if you don't bother me." In fact, the spirit of many schools alternates between oppressiveness and boredom, thoughtlessness and panic.[2] Professor Sizer's sentiments are echoed by another educator, who writes:

> Because education to the average child and adolescent of today is presented as such a sterile experience, with only the ephemeral future goal of making money (which they may not achieve), it is not surprising to me that those who find educational standards hard to meet wish to drop out. Nor is it surprising that the bright individual finds the mechanics of school work dull and wishes to seek fulfillment outside of the drudgery of school. Both groups find the world outside of the classroom as promising and much more exciting, as of the moment, than their routine studies.[3]

In a thorough study of contemporary education, still another educator concludes that many schools aspire to be "like shopping malls

. . . concerned with attracting customers who will purchase the stores' products and will be sufficiently satisfied to come back for more"[4] Unfortunately, "although there are some excellent programs and teachers, most educational materials are mediocre and without much content."[5]

Reforming Our Schools

School reform has always occupied educational practioners, and many changes have been made over the past hundred years. The contemporary reform movement begun in the early 1980s has been designed around attempts to get the grades and test scores up, to compete in the global market, and to establish credibility. Current efforts involve the creation of charter or self-governing schools; movements to lower class size to make the classroom more manageable; attempts to raise salaries to attract and retain a higher quality teacher; initiatives introduced to promote competition between schools to force them to justify their existence or to allow parents to use vouchers for those who wish to leave public schools in search of a private education; and movements to specialize in areas of special talent to attract a more unified and more "teachable" set of students. Some entrepreneurs have started gathering funding for for-profit institutions in which students can take classes by satellite so that administrators can view schools as businesses and therefore maximize economies of scale and minimize overhead.

Educational pundits promote an era of schools that choose a curriculum that can be duplicated in any classroom, regardless of the human being hired as the facilitator or the students as passive consumers. Candidates for political office extol the amorphous and alluring qualities of excellence, discipline, and standards, yet do not propose a specific plan. And, of course, some movements nostalgically attempt to resurrect programs of the past "when schools were good"—a back-to-basics mentality, in which "frivolity" has been surgically removed. Alas, what some call frivolous may be just those programs that enable students to remain connected.

The reform movement has required us to ask a series of essential questions. What can prevent a self-governing school from easily lapsing into the same recognizable sort of bureaucratic nightmare it has tried to avoid? Lowered class size may make the work for the teacher more manageable, but does the curriculum, the quality of relationships in the class, and the culture of the school make the work more meaningful for the kids? Justifiable and desperately needed in the teaching profession, does a higher salary guarantee competence? In the rush for a TV in every classroom and a computer at each desk, what ensures the kind of training that can help teachers connect technology to good teaching? R. G. Des Dixon, author of *Future Schools,* warns: "Worldwide, school is a pufferbelly locomotive chugging incongruously through a high-tech landscape."[6]

Although the jury is still out on voucher schools or the school choice program, no palpable evidence yet exists that our children and their teachers are in an environment that is safe and nurturing and stimulating. In fact, some efforts have already collapsed. How can "standards" be determined in the abstract if the nature of the school cannot live up to them or even understand their meaning? How can we provide the motivation to succeed when, as a young, promising man or woman living in poverty, school seems like a hopeless and elusive abstraction? In a "back-to-basics" movement, how do schools deal with the range of abilities and backgrounds? Who will be left behind? Does excellence allow for goodness?

Caught in a political quagmire, many reformers "figure out what's right for the grownups." We have a long history of using children to meet our social problems."[7] Dixon writes: "The education industry offers the public Band-Aids for whatever school wound is suppurating at the moment."[8] Many movements and policies feel like a headlong rush to build a house of cards; however, inertia and greed and hubris and an obsession with new structures tend to undermine new ideas. One is left having to shuffle the deck and deal again. Without examining fundamental assumptions about adolescence, we may end up constructing a better mouse-trap. Such efforts, like the restructuring of the school day, have practical implications, but the students (and their teachers) languish at the periphery, rather than at the center, of the discussion.

Dorothy Parker once wrote: "You can't teach an old dogma new tricks." Change must take place within this context of a thorough self-examination, however messy, frustrating, or daunting a task. When it comes to school, one size does not fit all.

Lest you despair, a great deal of interest in and encouragement for precisely those models that place children and teachers and their relationship in the center of the equation have cropped up. Public and private, these are learning communities capable of teaching skills, transmitting a cultural heritage, and preparing teens for global citizenry. "There is a clear recognition that young people will require a great range of habits of mind and a great number of complex skills if they are to have any meaningful job opportunities in a day of closing doors. To accomplish such an education requires reflective teachers who know them and can devise the modes of teaching that are appropriate for these persons, that can launch them in diverse ways into what we now understand as inquiry."[9]

We must match the school to the needs of the kids who inhabit it, and allow teachers the freedom and the opportunity to make that connection. To start, we must be willing to hear the voices from inside school walls:

The Kids

"This place hurts my spirit!"[10]

"Classes would be more interesting if they would make it fun and relate subjects to things going on around us. It would help us understand and want to learn. And I would like to know about my history, Mexican history! I know I live in the U.S. but I still want to learn about my background. The only way I learn of my background now is by my parents."[11]

"Don't just test me all the time. Talk with me! Care about me! Give me some time, man! Okay, I may act dumb, but don't just put me down all the time."

"I don't know what's with my math teacher. He's like stapled to the chair. He's either tired or afraid of us."

"Nobody's real here. You've got to be a statue or a good soldier or a perfect scholar. C'mon, I'm just a kid."

"Believe it or not, this classroom is the only place where I feel safe. I'm known. Somehow, I can stand up in front of my friends and explain my mold experiment and feel listened to."

"I feel like my mind is exploding. Sometimes it's a great thing, because I think a lot. Sometimes it's really depressing, because I don't particularly think the world is a friendly place."

"A great school is one where you don't sit in rows, like in a factory. I'm not an empty can to be filled up. I'm not a product, but more a process."

Their Teachers

"I don't want to spend my time preparing them for some state-mandated test. I'll never see the results. I want to spend my time with them—hearing them, knowing them, teaching them, caring for them."

"I came to this profession because I believe in kids. After more years than I care to admit, I still do. I know, though, that they live in a different world from mine. I know that they need me. I'm there for them."

"Maybe there will be a fire drill and second period will self-destruct. Maybe the entire morning will be drenched in bleary anxiety, filtered through chalk dust, recorded only in the incomplete circles my coffee cup leaves on the cover of my grade book. Or maybe the winter sun will shine with a summer's heat and on the very day that we are reading Frost, the world will exhibit its essential paradox in mud and snow and they will feel metaphor seep through the soles of their shoes and know it from the ground up."[12]

"Students need to know some basic information in order to take the next step, to inquire. They light up when they can *create* the experiment in science, rather than merely *duplicate* the one in the book. Somehow, when I see them struggling with real ideas, taking risks, getting feedback from peers, they take a giant leap in maturity. They have to have some say about their environment. They have to feel in charge, to feel good about something, to be validated for their efforts."

"I wish I had four hundred orphans and forty lovable teachers and thirty acres. I'd start from scratch."

A principal: "I've been around the block too many times. I've read insulting 'teacher-proof' lesson plans (so teachers can promote student achievement without 'screwing it up'), glitzy pre-packaged programs in self-esteem, workbooks, consultants, corporate bottom-line models. The list goes on and on. School is teachers and kids, kids and teachers—that's it. Make that good, make it real and meaningful, engaging and optimistic, and you've got something. We need to talk."

Adolescence has often conflicted with the structures, atmosphere, and assumptions of schools for quite some time, because many schools consider kids as intrusions, as cattle to move. One education professor laments that the reform reports "speak of those very children as 'human resources' for the expansion of productivity, but the world we inhabit is palpably deficient: there are unwarranted inequities, shattered communities, unfulfilled lives."[13]

Schools have taken on the role of families. They may be authoritarian, authoritative, or permissive. They may be dysfunctional or splintered. They may favor some children and not others. Some may try to protect themselves from these problems, even from the students themselves. Some schools hunker down and try to weather the storm, resisting change. They may dismiss honest attempts at change for fear that we will experiment with yet another generation of kids. These schools may, like some parents, take on the authoritarian model. Other, permissive schools, may latch onto the first easy distraction they can find; they may provide tacit and immediate approval for every pressing need or poorly-conceived innovation. Some may collude with teens to boost morale by capitulating to appetite or fad.

Schools are the test-tube in which many of us have located either the recipe for society's ills or the vaccine. Saturated by the demands of the society, if not the immediate neighborhood around them, they are often isolated and overwhelmed. Schools are also held responsible to help children answer that crucial question, popularized by Jesse Jackson: "Penn State or the state Pen?"

The pressure is intense—to educate, to maintain safety, to assist kids in constructing a reasonable moral life, and to help provide them with the skills they need to survive and flourish in the world outside of school, to see life as a worthwhile and meaningful enterprise, to be respected in the world and to find their way.

It is not an easy task. I am reminded of the Eastern European story of "The Mitten," in which a boy leaves a mitten out in the snow, while collecting wood for his grandmother.[14] At first, a series of animals come in to stay warm; everyone is accommodating. After a while, however, the animals are resentful of one another. A boar and a bear make the mitten full to almost bursting. A gnat wants to enter, but the animals resist him. Finally, he forces his way in; the mitten breaks, the gnat is blamed and scorned, and all the animals scurry away with as much of the mitten as they can carry. So it is with schools that find themselves adding more as the vicissitudes of interests and needs arise. As they do so, however, there is little evaluation of the big picture. Schools are almost bursting, like the mitten, because there simply is no other reliable place to go. It's cold out there. The symptoms of societal malaise make it difficult to educate for the adolescent syndrome. They have to change.

Although some argue that schools should not accommodate societal needs or transform themselves into little towns, many have decided to create the village that raises the child. As full-service operations, these schools combine innovative and culturally-aware teaching with free lunches, teen-parent and family counseling, guidance for latchkey kids, vocational as well as college counseling. Some schools are also gang mediation headquarters, multicultural resource centers, drug counseling, birth-control, and employment agencies. Some schools stay open at night, allowing for neighbors to use classrooms, the gym, the computer room, the library. Dedicated teachers, parents, and administrators have begun a design for K-20 schools, thereby creating a "seamless system for individuals and the community."[15] Researchers have found that "combining prevention interventions with school restructuring will create stronger institutions and schools will become neighborhood hubs, places where children's lives are enhanced and families want to go."[16] They require support from the home, the neighborhood, and the business community.

In short thousands of fabulous schools and teachers are out there—people and institutions that need you, and whom you need. Regardless of educational philosophy: traditional, progressive, comprehensive, or a hybrid of them all, successful schools believe in kids and teachers and in their own ability to make a difference.

I have discussed, in every chapter of this book, how schools can help nourish healthy growth throughout the syndrome of adolescence; I also believe that features of school design and approach to learning can make a difference and contribute to character, competence, confidence, and a sense of community—the necessary components of a great school—and a healthy teen. It's being done throughout the country. Most of all, it requires a fundamental and abiding partnership between school and home. Here are some of the features.

1. Respect intelligence. Kids really do want to enjoy the life of the mind. They object to patronizing, inconsequential, or touchy-feely learning. Paulo Freire, the great Brazilian educator, describes life in classrooms as a kind of "narration sickness"—one talking head, thirty-five passive recipients forced to assimilate facts they'll never use or incorporate into meaningful practice. Schools must see themselves as dynamic places of intelligence, rather than institutions of management.[17]

Above all else, schools must not develop intellectual strategies based solely on getting certificates from the mayor or a respectable standing in the test-score columns of the local newspaper. Rather than develop schools that cater to gifted kids, they should take up the challenge of recognizing kids' gifts. Kids may look and act and dress in ways that appear intimidating, but they are capable of greatness. Unless they're malnourished or abused, their brains have had to adjust to enormous amounts of stimulus, a commendable act. They're bright and want to be eager to learn. Imagine when they encounter teaching that Freire describes as "joyful and rigorous." And in that joy, rigor is connected inexorably with interaction, with human contact and with the exchange of ideas. We must allow teachers and parents to bring out the best, in an environment that allows such thinking to flourish.

Such a point of view requires that the teacher's intelligence and voice are respected as well. Students achieve, engage, and connect when in the company of professionals allowed to move beyond the cellular isolation of their classrooms to transform the practice of teaching to conceive curriculum that honors change, challenge, and shared experience. In a like manner, respecting a child's intelligence means allowing young people to monitor their own progress, to think about their own thinking. Students need opportunities to combine their intense reflectiveness with intellectual introspection. They need to participate in the learning process, for one does not find raw material in children; one must help them create it. And so "they need to interact with teachers to become researchers, together, examining not only the curriculum and the teaching methods, but learning itself, and how it happens."[18]

2. Foster the head, the hand, and the heart. Each school, like

each teenager, should be viewed as an organism, with parts that must work together for health. When one part is sick or unused, the whole system's immune system suffers. Schools must be intellectual places that respect inquiry, risk taking, and creative problem solving. Concentration on school achievement has traditionally been limited to information delivery and retrieval. This factory model, in existence for a century, is wearing out the moving parts.

Young people can demonstrate competence in a much wider range of ways.[19] They must build things and therefore leave their seats; they must show how their skill in art can illuminate their own understanding of geometry. And they need opportunities to be experts in something and to be depended upon accordingly. They must be engaged in projects with real tasks and real consequences. They must feel as though they are a part of a meaningful, intellectual apprenticeship. Teachers must therefore ask themselves: Is there something in the institution, in my classroom, with which a young man or woman can fall in love?

In addressing the need of teaching to the whole person, we must restore the arts to public education. Art is an academic enterprise. Art allows students to enter different realms of being, to see things differently, to interact with others in a noncompetitive environment, to find a means of expression that, coupled with their own internal resources, can produce something tangible and interesting and personal. Art enlarges perspective, enhances other subjects, honors diversity, celebrates freedom, encourages a feeling of ensemble, engages the heart. To remove arts from education is to tear the heart out of the patient.

3. Build community. Kids need to be reintroduced to the safety net. We live, according to essayist William H. Gass, in a world of "migration and displacement," even in the isolation of our own homes. "We go blank when the screen does. Our previous definition of the human—that we reason, that we reflect upon ourselves, that we make tools, that we speak—is in the shop for microchip repairs. We are really, when you count performance and tabulate behavior, not supercomputers, but a lot like locusts, little chafing dishes maybe, small woks, modest ovens, simple furnaces, barbecue pits, and picnic grills: we consume."[20]

Teens desperately hope to consume the social structure; they crave a sense of belonging; they want to be known as individuals, but also in association with a group and a place. Without a sense of community that welcomes them, they feel lost. They look within and turn their newly discovered powers of abstraction against themselves; they become slaves to narcissism and loneliness. "Why do this?" they ask. "What's it for? Where am I in this?" Teachers and parents must look at schools as learning communities. They must ask, "What can we do to make this school a community?" The structure of the school day, the nature of relationships, the distribution of power, the process of decision-making—in short, quality of life in schools should be reexamined to address this question. Kids want to practice democracy, to live with a true sense of obligation to others.

4. Attract, retain, and evaluate teachers who are passionate about the subject and compassionate toward children—teachers who teach with adolescence in mind. Our schools need true vitality. Age plays no role here whatsoever. In "rough" schools, I have seen teachers in their seventies, along with retired doctors or English professors, hold the material and students in high regard and get results; in "smooth" schools, I have observed young teachers who are filled with performance who entertain without substance. Principals need to throw in the circular file the checklists of "good" teaching and instead initiate meaningful dialogue with teachers about the nature of teaching and learning, and how and when it happens. Evaluation must therefore focus on the quality of intellectual and personal relationships. The intellectual classroom without the personal becomes flat and forgettable; the personal classroom without the intellectual is shallow and transitory. The profession needs teachers who are not only skilled in their subject, but talented with teenagers.

5. Respect difference in culture and background. Too many students feel invisible or disenfranchised. Their teachers may not know about their national, ethnic, or religious origins. More often than not, poor, minority children suffer the most, for they cannot sustain the resources, nor are they supported, to succeed.[21] Adolescents need schools that give them a sense of home, that acknowledge their presence and efforts.

6. At the same time, schools must avoid labeling students. All too often, students report having been "identified" and "sorted," as if they have just fallen out of some kind of misarticulated platoon formation. In the rush to find some kind of order in chaos, some

schools have slotted students into artificial classifications. Outside of that criteria that identifies "the gifted" are huge segments of the population left behind. Critics attack this artificial taxonomy as "a social invention," in which "children are the 'canaries in the mine' of modern-day education; they may be signaling us to transform our nation's classrooms into more dynamic, novel, and exciting learning environments."[22]

7. Make schooling manageable. Many small schools are more effective than the metropolises we have constructed. Perhaps some of our existing schools could be sold. We could use the money from all that real estate to purchase our strip malls and turn them into mini-schools where students are known and heard. Perhaps our existing schools can be broken down into smaller, more flexible schools or relocated into the spaces where neighbors work. Schools must be small enough so that students are not an afterthought. Only then can we enhance the quality of relationships, set tangible goals, experiment with the school day, its location, its services, and its functions.[23]

8. Create accessibility. The role of the parent in school cannot be reduced to career days, fund-raising, and campus cleanup. Your experiences of the life cycle, your culture or religion or ethnicity, your resources can be of immeasurable assistance in the classroom. Both parents and the school need to view themselves as advocates for the child, and must therefore have unobstructed access to each other. Accessibility involves providing the possibilities for close interaction between students and their teachers, and so the movement to lower class size is, indeed, essential.[24]

Furthermore, curriculum must change to establish access to human beings, to information, and to the parents' world of work outside of the schools' walls, precisely because society itself is changing—ethnically, economically, politically, geographically, socially, scientifically, morally. In form and in content, the present curriculum falls short of its connection to students and to the permeable boundaries between their lives and the world outside of school.

The late Ernest L. Boyer of the Carnegie Foundation for the Advancement of Teaching continued to maintain that good schools build connections that tie together community, a coherent curriculum, climate, and character. Much of his work resonates with current research that high schools need to be human places where learning is not so much individualized, in which students slog through a stilted curriculum at their own pace, but rather a personalized, in which they are challenged because their own inclinations and passions are given room to breathe.

Schools must spend more time leading the horse to water than in forcing it to drink, in guiding rather than governing, in evoking rather than invoking lessons. The work must come from teachers whose presence exudes a belief that students can master material and think on their own.

Rather than teach the material to children, schools that understand adolescence teach children the material. In the latter equation, kids come first. The word, education, originates from the Latin, *educare,* to rear or to bring up, to lead forth. And remember: Adolescence also originates from the Latin: *adolescere,* to grow, to be nourished. Public or private school, in one room or in a place that looks like General Motors, rural or urban, schools must see kids as their primary beneficiaries.

Preparation for the future cannot be reduced to learning larger and larger quantities of material. We may simply not know, in the next decade, what to learn. The Internet has created such easy access to a wide range of information that the conventional forms of knowledge, as we know it, have become superfluous. Besides, we have entered an era in which the sheer amount of knowledge has risen astronomically. No one is certain about the "truth" of a scientific fact. A teacher's obsession with course content coverage may result in work that is superficial, arbitrarily slavish, inorganic, and inconsequential. In short, motivation suffers. *Fuzzy logic,* a new development in computer thinking, does not rely on binary on-off functions. Rather, it points the way to more complex forms of thinking; instead of yes and no, there is maybe. Chaos Theory (or nonlinear dynamics), recently popularized in films and in economics, examines systems as wholes by mapping the patterns within them. Scientists working in these areas search to find order in "the irregular side of nature, discontinuous and erratic side."[25] These new scientific developments also tell us about modern life and about adolescence, and about how we can design schools that value a working and flexible knowledge base, along with playfulness and surprise, curiosity and innovation, respect and dignity.[26]

What to conclude? We must work toward establishing the physical and affective spaces that allow students to grow into adults who are articulate, literate, confident, and moral, who then can prepare for work in careers that can hold both success and gratification. We must interest them in pursuing a lifelong pleasure derived from the intellect and in personal health; we must help them with the means of making the world a better place for their having been a contributor. They must, in collaboration with their teachers, construct their learning. In short, it is our duty and moral obligation to connect the meaning of education with the meaning of adolescence. Interestingly enough, the language similar to my notion of the adolescent syndrome is particularly trenchant in a book by William Damon, professor of education at Brown University: "Like a broad-spectrum vaccine that can block the growth of many viruses at once, a child's whole-hearted engagement in schooling can stop destructive, wasteful activities before they begin to consume the child's life."[27]

Certainly it may appear as if the hope for schools as the catalyst for a new social order is utopian. But if you live on the inside, you see glimpses of brilliance: teachers and parents in a partnership, working with students and their communities to bring about a kind of heliotropic response, in which young people grow toward the sun. Let us shift the conversation from the quick fix, from the competitive spirit, to the students themselves. Let us create the kinds of schools that can harness the power of adolescents—their intelligence, their spirit, their will. Let us not let our own lethargy get in the way. If it impels us to create an entirely new way of educating our children, so be it. There is no more vital task.

11
Let's Get Motivated
Getting Them Up in the Morning

"Every wall is a door."
—Ralph Waldo Emerson

The adolescent syndrome can zap motivation. It may also be impossible to sort through the tea leaves of psychological data and behavior. What drives human beings to act, to maintain their will, and to persevere is inconclusive. Some say that the home determines everything; others say it's the school. Still others discuss the effect of numerous changes on a teenager's life and his or her coping mechanism. Academic circles are engaged in a whirlwind of debate about the role of culture and economics; some theories maintain that adolescent behavior is motivated by the satisfaction of basic drives or the seeking of rewards and the avoidance of punishments; still others have analyzed heart rate or other genetic factors or birth order. In short, motivation is comprised of a complex ebb and flow of energy and lethargy, hope and despair; disposition and direction. Parents and teachers are often left describing and observing the symptoms.[1]

Because the variables concerning motivation are so manifold, I would like to start with my own adolescence. When I was a preteen I was a voracious reader, but rarely of the books assigned. Depending upon my age, I'd slip baseball biographies or a tattered copy of *Lolita* or Marxist pamphlets into the covers of my textbooks. Deep in thought, I'd have to endure the embarrassment I created when, on repeated occasions, I was jolted from my reveries and had to ask the teacher to repeat the question. At one point, an exasperated teacher exclaimed, in front of the class, "Fred, (or perhaps she said Mr. Mednick, in that classic pejorative tone) you are an addled child."

I did not know what this invective—"addled"—meant, but I clearly knew that I was scum in her eyes. My face flushed; I could not think. Humiliated publicly, I rushed home and grabbed the Webster's only to learn that addled originated from the Old English *adela,* meaning mud. To addle is to make or become rotten or confused. I was addle-brained, I thought. Although I cannot blame the teacher for the observation, I have lived with her opprobrious tone and the sense of being dismissed.

I was pierced by her comment. I was leveled. Yet, though the medium was so destructive and inappropriate, I had felt that way anyway—confused in school, unable to integrate the lessons into something comprehensible and useful. Muddy in school, I simply found sports or politics more intriguing. I tried hard, but had difficulty piecing parts of the puzzle together. Without an advocate, I decided to suffer in silence. I looked around the class and found students who "got it" without significant studying and I compared myself to them. I wanted to prove to everyone, albeit unsuccessfully, that I was *not* addled, that I *could* achieve. After a while, I simply didn't feel like it anymore. I all but gave up.

I suppose my experience was not unusual. So many classrooms are webs of psychological intrigue. They are mired in complicated issues over authority and power and control or resentment toward wired boys like me; the nuances of the teacher-student relationship; school culture; a child's ability to date, or other distractions that get in the way. Was it me? My orientation to school? Was it the school itself? Most likely, the answer is that all were true.

While educators and psychologists and motivation experts struggle with the "key" to motivation, you may simply want your child to get up on time, or do his or her homework, and see the world as a reinforcing, hospitable place. Let's take a closer look.

At School

School can feel like a sedative. School can muddy the thinking, can addle the child. Kids wonder why they are there. They question where "it" is leading. "Why are we doing this?" "Where is my voice here?" "Why do I feel like cattle?" Schools cannot be blamed alone, but they may exacerbate the problem.

As kids enter junior high, they move from a structure of close supervision to a looser configuration of class after class, teacher after teacher, expectation after expectation. Such changes take place at the same time that puberty begins to take hold. Depending upon the severity of the case, some students' obsessive concentration on self, their changing self exposed to the public, and a surge in expectations can contribute to a sense of anomie and distraction.

In junior- and high-school, teenagers experience the nature of serious competition in academics and athletics. For many, the question: "Whadja get?" may serve as a cruel way of maintaining a pecking order. Kids who do consistently well, the *A* students, may fear that their success is alienating or conformist, and may engage in forms of sabotage. *D* students may enjoy their status as rebels or simply back out of the "school thing" because they are consistently humiliated by their failures and confirm their beliefs that they are incapable. Add more pressure by maintaining a tracking system[2] by which "homogeneous groupings" can theoretically "get the work done," and you have insiders and outsiders, successes and failures, and a considerable number of kids who question the very merits of the game. Environments that heighten social comparison and overassessment of self can help the competitive ones, but more often than not can lead to disengagement and enervation.

Schools are subject to intense scrutiny and their task is daunting, for they cannot be all things to all children. They must deal with their own funding and varying degrees of public support for education; with culture and ethnicity and discrepant income levels; with individual emotional makeup, temperament, and learning styles; with family dynamics; with peer pressures; with the neighborhood. Some kids and schools have defied all odds. Other situations, with all the "right" things going their way, may—through ennui, convention, and internal politics—produce students who fall through the cracks. And blame works both ways: An elementary school teacher once said, "If you can teach them to read, you're a genius. If you can't, it's their parents' fault."

Interesting Research on Intelligence

Conversations with teenagers about intelligence and motivation reveal that some kids believe they are naturally smart. Others believe they have to work at it, and when they get it, they've earned the right to be smart. Professors Carol Dweck and Valanne Henderson have reported remarkably similar findings. They have centered their efforts on an one's orientation to intelligence and schoolwork that can help parents and teachers move students beyond those muddy quagmires. Dweck and Henderson have investigated the ways in which young people perceive their own abilities as a measure of how they do in school. They looked at successful students, the "smart ones" in elementary school who, in junior high and high school, hit a wall and back down. They found those students who "get it" immediately, and those who "get it" eventually, after a struggle. The students who are first to raise their hands with the right answer, the ones who simply seem to be born intelligent are, in their terms, "entity theorists."[3] The students who work at it to make the grade are "incremental theorists." When asked the question, "When do you feel smart?" "entity theorists "point to times when a task is easy for them, when not much effort is required, when they do not make mistakes, or when they finish first."[4] Incremental theorists discuss effort that pays off or the intrigue of figuring the work out. Entity theorists have it; incremental theorists earn it. Entity theorists believe that intelligence is fixed; incremental theorists believe that intelligence is developed.

Though entity theorists consider learning easy initially, they run into trouble when intellectual risks are required. These students often avoid unfamiliar territory because they fear failure. Incrementalists take those steps until the *"aha"* experience arises; they adapt to new situations, and they understand that failure is an integral part of learning. They may view their academic challenges as a chance to "get smarter."

The intelligence-is-born-versus-made research is one of many ways the educational community is trying to come to terms with the causes of motivation. Although kids can change from being one sort of theorist to another, this framework can serve as a model and structure for your own observations of your child's progress. This is especially evident at around fifteen years old, when they hit a series of abstractions in school. Watch their responses to the work; you may get clues to help you help them. Finally, such a framework can help teachers design schools or establish pedagogies and curriculum that can both respect the ones who "get it" and the late-bloomers, help the ones who have been used to success and who may—in light of new, harder work—back down.

Learning Styles

Howard Gardner, professor of education at Harvard Graduate School, considers intelligence "the ability to solve problems, or to create products, that are valued within one or more cultural settings. Note that nothing has been said here about the sources of these abilities, or about the proper means of 'testing' these capacities."[5] He believes that standardized tests are only one narrow way of determining student capacity for learning. Rather than consider intelligence as one piece of quantity, Gardner maintains that intelligence is multifaceted, molded by innumerable factors such as biology and culture and proclivity. He elaborates on the work of the great Swiss psychologist, Jean Piaget, whose contributions to our understanding of intellectual growth and development are the cornerstone of teacher education. Whereas Piaget maintained that intelligence is a ladder one climbs toward increasing layers of abstraction, Gardner has augmented this perspective a more flexible view of thinking, that each of us has different forms of intelligence. He quotes Lillian Hellman's *An Unfinished Woman*: "'When writing, all the natural instincts are at work the way some people play a musical instrument without a lesson and, others, even as children, understand an engine."[6] After having studied "prodigies, gifted individuals, brain-damaged children, 'normal' children and adults, experts in different lines of work, and individuals from diverse cultures," Gardner identifies these various kinds of intelligences: linguistic, musical, logical-mathematical, spatial, bodily-kinesthetic, and personal. Gardner's work helps parents by asking them to look at the how as much as the what. How does my child approach work? He helps schools by providing the theoretical background with the challenge to teach to various intelligences rather than establish rigid, stratified structures that narrow the focus of teaching to facts to be learned for Friday's test.[7] Rather than classify students by how smart they are, we should focus our attention on how students are smart, how one's intelligence can be educated and nurtured, how we can develop schools that validate multiple intelligences. And a child whose intelligence is validated is motivated.

Intrinsic versus Extrinsic Motivation

Many books on teenagers discuss motivation in terms of rewards and punishments. They go something like this: Let them earn privileges; take them away when they're out of line. If homework is completed on time, then give them phone time; if they abuse the "contract," rip it out of the wall. Get good grades and by ____ (you fill in the age), you can take out the car. Here's your allowance, should you clean your room or the dishes or take out the trash. Most parent-teen relationships, like most relationships in general, are based upon informal or formal quid pro quos. You scratch my back; I'll scratch yours. Earn it or lose it.

The models for this conduct are numerous. Human beings are motivated by the gratification of needs or the avoidance of punishment, say many. We work to pay off our credit card purchases. Because families and schools are compulsory institutions, behavior is motivated by carrots and sticks. At school, (for those students still connected) grades are the currency of acknowledgment and the ticket to a future. Outside of school, if you've got cash, you've made the grade. But there's a price, a law of diminishing returns, especially if the operation of a home or classroom is reduced to an overly competitive and rigid structure of rewards and punishments devoid of conversation or intelligence. Just as kids work when their eyes are on the prize, they can also appreciate the value of work or certain behavior for its inherent value. Although kids may work for the reward, they can also feel rewarded by the work. They may learn a poem because it will be on test; they may also be struck by its beauty and learn it because it strikes a deep and responsive chord.

Schools fall into the trap of one or the other extreme. Those that focus their efforts on product only—test scores and college-entrance records—may diminish the joy of learning for all students and discourage those who "make the grade." The schools that focus their efforts on process only in the name of progressive ideology, or the belief that facts are useless clutter, tend to lose kids who are looking for direction. A teacher writes about the dichotomy often posed between the well-filled and the well-made head. "The distinction is clear: for the former, a mind that commands wide-ranging knowledge and ready facts is the sure mark of a clever and successful student; for the latter, it is the *way* in which a student's mind works that is essential.[8] Good teaching involves both.

Let's take a moment and look more specifically at the downside of the carrot and stick approach. Studies are showing that, for children trained to accumulate facts, gains are short-term. The kid does get the assignment done, but resents the maze in which he or she must scurry. Many young people find themselves a part of a game plan they did not help create. Although competition has motivated behavior and has brought out one's "personal best," an excessive dependence on competition ignores the individual who can, if internally motivated, achieve in ways far greater than if programmed. In fact, after a while, the rat gets tired of the maze and does not want to move.

I have seen kids "get into" the homework assignment, having found a way to make it accessible. Once that occurs, the results are clearer and more substantial. More work or rewards do not necessarily make it better; better quality work makes kids want to do more. When they are engaged, they soar. I see the effectiveness of internal motivation when teenagers, once conscripted into community service, suddenly experience the energy that accompanies giving and far surpass the hours they must complete for their particular school's graduation requirement. A prominent psychologist has written, "enjoyment motivates us to do things that push us beyond the present and into the future."[9]

On the other hand, a completely deprogrammed state in which traditional incentives play no role can result in an ebbing away of energy. Schools that adhere rigidly to sentimental indulgences in process for it's own sake may end up wondering why they muddle about.

Process and product, internal and external incentives, cooperation and competition, expectation coupled with accountability create a rich learning environment. A classroom can be structured for young people to use their peers' collective wisdom and achieve independently. Student artwork can be displayed around schools to celebrate individual efforts; at the same time, young people can work on a mural and enjoy the group accomplishment. A child who must study for a test and earn the grade can also participate in those kinds of projects where he or she develops a portfolio of his or her best works in progress—the challenges and the successes—to demonstrate a mind at work. Students may turn in their work to meet a teacher's minimum demands, but can also revel in an opportunity to demonstrate how one has learned. At the middle school level, intramural rather than interscholastic sports seem much more developmentally sound, in which students can compete in a friendly setting, rather than one filled with tension; the twelve or thirteen-year old, internalizing humiliation on the ball field where the stakes are high, the parents screaming, the coach pacing.

Motivation: A Short Guide for Parents

The factors contributing to or detracting from motivation are complicated at school, they are no less so at home. Here are my suggestions.

1. Watch the peer group. Even though you may not be able to make conclusions about one-to-one connections between surliness and surly-looking friends, it's important that you find out, in informal ways, about the members of your child's "crowd." You cannot inoculate your child against certain strains of friends, but you need to pay attention. Kids confide that the key to motivation (or the lack thereof) was the "crowd I hung with." Sometimes, your son or daughter may be attracted to an image other kids might represent, and that may not include doing well in school.

2. Minimize a single-minded emphasis on achievement-at-all-costs. Some parents push their kids too hard. Their motivations may be many. Some compensate for an unfortunate past. Others believe that their child is "severely gifted" and can accomplish anything—straight As, admission to the Ivy League, a cure for cancer. Authoritarian parents are particularly prone to falling into this trap; disappointed with the quality of their child's accomplishments, "educators and parents respond with disapproval and, to a degree,

with withdrawal of affection, thus ensuring that the child's confidence and growth toward self-sufficiency will be impaired."[10] One child complained: "I am not just a student, I am a kid, too! Why don't they ever talk with me about anything besides school?" A great deal of contemporary research has focused on the burn-out syndrome in children consumed with the desire to excel. This syndrome exacerbates the syndrome of adolescence, for teens will therefore be unable to treat their own symptoms. Robbed of their childhood, these "little adults" may—indeed—demonstrate inflammations at another date, in forms that may be inappropriate, depressing, or self-defeating.

3. Minimize conflicts over schoolwork. Additional symptoms of stress crop up when kids and their parents turn school performance into a cause for personal scud missile attacks. In *Winning with Kids,* two analysts write: "Do not imagine that your child is indifferent to his school progress. Indeed, kids compare grades the way adults compare incomes, and it is nearly impossible to overstate their importance to teenagers. Your child is acutely aware of his class rank. He's discussed it with his teacher, his guidance counselor, his coach, his friends, his friends' parents. He *knows,* and your lecturing, or arguing, or punishing will not help him take on the responsibility for studying if he is not prepared to do so."[11]

4. Stay connected, even when they're pushing you away. Kids who are overlooked often have motivation problems. Some may simply not have enough structure and therefore feel lost, aimless, and unfocused. These are kids who surprise you because they may suddenly and desperately want you to stay in the same room while they're studying for finals, even though they usually spend a great deal of energy pushing you away.

5. Help them get organized. It starts with you and your family. Though kids can tolerate (and create) a great deal of chaos, it gets old quickly and they begin to feel uneasy. Life cannot be hectic all the time. Try to establish routines. You'd be surprised how such a structure allows kids to get back on course again. You may not be able to help them on their homework, except if they ask you to quiz them. However, you can arrange for a clean, well-lighted place and a consistent expectation for work. Some kids have commented that when parents set the parameters, they feel safe. This is particularly important in split homes, where parents are often pitted against one

another, and expectations at each home are so discrepant. Finally, watch the distractions: Some parents provide strict limits on television and phone time. Often kids complain, "But we were doing homework on the phone!" or "My brain is fried, c'mon, let me just veg."

6. If your child will let you, help him or her make studying more efficient. If your child's school stresses the swallowing of large amounts of material, remember that kids report feeling stupid if they cannot recall the facts they are asked to regurgitate. They appreciate simple mnemonic techniques, for example, which can restore a burst of confidence in their competence as learners. When kids are spinning their wheels on vocabulary or scientific memorization, help them break things down into manageable chunks. There are wonderful and readable books that provide help in attaching an image to a word, play with sounds, or establish a chain of thinking easy to recall. Often, if the hurdle of memory is overcome, adolescents can enjoy the bigger picture and even the discipline. It is what the Japanese call *gambaru,* the calming quality of persistence and practice.

7. Pay attention to the way in which your child approaches the work. Certainly, for one, your child's orientation toward intelligence can give you a clue. If you have an entity theorist whose harelike speed suddenly screeches to a halt because he or she has reached a "limit," or you have an incremental theorist whose tortoise-like steps don't seem to be leading anywhere, you are bound to have a motivation problem. You may want to bring your observations to the attention of your child's teachers or school counselor. Materials are available that can help you determine what kind of intelligence your child has.

8. Kids may not be "lazy" or "stupid," but frustrated. Note the anxiety level associated with schoolwork and the whole quality of experience. You may watch your kids read the same section over and over again and seem to get nowhere. The notes from class may be disjointed. There may be significant pieces missing in what your child hears at and reports from school. According to learning specialist Dr. Priscilla Vail, many kids are "gifted and learning disabled, academic ugly ducklings, street smart and school dumb, atypical learners, or smart kids with school problems." If your child is unusually agitated or hyper and faces schoolwork with trepidation

and avoidance, if you find yourself throwing tutors at the problem, you might want to describe the symptoms to your child's teachers or the school counselor. You may be describing "normal" adolescence; your child may benefit from a peer-tutor or extra attention. Perhaps, in comparing notes with school personnel, there may be a need for a comprehensive evaluation conducted by an educational therapist or psychologist. These professionals are trained in identifying divergent learning styles and zeroing in on your child's particular struggles.[12] As a result of this closer look, you might gain confirmation of your instincts. Your child may, indeed, have bonafide learning disabilities and may need specific and calculated learning strategies, such as: taking more time on tests and papers, taping classroom sessions to reinforce the lesson or listening to books already prerecorded, enlarging a repertoire of skills in note-taking, organization, time-management, and listening that relate more closely to one's learning style and which can facilitate the recall and integration of information; hearing feedback from a source other than parents. In some cases, teachers and learning specialists can be enlisted creatively in developing a parallel, alternative curriculum that may involve "multiple examples of the lesson, rationales, varied formats and materials," for an extra boost.[13] You may also learn that your child has deficits in social interaction and has begun to avoid anything associated with school. Here, too, attention to your child's orientation to school, and the social fabric that he or she may have constructed, may indicate a direction for remediation.

9. Check your child's health. Teens may light candles in their room half the night writing heavy, expressive feelings in their journals and so weaken resistance to infection. Teenagers get strong cases of flu, strep throat, and mononucleosis. They get run down, and health may be as much a cause as a symptom. I have observed, for example, kids with persistent allergies who have hearing difficulty or miss portions of a teacher's directions. Others are perpetually sleepy.[14] Some who have persistent medical difficulties or prolonged illnesses can become passive and helpless. A professional medical examination may help identify those health problems that may lead to disengagement or learning disabilities.[15] I once witnessed a dramatic reversal of a young woman's academic downward spiral, after she had been seen by a developmental opthamologist, whose treatment helped her give new life to her reading.

There are also features of your child's life, such as humiliation in school, difficulty working a way into a favored peer group, family issues, or poor academic performance—that can lead to psychosomatic illnesses which, in turn, certainly impede motivation. School nurses generally agree that when students come in with medical complaints, many will allude to family problems. When things are bad, there are more cases of stomach disorders, headaches, sleep disorders, lack of appetite, itching, and breathing problems. Studies have correlated stresses from "failure in school—or, more generally, the risk of downward mobility"—to declining health, "particularly in cases where no favorable familial conditions exist that might lessen the impact of failure."[16] A self-defeating cycle occurs. They feel stress, then they get sick; they get sick, then they feel stress. And motivation suffers.

10. Respect each child, individually. Kids often report feeling inferior to higher-achieving siblings. They can't stand the comparisons. They are repulsed by those teachers who say, "You're certainly not the same worker as ____ (fill in the name of the brother or sister);" their radar is sensitive enough to pick up the signals you send. Each child craves respects for his or her ideas.

11. Motivation is a function of self-respect and personal pride, which is nothing short of a positive construction of self. In *tangible,* rather than touchy-feely ways, we educators and parents must establish and nourish programs that provide a sense of pride, that respect kids' thoughts and feelings. In so doing, we must give them an opportunity to demonstrate intelligence and good will, something they can feel proud of. These involve opportunities for real academic achievement, responsibility, resources, respect, and reliability. Kids attended to in this way often report: "I believe in myself," or "They believe in me." These are the teenage mothers who find an inner resolve to get a high-school diploma; the young black males who transcend the disrespect they must face and succeed in school; children with learning disabilities who take the extra time to drill themselves late at night. It's not easy; for empty feel-good school assemblies don't provide lasting relief or long-term benefits for the adolescent syndrome. An educator writes: "A child cannot be quickly inoculated with self-confidence."[17]

All too often, young people become helpless because they do not understand or experience pride. The famous University of

Pennsylvania psychologist Martin E. P. Seligman has discussed such notions in his landmark studies of "learned helplessness."[18] Seligman harnessed dogs in electrified cages or a "two-compartment shuttlebox" where "they were supposed to learn to escape shock by jumping across the barrier separating the compartments. Upon the onset of a shock, a dog quickly jumps over the barrier into the next compartment. Seligman would conduct a series of trails until the dogs simply gave up, taking the shocks, "whining quietly." They gave up. They learned that they were helpless. It wasn't so much the shocks that so debilitated these animals, more than it was the harness, the inability to escape, the loss of control. They were not in charge of their own fate. As caregivers, parents and teachers need to rely less on external reinforcements and punishments and more on structuring and encouraging concrete strategies so that teens feel that the locus of control resides with them. They need to set goals, develop plans, monitor and evaluate their own progress and, at the same time, receive validation for that which they can identify and celebrate. Teens also need to hear from teachers and parents, once in a while, when real progress is being made, for—all too often—conversations and interactions focus on the "problems."

12. Build an alliance with the school. Success is a function both of a child's will (without which all efforts are fruitless) and your own willingness to work in concert with the educators who see your children every day. You are not a failure if your child is hyperactive or a bully or a loner or a neurotic. Your job, though, is to recognize the symptoms. Real failure comes when the school and the home find themselves in a blaming game. Both parents and teachers are experts, well intentioned and invested and responsible.[19]

· · ·

Kids want to be useful and needed. Counselors at the Youth Authorities, who work with teen and young-adult offenders, report a common theme. Kids tell them repeatedly that no one ever patted them on the back or told them that they were worth anything. No one every gave them responsibility and supported it with gratitude. They feel lost and alone. After they're released from youth homes or detention centers, many return because the food is better and the bed is clean, the expectations are consistent and clear and there are people to talk with them.

Kids crave validation in school and they crave it at home. I see this each time I listen to students talk about how teachers stayed with them, when their words and thoughts are given substance and credence and serve as a source for celebration; where community-service opportunities have allowed them to express their dependability; when they are acknowledged and encouraged and empowered to make change in their communities. I witness—each day—the connection between this construction of character and the internal mechanisms that make kids want to work and achieve.

Just as one teacher in my early adolescence humiliated me and sent me into paroxysms of despair and self-loathing, another teacher validated my intelligence. At a crucial time in my late teens, in my first year of college, a literature teacher came along who almost singlehandedly lifted me out of the doldrums of schooling, and who pushed me in the direction I was going. She claimed that she was one of William Faulkner's mistresses. She was huge and wore iridescent, flowered moo-moos to class. She chain-smoked through a black-plastic cigarette holder she found in an ambulance in Barcelona during the Spanish Civil War. In class she cried when she read poetry or self-selected passages of literature. There were those delicious moments of silence afterwards in which all of our thinking took place, her smoke hanging in the air. We were all suddenly a part of something very large and palpable and affectionate and electric in that classroom. We all felt it—auto-workers at the Hayward, California auto plant trying to eke out a bachelor's degree, kids like me, senior citizens auditing the course. She found the time to notice me. She told the class that my paper was insightful and creative and alive. I was awakened. I was noticed. Her words and her images rest within me powerfully. I felt that the walls I had built, and the halls though which I walked, finally opened and became, in Emerson's words, a door. Because of her, I am a teacher.

Conclusion
Chasing the Light at the End of the Tunnel

When I was fourteen, my father was so stupid I could hardly
stand to have him around. At twenty-one, I was astonished
at how much he had learned in the past seven years.
—Mark Twain

Adolescence as a syndrome is not synonymous with adolescence as sickness. The dis-ease to which I referred earlier is a natural course of events. It is a part of life. It doesn't go away. It's fluid. It happens to them and it happens to you.

At the onset of adolescence, most parents report feeling out of sorts, anxious about the effectiveness of their parenting practices and impulses, unsure of their own intuition. Although we can easily acknowledge the complex and confusing world adolescents face, it is no less difficult for the parent of one, because many report that the storm and stress of the period haunts them with their own fallibility over household scenes, the "mishandled" crisis, the exasperations, the powerlessness.

After a while, parents of adolescents report, in their words: "a wrenching loss of self" "an emotional gulag," "a strange sensation at the onset" "a kind of psychic numbing" or "panic" or "ache." It may come from the loss of intimacy with and of your child's childhood; it may also come from the new forms your marriage must create—even now when you're waiting up—or when your teenager has left your home for good and you must face your mate without distraction. In a long letter to her children, Marion Wright Edelman, director of the Children's Defense Fund, confesses: "Most of all, I am sorry for all the times I did not affirm all the wonderful things you are and did that got lost in parental admonitions about things left undone or thought not well enough done."[1]

You might remember how, when you were younger, you thought most adults were phonies, a notion popularized by J.D. Salinger's *Catcher in the Rye*. Holden's adolescence was painful, and he hoped to stave off the disastrous "plunge" into adulthood by protecting his sister, Phoebe, and others her age. He knew, however, that the inevitable could not be stopped, and so he looked for ways to preserve childhood, to freeze it in time, to protect it from the influences of modern life. He hoped to "catch" her before she fell into the abyss of adulthood.

As an adult, you may have sworn that you would not make the same mistakes as your parents. You may have thought you could relate when the time came. A *New Yorker* magazine cartoon says it all; a pudgy middle-aged man in a cap and gown gives a speech to the new graduating class. He points to the crowd and says, "First, off, by way of establishing some credibility, I'd like to note that twenty years ago I was living in a fur-lined van." Alas, the faces in the cartoon audience are blank. Now you are the parent of an adolescent, perpetuating notions you so abhorred just a mere decade and a half or so earlier. Adulthood, like adolescence, has suddenly come as one big surprise. You may feel as though you are chasing parts of yourself on the frieze of an ancient urn.[2] Suddenly, your child begins experiencing various symptoms of the adolescent syndrome, and you find yourself trying to determine the most appropriate treatment, regardless of how hip or young you might feel. (You might take some consolation in one American-Indian tradition that adulthood does not begin until age 52.)

Parenting an adolescent may feel lonely. Contemporary adolescence is lonely, too. It is unfortunate, *because human growth is bound so closely with connection*. If we took the roof off the modern American home housing a teenager, we would see, for the most part, little dependence of family members on each other, except for the details of survival.

That acute sense of loneliness is described in Mihaly Csikszentmihalyi and Reed Larson's extraordinarily insightful book, *Being Adolescent*, in which seventy-five suburban teens were issued beepers. At the moment when the beepers sounded, these young people were asked to jot down immediately what they were doing at that moment, with whom, and their feelings at the time. Essentially, the adolescents report their own "findings," from which conclusions are drawn. The intention of the study was to track adolescents in a unique study that allowed them the opportunity to "do their thing." Their thing does not necessarily include adults. In fact, a great deal of time is spent alone—grooming, idling, puttering, sulking, listening to music. Sadly enough, the study—a look at internal and external adolescence—showed that teenagers feel the most upset or depressed when in the company of adults. Psychologists calls this phenomenon "psychic entropy," a sudden sense that things break down. Though there were exceptions: rich conversations at the dinner table where everyone's voice is heard, many teenagers are disconnected and alienated from the joy of inclusion.[3]

As I discussed in chapter 7, "Crossing the Line," kids left alone or unsupervised are "more likely to smoke cigarettes or marijuana, drink alcohol, exhibit symptoms of depressed mood, and see themselves as risk-takers," regardless of whether these teens come from single- or two-parent homes.[4] They hope to anesthetize their symptoms. Teenagers have come to seek, and perhaps find solace from, increasingly dangerous thrills. "Doing it, long a teen colloquialism for having premarital sex," has also come to mean killing oneself.[5]

As a parent, you may also feel a sense of isolation. Teenagers are often isolated, too, from their culture, from their family, from history, from adults, and from themselves. They do not experience as real any of the cultural rituals that have bound generations together. Christmas, for example, is for them a series of fabricated images and "stuff." Interestingly enough, the New York City Post Office has reported a dramatic increase in desperate letters written to Santa Claus, in care of the North Pole. Workers at the post office have read that teenagers do not necessarily write to get something, but rather to feel something—a sense of connection, of family, and of stability.

You might be unsure of your own direction. Teenagers, too, do not know where they came from or why they're here, or what they are on earth to accomplish. Adolescents are pushed out of childhood by their exposure to the adult world, yet must also experience, firsthand, its sickness. More often than not, they are initiated into the adult world as victims. They watch divorce firsthand; they are the victims of drive-by shootings; many long to be mothers and fathers with someone to love, and many achieve this goal. In short, they live in a world that challenges their very existence as youth. And as far as the future, the world of work does not emerge as the profession to which young people may aspire, but rather as a stint in a low-wage fast-food chain intended to make ends meet or to spend.[6]

Historians tell us that childhood today does not look like childhood of earlier centuries. In the seventeenth century, particularly in Europe, children dressed like adults and played like adults. They were smaller workers in the adult work force, and they participated in adult life. They were little adults. As it turns out, the separation of children from their parents took place in and around the time when formal schooling emerged. Philosophers like John Locke and Jean-Jaccques Rousseau, in the late seventeenth and throughout the eighteenth century, began to provide advice to parents about the necessity for the distinct qualities of childhood. Rousseau's advice to parents was "Leave childhood to ripen in your children." In his book, *Emíle*, he discussed the importance of what children bring to learning, their own desires and curiosities. In his day, many children were not expected to lead long lives. Therefore, children should live free, wear loose clothing, and appreciate nature. (The only similarity to our generation of children is the bit about loose clothing.)

Time marches on, technological science takes hold, and the child is seen as "the future," a way in which societies are improved. In short, adults figured they could make improvements, intellectually and morally. They could protect children from the depravity and muck of adulthood. When we move on into the twentieth century, the child is no longer a simple being, but a complex one. We come to wonder what's inside, what the features are which give rise to this or that response, what the role is of instinct, of background, of genetic predisposition. After a while, the child is hardly seen as just "the next generation," but rather a symbol of hope, a new generation that will not screw it up.

Contemporary teens are neither children nor adults. They are fundamentally isolated between these two states of being. In the end, they are separated both from their childhood and from adulthood. The institutions to which they belong promote this betwixt and between quality. The church and the neighborhood club do not help to provide definition and clarity; they neither see themselves as creators of a livelihood nor the means of sustaining life or as useful members of society. Television skews experience itself and heightens fear, even as it titillates the senses in an artificial construct of feeling. As a society, we are isolated from ourselves and unclear where we're going. One of my literature professors once claimed that, in Dante's day, one spoke about the sadness of hell. In our day, we feel the hell of sadness. There is a personal disquiet and anomie about us. The information revolution provides us access with information such that we know more about Russians than our neighbors. "Technology has eroded the bonds of neighborly interdependence."[7] We teach teenagers in school how to perform on standardized tests, to write the five-paragraph essay, to sort and classify by color or shape, but we may not be able to teach them how to relate the essential narratives of their own lives or their connection to those around them. Although Rousseau's notion of a naturally-ripening childhood may seem hopelessly naïve—even dangerous—in the late twentieth century, he does give us pause when we realize how little time is reserved for childhood itself. This generation has seen it all: war, a soaring national debt, the suicides of their young heroes, natural disasters, oil-slicked birds from millions of gallons of spilled oil. On live television—and most likely alone—they've watched a school teacher blown out of the sky, police brutality, indiscriminate urban terrorism, and the fall of their local and national politicians and preachers.

Our contemporary life seems like a race for more. More cable stations, more pentium power, more brands of cereal. Although teenagers may wish to control time—to stall, to race, to sleep through it— time controls them. As it controls all of us. Sometimes, in the middle of discussions with teenagers, I ask myself: Where is the Sabbath? Time for observation and deliberation? Time to sort out all the stimulus and the pressure? The prevailing notions of Western culture—I want more and I want it now—disconnect kids from both a continuity with time and a set of consequences of their actions.

None of us can forecast what lies before us. Years ago, we used to open up our biology textbooks and turn to the overlays of the various systems of the frog—the digestive, reproductive, skeletal, circulatory, respiratory. Each page was distinct, leading to something, and when all the pages rested on top of one another, the frog was evident, even in all its complexity. Clarity revealed itself. That may no longer be the case. There are thousands of overlays for the human being—the physiological, certainly, but also the emotional and social and technical and educational and parental. We do not know what the future will look like. It does not all compute according to predictable patterns. Scientists talk of how a certain phenomenon can be 40 percent true. Teens now will live in a world of e-mail and instant information access and will conduct electronic meetings without sitting next to anyone. The 1990s have been called "the decade of the brain." According to a major Internet access provider, "Experts forecast that by the year 2010, the world's knowledge base will double every 70 days."[8] Some say the future will consist of a set of internal experiences, like one's own manufactured virtual reality.

The future as our children will experience it may already have begun with the introduction of the Walkman, in which young people can simultaneously hold a basic conversation and listen to a rap song. And now, catalogues boast a pair of bifocal glasses; in which the upper part serves as a television, controlled by a device worn on the belt, and the lower part serves as sunglasses, enabling the pedestrian to walk and watch television at the same time. One can alternate, therefore, between the fabricated and the nonfabricated, the fantasy and the real. A divided attention is acceptable.

A Word about Grandparents

Modern life is overwhelming and confusing, like the popular Magic Eye optical illusion books, in which one hopes to find a picture among a thousand dots and diversions. But one thing is certain, if teenage life is a syndrome, it is fundamental that we listen to the ones that have experienced it before, grandparents.

There is something about the relationship between teenagers and their grandparents that takes issue with the notion of an adolescent's automatic "aversion" to authority. It's simply not true. Generally, grandparents do not admonish kids to hurry up or to clean their room. They intend to enjoy their grandchildren, and nothing else matters. To many teenagers, life with grandparents may mean that the pressure is off. Elders provide comfort and stability precisely because they have survived. They provide insights to teenagers about their parents, because these grandparents have seen those parents' vulnerabilities and youth. Teenagers often feel a grandparent's affection for them, precisely because grandparents have witnessed the passage of time. Invariably, when adolescents talk personally about their lives, their grandparents enter in—with enormous feelings of fondness, of safety, of advocacy. They crave that solid run of years. They know it is easier because they don't live together—they know that the grandparents return home when the going gets rough—but they know they are loved, more often than not, unconditionally.

Perhaps more than ever, children need to be connected to those who can tie them to a vital past, a living history, a quality of inheritance that reverberates a lifetime. Kids remember their grandparents' kitchens, their furniture, their idiosyncrasies, the way they smell and move and see the world. Grandparents have nothing to gain but life itself, for their light is limited, and many are not about to give that up. And that is an enormous gift.

• • •

Go back for a moment to the time when you read children's books to your kids. All the messages are there. Here's one from E.B. White, author of *Stuart Little:*

"A person who is looking for something doesn't travel very fast . . . Stuart rose from the road that led toward the north. The sun was coming up over the hills on his right. As he peered ahead into the great land that stretched before him, the way seemed long. But the sky was bright, and somehow he felt he was headed in the right direction."[9]

The great philosopher, Sören Kierkegaard, once wrote: "Life must be lived forwards, but can only be understood backwards." And though this statement may leave vision to hindsight, my experience, and that of generations before me, tells me that with care now, young people will rise to any occasion, take charge of their lives, create meaning.

Parenting is difficult. Hindsight truly is 20-20. Life is short, indeed, and although lives with teenagers are often entangled, the prognosis is good. The light at the end of the tunnel may seem like the blinding light of an oncoming and runaway train, but those momentary crises do fade in the scheme of things, in the long view. The turbulence and lightning may be the storm before the calm.

This was the case in Dante's *Divina Commedia,* and it is the case now: Your crisis will pass. Parent after parent tells me: "It goes quickly. Enjoy it, if you can."

But adolescence is even more than an endurance contest. Adolescence heals itself; it runs its tormented and inspiring, fragmented and creative course. It cannot be avoided or coerced into submission. It is a territory, inevitably entered into regardless of one's omnipotent desire to control fate. It is an acknowledgment that life is fragile and fleeting and that parenting requires a leap of faith. It also requires that you be there. I hope you have gained a greater understanding of adolescence as a syndrome and your role in it; you are ultimately the parent, the adult, the one in charge. Nothing I have said here, while you are waiting up, is an excuse not to do the job. Now that you know more about adolescence, it is all the more reason that you stay engaged. You may not know if your parenting is overly concentrated or overly diluted. You may not have any perspective on your job as parents. Parenting is the hardest job of all, for it takes great will; you have to let go but still care; acknowledge the past yet find meaning in the present, and prepare for the future; balance your life with that of an emerging adult.

Your own life may mirror the uncertainty of your child. You may be working with stress in a business experiencing acute corporate anorexia (downsizing). You may feel as if life is reduced to numbers and quantity instead of quality. You may find yourself in a frenetic state like the man on the Ed Sullivan show spinning plates. In the end, your child is more important. As one colleague put it: "So much depends on the degree to which parents can keep their souls and their soles in the room." You won't regret it.

An educator once reported: "After all these years, I still feel a little like the queen in *Alice in Wonderland* who practiced believing six impossible things before breakfast."[10] I agree. I am in the business of educating young people because I, like thousands of teachers and school administrators, believe in them. I find evidence of this magic and a teenager's spirit in all the most unlikely places—in the car, at the lockers, in a collective uninhibited singing of the popular song "YMCA" at a dance, after a good cry, at graduation. Teenagers are a kind of jazz, for they embody the components of improvisation and free form, yet with an elegant structure underneath, one that teachers and parents should recognize and appreciate.

And while you're waiting up for your child to come home, let me add this about families. Children blossom most evocatively at those moments of mutual recognition, when parent and child tell the truth, when they are capable of acknowledging each other's dark side, in struggle mixed with affection. At these moments, the family—in whatever form it takes—emerges like some ineffable safety net. Recent evidence suggests that teenagers are *looking* to reestablish that connective tissue that binds families together.[11] Families are both terrible and wonderful structures; their love and commitment is, in the end, the only thing we've got that can ensure, by any degree, a child's survival. Aeschylus wrote: "Especially in times of darkness, that is the time to love, that an act of love might tip the balance."[12]

Notes

Introduction

1. Irene M. Josselyn, "The Adolescent Today," quoted William C. Sze, *The Human Life* Cycle, 258. She writes: "It is important to bear in mind that when a therapist discusses any problem or any personality group, he does so primarily through a distorted glass. We see, in some depth, the disturbed person. Our social contacts provide us experiences with less confused people, but we rarely know them as deeply as we know the disturbed person with whom we are working. Thus, the remarks I will make are related to what, in essence, is a caricature of adolescents."

2. Again, I must acknowledge the enormous assistance and research of the professional psychological community, both in the preparation of this book and in the role they play in illuminating the work of educators and parents.

3. This notion of windows and mirrors was developed by Emily Style, an English teacher and Diversity Coordinator for Madison (N.J.) High School, and Co-Director with Dr. Peggy McIntosh of the National SEED Project (Seeking Educational Equity and Diversity). Her essay, "Curriculum as Window and Mirror," was published in an OakKnoll School monograph, *Listening for All Voices* (Summit, N.J., 1988.)

4. My favorite description of adolescence comes from a psychoanalyst, Peter Blos, who, in "The Child Analyst Looks at the Young Adolescent," writes: "What we witness is a regression manifested in oral greed, rapaciousness, smuttiness, oblivion to unkemptness, dirtiness and body odors, motoric restlessness, and experimentation in every direction of action and sensation." *From 12 to 16: Early Adolescence,* Jerome Kagan and Robert Coles, eds. (New York: Norton, 1972), 54.

5. Reported in Jerry Adler, "Kids Growing Up Scared." *Newsweek*, 10 January, 1994, 44.

6. Ibid., 45.

Chapter 1

1. *Oxford English Dictionary* (Oxford: Oxford University Press, 1971), 748.

2. Anna Freud has written a psychoanalytic view of mental health and illness. *In Adolescence as a Developmental Disturbance*, she writes: "Our psychoanalytic investigations of individuals have convinced us that the line of demarcation between mental health and illness cannot be drawn as sharply as had been thought before. Especially so far as the neuroses are concerned, neurotic nuclei are found in the minds of normal people as regularly as large areas of normal functioning are

part of the makeup of every neurotic. Also, people cross and record the border between mental health and illness many times during their lives." Excerpted from William C. Sze, *The Human Life Cycle* (New York: Aronson, 1975), 245. Encouraging, eh?

3. Western thought is obsessed with the notion of categories and boxes and stages, each labeled and defined. It makes for clarity, no doubt, but these mechanistic paradigms pose a problem; human beings' lives do not move as if on a steady course. Although there are some quite recognizable predictors—the onset of menarche or the entrance into junior high, human development is much more bumpy than a one-to-one, time-locked correlation between an age and a stage. Rather, it is embedded in a complex web of being. In short, nurture and nature are still alive and well.

4. Rolf E. Muuss, *Theories of Adolescence*, 3rd Edition (New York: Random House, 1975), 233.

5. N. Krell. *The Universal Experience of Adolescence* (London: University of London Press, 1969), 9.

6. Gail Sheehy, *New Passages: Mapping Your Life across Time* (New York: Random House, 1995), 67.

7. For more on the nature of contemporary adolescence and narcissism, please read Neil Postman's *The Disappearance of Childhood* (New York: Vintage, 1994). Postman takes a hard look at how "in having access to the previously hidden fruit of adult information, [adolescents] are expelled from the garden of childhood," 97. He describes the condition of the "adultified child" and the "childified adult."

Chapter 2

1. David Byrne, "The Great Curve," from *Remain in Light,* RZO (Rascoff, Zysblat Organization, Inc., 1990).

2. There is no intention here to draw true parallels to clinical cases. The syndrome I describe reflects "normal" symptoms of a childhood disease, however exasperating they might be, however difficult to distinguish from real trouble. Much more serious cases require a whole new form of remediation and intervention.

3. I suggest you read a wonderful book the title of which is explanation enough: Anthony E. Wolf, Ph.D., *Get Out of My Life: But Could You Drive Me and Cheryl to the Mall?: A Parent's Guide to the New Teenager* (New York: Noonday, 1992).

4. The news reports of the Branch Dividian cult compound residents in Waco, Texas, and the foiled plot of skinheads and members of the Fourth Reich to kill Rodney King and blow up a well-known African-American church in Los Angeles have revealed self-sacrificing devotion to adults who talk of doctrines as sacred covenants, of demands for purity, of rites of passage, of the need to give up one's individual identity. Please see chapter 7, "Crossing the Line," where I address this issue in greater detail.

5. Theodore Lidz, *The Person: His Development Throughout the Life Cycle* (New York: Basic Books, Inc., 1968), 299.

6. Nathan W. Ackerman, M.D., *The Psychodynamics of Family Life* (New York: Basic Books, Inc., 1958), 269.

7. Alex J. Packer, *Bringing Up Parents* (Washington, D.C.: Acropolis Books, Inc., 1985), 38.

Chapter 3

1. Benjamin Spock, M.D., and Michael B Rothenberg. *Baby and Child Care* (New York: Pocket Books, 1971).

2. William Damon, *The Moral Child* (New York: The Free Press, 1988), 112. Damon discusses the differences between permissive, authoritarian, and authoritative parenting.

3. Lucinda Franks, "Little Big People," *New York Times Magazine*, 10 October, 1993, 34. Though the author speaks mostly about affluent youth, I have witnessed the characteristics of a generation that transcends class lines.

4. Robert Bly, *No Sibling Society* (Reading, Mass.: Addison-Wesley Publishing Company, 1996), 3-44.

5. Certainly, standards for behavior must be determined, discussed, and displayed. However, the facts of life with a teenager are such that the standards cannot turn into a set or rigid "should's," for you will be sorely disappointed.

6. John Holt, *Why Children Fail* (New York: Dell Publishing Company, 1964), 168.

7. Refer to chapter 6: "Lying, Cheating, and Stealing: A Guide to the Ethically Challenged," for more on consequences.

8. Andrew G. Yellen, Ph.D., *The Art of Perfect Parenting: And Other Absurd Ideas* (Northridge, Calif.: Yellen and Associates, 1993), 27-32.

9. Jim Astman, headmaster of The Oakwood School in North Hollywood, California, and adjunct professor of Education at Claremont Graduate School.

10. Lori Stern, "Conceptions of Separation and Connection in Female Adolescents," *Making Connections: The Relational Worlds of Adolescent Girls at Emma Willard School,* eds. Carol Gilligan, Nona P. Lyons, and Trudy J. Hanmer (Cambridge, Mass.: Harvard University Press, 1990).

11. Deborah Tannen, *You Just Don't Understand* (New York: William Morrow and Co., 1991).

12. Students at The Oakwood School, in North Hollywood, California, interviewed by Jim Astman and author, 1980-1994; and The Bush School, Seattle, Washington, interviewed by author, 1994-1996.

13. KCET, Los Angeles: The Public Television Outreach Alliance campaign poster: The Year of the Family, 1991.

14. Elizabeth Mehren and Lynn Smith, "Stretching The Family Circle," *Los Angeles Times,* View, 1-2.

Chapter 4

1. The American Academy of Pediatrics, *Caring for Your Adolescent: Ages 12-21.* Donald E. Greydanus, M.D., Editor, 138.

2. Philip Elmer-Dewitt, "On a Screen Near You: Cyberporn," *Time,* 3 July 1995, 38–45.

3. Committe on Adolescence, Group for the Advancement of Psychiatry; Normal Adolescence, introduction by Katherine B. Oettinger.

4. Here's a frightening notion from Neil Postman's The Disappearance of Childhood: "As I write, twelve- and thirteen-year old girls are among the highest-paid models in America. In advertisements in all the visual media, they are presented to the public in the guise of knowing and sexually-enticing adults, entirely com-

fortable in the milieu of eroticism. After seeing such displays of soft-core pornography, those of us not yet fully conditioned to the new American attitudes towards children yearn for the charm and seductive innocence of Lolita" (New York: Vintage, 1994).

5. Andrea Warren and Jay Wiedenkeller, *Everybody's Doing It: How to Survive Your Teenagers' Sex Life (and Help Them Survive It, Too)* (New York: Penguin Books, 1993), xviii, xix.

6. William Carlos Williams, "This is Just To Say," from *The American Tradition in Literature*, 6th ed. (New York: Random House, 1985).

7. "Hostile Hallways: The American Association of University Women Survey on Sexual Harassment in America's Schools" (June, 1993), 5.

8. Mark Walsh, "Judge Rules Students Sexually Harassed by Peers May Collect District Damages," reported in *Education Week*, 15 September 1993, 13.

9. From Harry Maurer, ed,. *Sex: An Oral History* (New York: Viking, 1994).

10. Thomas Lickona, "Where Sex Education Went Wrong," *Educational Leadership*, Vol. 51, Number 3, (November 1993), 84–89.

11. A word coined in the feature film, *Clueless*, Robert Lawrence and Scott Rudin, producers, Paramount Pictures, 1995.

12. By the way, only 34 percent of adolescents alter their behavior as a result of fear of the disease. Bruce Roscoe, and Tammy L. Kruger, *Adolescence* 25, no. 97 (Spring 1990), 39–48.

13. In some parts of the country, there really is no turning back. The New Haven, Connecticut, School District, as of 1993, began offering condoms to fifth graders.

14. Child Health, U.S.A. '92, reported in *America's Agenda* (Winter, 1994) "Graphic Facts of Adolescent Life."

15. "Norplant Wins Teenage Fans," *Los Angeles Times,* Section B, 9 September, 1993, 16.

16. Please see chapter 9, "Difference in the 1990s" for a discussion on gay and lesbian issues in adolescence.

17. Michael Granberry, "Backlash to Teaching Chastity," *Los Angeles Times*, Section C, 15 February, 1994, 1.

18. I strongly suggest that you read a wonderful book by Harvard professor Carol Gilligan, entitled *A Different Voice* (Boston: Harvard University Press), 1992. Ms. Gilligan's book provides detailed insights into the nature of young women's experiences. Please also see chapter 8, "Young Women: Finding Voice and Heart."

19. "When It Happens," publication of the Santa Monica Hospital Medical Center, Rape Treatment Center, 1994.

20. Michelle Stacey, "Bad Boys," *Seventeen* (November, 1993) 126. Stacey reports the findings of Michael Resnick, Ph.D., who describes young boys in groups who submerge their sense of self. "Adolescents have what's called a porous sense of self, which means that at any moment who you think you are is very fluid." A young man with such a porous sense is vulnerable to all the basest elements of behavior.

21. Irene Lacher, "The Rape Debate," *Los Angeles Times*, Metro, 17 October 1993, 1

22. Betty W. Phillips, Ph.D., "Ignore Child Abuse Now, Attend to Adult Social Problems Later." *Child and Adolescent Behavior Letter* (Brown University, Oct. 1993): 1–4.

23. "Fallout from child-abuse cases is taking its toll: Teachers and others are

scared to reach out—and kids miss hugs that used to come so freely." Bettijane Levine, "The Forbidden Touch," *Los Angeles Times*, View, 18 November, 1993

24. "Beyond the Condom Wars: A Comprehensive Approach to AIDS Education," *The Harvard Education Letter* (September/October, 1993), 6.

25. Carol Brzozowski-Gardner, "Teachers, Trust, and AIDS Information," *Education Week*, 18 October, 1995, 32.

26. "School Administrators, Parents, and Sex Education: A Resolvable Paradox?" *Adolescence* 24, 1989 (Fall), 95.

Chapter 5

1. "Students Plot Against The Teacher" *Los Angeles Times*, Section A, 10 July, 1993, 45.

2. Melinda Henneberger, "Gang Membership Grows In Middle-Class Suburbs," *New York Times*, July 24, 1993.

3. Please see chapter 6: "Lying, Cheating, and Stealing: A Short Guide to the Ethically Challenged" for more on cheating.

4. William Kilpatrick, "Turning Out Moral Illiterates," *Los Angeles Times*, 20 July, 1993, View, 48

5. Jill Smolowe, "Crusade for the Classroom," *Time*, 1 November, 1993, 34.

6. For a little inspiration here, I suggest you flip through a book entitled: *No Kidding Around!: America's Young Activists Are Changing Our World, And you Can Too*, by Wendy Schaetzel Lesko, from the Activism 2000 Project, Co. 1992.

7. David L. Kirp, *Learning by Heart: Aids and Schoolchildren in America's Communities* (Rutgers University Press, 1989).

8. David Elkind, *Children and Adolescents; Interpretive Essays on Jean Piaget* (New York: Oxford University Press, 1970), 50.

9. Carol Gilligan, *A Different Voice: Psychological Theory and Women's Development* (Cambridge, Mass.: Harvard University Press, 1982), 29.

10. Please see chapter 8, "Young Women: Finding Voice and Heart," for more information on young women's development, seen from an educator's perspective.

11. William Kilpatrick, *Why Johnny Can't Tell Right from Wrong: and What We Can Do about It* (New York: Touchstone Books, 1993), 150.

12. From Eleazar Moody, *The School of Good Manners, Composed for the Help of Parents in Teaching Their Children How to Carry It in Their Places During Their Minority* (Boston, 1772).

13. From Todd Eckerson, "Teaching Ethics: A Sacred Responsibility," *CRIS Newsletter* (Council for Religion in Independent Schools) Vol. 12, Number 6, February, 1993.

14. Joan DelFattore, *What Johnny Shouldn't Read: Textbook Censorship in America* (New Haven, Conn.: Yale University Press, 1992), 47.

15. See chapter 9: "Difference in the 1990s" for more information on the effect of textbook censorship on adolescents.

16. The great sages themselves bitched and moaned about their youth. In the 8th century, B.C., Hesiod wrote: "I see no hope for the future for our people if they are dependent on the frivolous youth of today, for certainly all youth are reckless beyond words . . . When I was a boy, we were taught to be discreet and respectful of elders, but the present youth are exceedingly wise and impatient of restraint."

17. Aristotle, *Ethics* (London: Longmans, Green, 1886). Such admonitions are perennial. Aristotle urged the generation of youth in his day to cool their passions.

18. G. Fenstermacher, "Some Moral Considerations on Teaching as a Profession," in J. Goodlad, R. Soder, & K.A. Sirotnik (Eds.), 1990.

19. Martha Strauss, "Moral Development in Adolescents," from *Independent School* 3, Fall, 1987, 25.

20. Reported in "South-Central's Garden of Pride," in *Los Angeles Times* Editorial, pg. B6, January 3, 1994.

21. John W. Layman, *Inquiry and Learning: Realizing Science Standards in the Classroom,* "The Thinking Series," from the National Center for Cross Disciplinary Teaching and Learning (New York: The College Board, 1966), 14.

22. Amelie Rorty, "What It Takes To Be Good," in *The Moral Self: Building a Better Paradigm,* Gil Noam, Thomas Wren, eds. (Cambridge, Mass.: MIT Press, 1993), 33. Reviewed by Arthur J. Schwartz, in *Harvard Educational Review* 63, No. 4, Winter, 1993, 498.

23. John Dewey, *Experience and Education* (New York: Collier Books, 1972), 16.

24. William Damon, Greater Expectations: Overcoming the Culture of Indulgence in America's Homes and Schools (New York: Free Press, 1995).

25. For more discussion on issues of difference, please see chapter 9, "Difference in the 1990s."

26. For more on cults, please see chapter 7, "Crossing the Line: When Behaviors Go Too Far."

Chapter 6

1. The list of reasons for our lack of moral conscience is daunting. "The news suggests that guns, drugs, television, moral relativism, welfare, violence, sheer viciousness, careerism, testosterone, greed, hedonism, selfishness, loss of community, isolation and loneliness, too much wealth, too much poverty, racism, the victim's mentality, the death of shame, the dismantling of expectations, or other forces have moronized the culture and obliterated the moral center of the American brain." Lance Morrow, "Yin and Yang: Sleaze and Moralizing," *Time,* 26 December 1994—3 January, 1995, 150.

2. Toch Thomas and Betsy Wagner, "Schools for Scandal," *US News and World Report,* 27 April 1992, 66–72.

3. I see this as a particular problem in private schools, where the stakes are quite high. "I pay a fortune for you to go to that school; the least you can do is succeed."

4. The word plagiarism comes from the Latin word for kidnapping.

Chapter 7

1. Benjamin R. Barber, "America Skips School," *Harpers,* November 1993, 40.

2. This is an area under considerable scrutiny. Childhood depression can emerge as a result of innumerable factors. One doctor claims that there is "no reliable evidence for any theory of childhood depression, whether biological, psychological, or social." Reported in "Mood Disorders in Childhood and Adolescence— Part I," *The Harvard Mental Health Letter,* published by Harvard Medical School, November 1993, 2.

3. A wide variety of help is available, ranging from outpatient programs for

individuals and groups, daycare, and longer-term resident programs. Though the very notion of psychiatric intervention may be frightening, research has shown that competent psychiatric hospitals can help teenagers considerably.

4. I am also including cigarette use under the category of drugs, for cigarettes are a widely used and abused substance.

5. Interestingly enough, recent court rulings have placed liability in the hands of those parents who are absent at parties held in their homes where illegal activities may lead to dangers.

6. National Institute on Drug Abuse, reported in "Illicit Drug Use by Youths Shows Marked Increase," Marlene Cimons and Ronald J. Ostrow, *Los Angeles Times,* Tuesday, 1 February 1994, A10.

7. M.A.D.D. (Mothers Against Drunk Driving) report, 1993.

8. L. D. Johnston, et al., "Drug Use, Drinking and Smoking: National Survey Results from High School, College and Beyond Adult Populations," 1975-1988, NIDA, 38.

9. National Center for Education Statistics and Westat, Inc., 1993.

10. Inhalants are extremely dangerous. After an initial euphoria, hallucinations light-headedness, and a sense of empowerment, dangerous behaviors can result, including paranoia, mental fatigue, hostility. First-time use can be fatal.

11. Johnston, Bachman, and O'Malley, National Household Survey, 1988, reported in "Fourth Biennial Statewide Survey of Drug and Alcohol Use among California Students in Grades 7, 9, and 11," June, 1993.

12. Survey, commissioned by the Partnership for a Drug-Free America, 1996.

13. P.R.I.D.E. (from National Parents' Resource Institute for Drug Education—survey), 2 Nov., 1995.

14. Adapted from the partnership for a Drug-Free Greater New York and the National Council on Alcoholism and Drug Dependency.

15. Melinda Henneberger, "'Pot Surges Back, But It's Like, a Whole New World," *New York Times,* 7 February, 1994, E18.

16. Janet Cox, "The Bacchus Beat," the official monthly newsletter of the Bacchus & Bamma Peer Education Network, Internet: http://www.linkmag.com/bacchus/bb_october/cover.html

17. "How Nicotine Tricks the Brain," *The Seattle Times,* Science section, 9 April, 1996, A6, provided by Knight-Ridder Newspapers.

18. Jean L. Richardson, et al., "Relationship Between After-School Care of Adolescents and Substance Use, Risk Taking, Depressed Mood, and Academic Achievement," *Pediatrics,* (92): 31–38, 1993.

19. Please see chapter 11, "Let's Get Motivated: Getting Them Up in the Morning."

20. Much useful information about drug and alcohol abuse comes from Sharry Heckt-Deszo, a drug information speaker. Ms. Heckt-Deszo can be reached by phone at: (206) 772–4136.

21. D.A. Cole, "Suicide, Adolescent," from *Encyclopedia of Adolescence* 2, edited by Richard M. Lerner, Anne C. Peterson, and Jeanne Brooks-Gunn, (New York and London: Garland Publishing Inc, 1991), 1113.

22. Ibid., 1114.

23. "A Concern For Every American," from *Information Plus: An Information Series on Current Topics.* 1993 Edition, 152.

24. Mary Giffin and Carol Felsenthal, A Cry For Help. Exploring and Exploding the Myths about Teenage Suicide: A Guide for all Parents of

Adolescents. (Garden City N.Y.: Doubleday, 1983), reported in Glen Evans and Farberow, Norman L., Ph.D., *The Encyclopedia of Suicide* (New York: Fact on File, 1988), 5.

25. From "Preventing Adolescent Suicide" in *The Harvard Education Letter* 3, No.6; Nov. 1987. A focus on the work of David Shaffer and Madelyn Gould of Columbia University.

26. Report of the Secretary's Task Force on Youth Suicide, edited by Marcia R. Feinleib, published by the U.S. Department of Health and Human Services.

27. Susan Eaton, "A Culture Obsessed with Thinness Pushes Some Adolescents into Eating Disorders," *Harvard Education Letter*, 7 Nov/Dec., 1993

28. Ibid., 7.

29. Kathy Bowen-Woodward, Ph.D., *Coping with a Negative Body Image* (New York: The Rosen Publishing Group, 1989), 66–68.

30. Steven Levenkron, *Treating and Overcoming Anorexia Nervosa* (New York: Warner Books, 1982), 7–8.

31. H.Bruch, *Eating Disorders: Obesity, Anorexia Nervosa, and the Person Within* (New York: Basic Books, 1973), 66.

32. Saul Levine, "Radical Departures," *Psychology Today*, August, 1984, 21

33. Ibid., 25.

34. A. L Mauss, and D. Peterson, *Prodigals as Preachers: The Jesus Freaks and the Return to Respectability*, Paper presented at the Convention of the Society for the Scientific Study of Religion, San Francisco, October, 1973.

35. A phrase coined by psychologist and spiritual guru, Fritz Perls.

36. Leon Bing, "When You're a Crip (or a Blood)," *What Are We Talking about?* (New York: Harper's, 1993), 189.

37. Ibid., 205.

38. Luis J. Rodriguez, *Always Running: La Vida Loca—Gang Days in L.A.* (Willimantic, Conn.: Curbstone Press, 1992), 250.

39. "Today's Gangs Cross Cultural and Geographic Bounds," excerpted from *School Safety Update*, Nov. 1991, 1, and included in *Education Digest*, May 1992, 8.

40. Ibid., 9.

41. "Youth Gangs," *CQ Researcher*, published by the Congressional Quarterly, Inc. (Vol. 1, No. 22),11 October, 1991, 761.

42. Andrew Murr, "When Gangs Meet the Handicapped," *Newsweek*, 7 May 1990, 7.

43. National Public Radio report, in "All Things Considered," April 11, 1995

44. Susan S. Lang, *Extremist Groups in America* (New York: Franklin Watts Co., 1990), 91.

45. Ibid., 116.

46. C.P. Vey, cartoon, *New York Times*, 12 May, 1993.

Chapter 8

1. From A. Poulin, Jr., editor: *Contemporary American Poetry*, 4th ed. (New York: Houghton Mifflin, 1985), 84.

2. Carol Gilligan, Annie Rogers, and Deborah Tolman, eds. *Women, Girls, and Psychotherapy: Reframing Resistance* (New York: Harrington Park Press, 1991), 105.

3. Author interview with Rebecca Figueroa, English teacher at The Oakwood School.

4. Such stories can be found in Annie G. Rogers, "Voice, Play, and a Practice

of Ordinary Courage in Girls' and Women's Lives," *Harvard Educational Review* 63, no. 3, Fall, 1993, 271.

5. Zora Neale Hurston, *Their Eyes Were Watching God* (New York: Harper and Row, 1957, 1990), 72.

6. Harvard Educational Review, op cit., 281.

7. "Girls Talk; Boys Talk More," from *Harvard Educational Review,* Jan/Feb., 1991, 6.

8. Ibid., 7.

9. Anne Chapman, *The Difference It Makes: A Resource Book on Gender for Educators* (Boston: National Association of Independent Schools, 1988), 21.

10. The problem is compounded when it comes to ethnicity. In one report, African-American girls have fewer interactions with teachers than white girls *School Library Journal,* April, 1992, 18.

11. American Association of University Women report, 1992.

12. All interviews, except for those attributed to other sources, were conducted by the author in public and private schools in Los Angeles and Seattle.

13. Alice Walker, *The Color Purple* (New York: Harcourt Brace & Company, 1992), 11.

14. For a thorough treatment of girls and leadership, please see Carol Gilligan, ed. *Making Connections: The Relational Worlds of Adolescent Girls* (Boston: Harvard University Press, 1990), especially the chapter: "Competencies and Visions: Emma Willard Girls Talk about Being Leaders," by Nona P. Lyons, Jane Forbes Saltonstall, and Trudy J. Hanmer.

15. This quotation comes from "Sheila," in Lori Stern's "Disavowing the Self in Female Adolescence," from *Women, Girls and Psychotherapy: Reframing Resistance,* Carol Gilligan, Annie Rogers, Deborah Tolman (New York: Harrington Park Press, 1991), 111. Writer Natalie Goldberg writes: "I never felt that I fit in. I was uncomfortable with the idea of mascara, flirting with boys. I hated the idea that I had to have children, that I would be a housewife . . . I rebelled, but I turned it on myself, and instead of feeling the energy that rebellion can produce, I became repressed and felt bland, unemotional inside." From *Long Quiet Highway* (New York: Bantam Books, 1993), 6.

16. Many African-American students report a feeling of resentment and discomfort every February, when posters suddenly appear in celebration Black History Month. They feel as if black history, even themselves, are tokenized and therefore trivialized. Although they acknowledge the importance of recognition, they feel as if they have been separated. A number of students complain that the issues lightly covered during this period are invasive, rather than generic and pervasive.

17. Peggy McIntosh, "Interactive Phases of Curricular and Personal Re-Visions with Regard to Race." Working Paper, No. 219, Wellesley College Center for Research on Women, 1990.

18. from Elizabeth Debold, LaurieWilson, and Idelisse Malave, *Mother Daughter Revolution* quoted in review by Anna Quindlen, "Birthday Girl," *New York Times,* 21 November 1993.

19. Ann F. Caron, *Don't Stop Loving Me: A Reassuring Guide for Mothers of Adolescent Daughters* (New York: Henry Holt and Company, 1990), excerpted in *Good Housekeeping,* Nov. 1990, 87.

20. Sally L. Archer, "Gender Differences in Identity Development: Issues of Process, Domain, and Timing," *Journal of Adolescence,* December 1989, 120.

21. Ibid., 130.

22. White males in positions of leadership, according to recent studies, have the most to lose, as affirmative action programs assist women and persons of color in promotions. Some researchers forecast increased tension as the numbers reach a critical mass.

23. Mary Pipher, Ph.D, *Reviving Ophelia: Saving the Selves of Adolescent Girls* (New York: Ballantine Books, 1994), 281. Ophelia, from Shakespeare's *Hamlet,* is destroyed by societal expectation and a loss of self. Pipher eloquently describes Ophelia's demise: "Dressed in elegant clothes that weigh her down, she drowns in a stream filled with flowers."

Chapter 9

1. Some experts believe that such actions are "fueled as often by insecurity and frustration as by hostility." (*New York Times* editorial, July 1, 1995); furthermore, "the coarser language that now permeates popular movies and music directed at young people may give those young people a greater sense of license to use such terms more widely. In addition, many students do not comprehend the history and persistence of oppression against particular groups." Nevethless, such hate messages are sinking in and have resulted in tangible acts of cruelty against those not perceived as part of the mainstream.

2. Edward Dolnick, "Deafness as Culture," *Atlantic Monthly,* September, 1993, 37.

3. Though the official U.S. Attorney General reports on "hate crimes" do not include those against persons with disabilities, "states which have passed hate crime data collection legislation . . . included disability as a characteristic which places those individuals at risk." From Waxman, Barbara Faye. "Hatred: The Unacknowledged Dimension in Violence against Disabled People," in *Sexuality and Disability* 9, no. 3, 1991, 186.

4. "Project 10: Gay and Lesbian Students Find Acceptance in Their School Community," Arthur Lipkin, from *Teaching Tolerance,* Fall, 1992.

5. Dan Woog, *School's Out: The Impact of Gay and Lesbian Issues on America's Schools* (Boston, Mass.: Alyson Publications, 1996). Mr. Woog writes: "An invisible minority has suddenly turned up in all 50 states—and if they haven't already, they'll be coming out soon, at a school near you."

6. There's an infamous history behind this. During the Inquisition in fifteenth and sixteenth century France, executions of homosexuals for heresy involved burning at the stake. Faggots, or small bundles of sticks, were used to start the fire. On the priority list, lesbians were rated as worse offenders than gay men; therefore, women were burned first. After a while, the homosexual males were wrapped around the female and served as faggots themselves to start the fire.

7. Donovan R. Walling, "Gay Teens at Risk," *Fastback 357*, Phi Delta Kappa Educational Foundation, 1993, 16.

8. From Susan Eaton, "Gay Students Find Little Support in Most Schools." *Harvard Education Letter,* August, 1993, 186.

9. From gay student responding to interviewer for film on the Secretary's Task Force on Suicide, 1992.

10. Robert J. Bidwell, Ph.D., Senior Fellow in Adolescent Medicine of the Department of Pediatrics, University of Washington School of Medicine. *Journal of Pediatric Health Care* (Vol. 2, 3-8) 1988.

11. Robert Jones, "Dangerous Liaisons," from *Los Angeles Times Magazine,* 25 July 1993, 36.

12. In my experience with students, the discovery of gayness occurs earlier for boys than for girls. Such realizations are accompanied, very clearly, by enormous discomfort, especially as they compare themselves with their friends, who begin an open expression of attraction to the opposite sex. As gay boys discover their sexuality and the camaraderie that accompanies it, they feel at a special disadvantage. They are also subject to extraordinary ridicule if they act in an "effeminate" manner.

13. I have heard numerous parents blame the atmosphere of colleges these days for their son's or daughter's new assertiveness about being gay. I am convinced, however, that the strictures—moral and social—that gay teens experience in high school may be too great. They may simply wish to wait until for the time and place that will make them feel the most supported.

14. Paul Monette, *Becoming a Man—Half a Life Story* (New York: Harcourt, Brace, Jovanovich, 1992), 278.

15. Carol J. Gill, "Cultivating Common Ground: Women with Disabilities," *Health/PAC Bulletin,* Winter, 1992, 34.

16. Though this notion of sympathy and pity may be true, there is a harrowing private story. The Associated Press has found that disabled children are abused (sexually or physically) and neglected at rates much higher than other children. Many may be carrying around secrets. Reported in *The Brown University Child and Adolescent Behavior Letter* 9, no. 12, December 1993, 6.

17. Joseph R. Shapiro, *No Pity: People with Disabilities Forging a New Civil Rights Movement* (New York: Times Books, 1993), 14.

18. Ibid., 14.

19. Education for All Handicapped Children Act, 1975, renamed the Individuals with Disabilities Education Act. Shapiro writes: "Like black Americans, disabled ones were looking to the schools for equity and social justice," 166.

20. Harilyn Rousso, "Positive Female Images at Last!," *The Exceptional Parent,* April 1986, 14.

21. Marion Wright Edelman, *The Measure of Our Success: A Letter to My Children and Yours* (Boston: Beacon Press, 1992).

22. bell hooks, professor of English at City College in New York, has written longingly about how her all-black school nurtured her intellect "so that we could become scholars, thinkers, and cultural workers—black folks who used our 'minds.' bell hooks, *Teaching to Transgress: Education as the Practice of Freedom* (New York: Routledge, 1994), 2.

23. James S. Kunen, "The End of Integration," *Time,* 29 April 1996, 39–46.

24. Dana Zohar and Ian Marshall, *The Quantum Society: Mind, Physics, and a New Social Vision* (New York: William Morrow and Company, Inc, 1996), 326-27.

25. Lisa Delpit, "Skills and Other Dilemmas of a Progressive Black Educator," Harvard Educational Review, 56, (4), 379–85. Also discussed in: Debra Viadero, "Unconvential Wisdom," *Teacher Magazine,* April, 1996, 46-51.

26. Stephen Bates, "The Next Front in the Book Wars," *New York Times*—Education Life supplement, 6 November 1994, 22-23.

27. Robert Pirsig, *Zen and the Art of Motorcycle Maintenance* (New York: William Morrow and Company, Inc., 1984), 312.

28. The media sends conflicting messages. Though the advertising world has

made attempts to acknowledge difference, the television and feature film industry continues to exploit stereotypes.

29. Robert Coles, *The Spiritual Life of Children* (Boston: Houghton Mifflin Company, 1990), 88.

Chapter 10

1. Jillian Roberts, *I'd Rather Be in Philadelphia* (New York: Ballantine Books, 1992), 191.

2. Part of William H. Gass' prose poem, "In the Heart of the Heart of the Country" (1968) describes school which, to him, is a petri dish of "croaking jealousy; bloated bigotry; coiling suspicion; wormish blindness; crocodile malice." From *The American Tradition in Literature,* Sixth Edition. Perkins, Bradley, Beatty, and Long, eds. (New York: Random House, 1985), 642.

3. Irene M Josselyn, "The Adolescent Today," in William C. Sze, *The Human Cycle* (New York, Jason Aronson, Inc., 1975), 260.

4. Review of "A Study of High Schools," *Harvard Educational Review* (Vol. 56, No. 1) February 1986, 37.

5. Ibid., 37.

6. R. B. Des Dixon, "Future Schools: And How to Get There from Here," *Phi Delta Kappan,* January 1994, 360. Of late, words like "slow," "haphazard," "spotty," "inconclusive," "quixotic," and "restless" are used to describe the impact of the school reform movements of the last fifteen years.

7. Reported in Elizabeth Mehren, "Taming the Blackboard Jungle," *Los Angeles Times* View, E3, 13 January, 1994.

8. Dixon, op cit., 37.

9. Maxine Greene, *Releasing the Imagination: Essays on Education, the Arts, and Social Change* (San Francisco: Jossey Bass Publishers, 1995), 13.

10. "Voices from the Inside: A Report on Schooling from Inside the Classroom." The Institute for Education in Transformation at the Claremont Graduate School, 1992, 11.

11. Ibid., 10.

12. Madeline R Grumet, *Bitter Milk: Women and Teaching* (Amherst, Mass.: University of Massachusetts Press, 1988), 163.

13. Maxine Greene, "In Search of a Critical Pedagogy," *Harvard Educational Review* 56, No. 4, November 1986, 427.

14. Alvin Tresselt, *The Mitten: An Old Ukrainian Folktale* (New York: Mulberry Books, 1989).

15. "Bridging the Gap," *Seattle Times,* Focus section—E, 28 April, 1996, E3.

16. Joy G. Dryfoos, "Full-Service Schools," *Educational Leadership* (Vol. 53, No.7), April 1996, 18–23

17. For a fascinating treatment of society's and education's affect on its students, please see Paulo Freire, *The Pedagogy of the Oppressed* (New York: Continuum, 1970), 88.

18. James Alan Astman, "How to Keep Our Dreams from Dragging in the Dust," *Oakwood School Monograph,* address to faculty, 1988, 13.

19. I strongly recommend Dr. Howard Gardner's *Frames of Mind: The Theory of Multiple Intelligences* (New York: Basic Books, Inc., 1983), a fascinating look at the various forms of intelligence—artistic and kinetic intelligence and spatial intel-

ligences, for example, which impel teachers to determine not so much how smart the students are, but rather how the students are smart. You will certainly recognize your child in his chapters.

20. William H. Gass, "Exile," *The Best American Essays—1992* (New York: Ticknor and Fields, 1992), 120.

21. James S. Kunen, "The End of Integration," *Time,* 29 April, 1996, 39–45.

22. Thomas Armstrong, "ADD as a Social Invention," *Education Week* 15, no. 7, October, 1995, 33, 40.

23. Theodore Sizer, the director of the Coalition of Essential Schools, has written extraordinary books on problems facing school and the reform movement—*Horace's Compromise* and *Horace's School,* which examine those features of contemporary schooling which undermine intellectual inquiry. He sets a specific path for contemporary school reform which acknowledges both the importance of a personalized education and of structures that respect the need to demonstrate competency.

24. My experience, corroborated by numerous research studies, indicates that underrepresented students benefit the most from lowered class size. Of course, lowering the teacher-student ratio is not enough; there must be a concomitant change in approach, curriculum vision, and pedagogical strategy. In other words, once the numbers get manageable, the space must open for possibilities that can enhance the growth and development of an adolescent's mind. I am referring to studies cited in "Synthesis of Research on the Effects of Class Size" in *Educational Leadership,* April 1990, 13.

25. James Gleick, *Chaos: Making a New Science* (New York: Viking, 1988), 3.

26. Alfred North Whitehead writes: "Inventive genius requires pleasurable mental activity as a condition for its vigorous exercises." *The Aims of Education* (New York: Free Press, 1929/1957), 45.

27. William Damon, *Greater Expectations: Overcoming the Culture of Indulgence in America's Homes and Schools* (New York: Free Press, 1995).

Chapter 11

1. Jerome Bruner, the noted psychologist and educator writes: "Somewhere between apathy and wild excitement there is an optimum level of aroused attention that is ideal for classroom activity." *The Process of Education* (Cambridge, Mass.: Harvard University Press, 1963), 72. It's not easy; the adolescent syndrome, however, can make teaching both a challenge and an inspiration.

2. Please see chapter 9, Difference in the 1990s, for more information on the pernicious effects of tracking on adolescents of color. "Homogenous" may, in theory, refer to "equal ability"; however, in many settings, the term refers to white students who tend to comprise the upper tracks.

3. Reported in "When Bright Kids Get Bad Grades" *Harvard Education Letter* 8, no. 6, Nov./Dec., 1992, 1–3.

4. Ibid., 3.

5. Howard Gardner. *Frames of Mind: The Theory of Multiplie Intelligences* (New York: Basic Books, 1985), x.

6. Ibid., 73.

7. Such notions are at the center of a national debate about standards, about how we assess children, about the nature and structure of our current educational system. Some educators believe that theories of intelligence are a smoke-screen for

avoiding the direct teaching of our cultural and scientific heritage, that schools that address such variety will dissemble into scattered elements of a fragmented education. You might refer to E.D. Hirsch's Cultural Literacy for an in-depth critique of such schools.

8. Jon Smith, "Filling Children's Heads," from The Oakwood School *Annual Report: 1992–1993,* 13.

9. Mihaly Csikzentmihaly, *Flow: The Psychology of Optimal Experience* (New York: Harper and Row Publishers, 1990), 261.

10. Jerome H. Bruns, Ed. *They Can But They Don't: Helping Students Overcome Work Inhibition* (New York: Viking, 1992), 49.

11. Dr. Tessa Albert Warschaw and Victoria Secunda, *Winning with Kids* (New York: Bantam Books, 1990), 285.

12. Recent attention has been paid to the increase of Attention-Deficit Hyperactivity Disorder (ADHD), which transcends class or racial or gender or economic bounds. A kid can be raised in a warm and authoritative family and attend a competent school, yet suffer from chronic inattention and disorganization, motor hyperactivity and impulsivity, and academic underachievement. They can't concentrate; they're easily distracted; they frequently call out at the dinner table or in the classroom. And they may start to give up. Such young people are frustrating for parents and teachers because they appear so bright. Though the discovery of ADHD is, in most cases, made much earlier in kids' lives, adolescence itself may mask the condition if it has not been previously diagnosed. A young man's or woman's moods may fluctuate widely. He/she may have outbursts of temper, learning deficits, a low frustration tolerance, and low self-esteem. If you are concerned about the possibility of ADHD, please contact your child's school and compare your own observations of your child with those who see him/her during the day. Once again, this is where the partnership between school and home is essential.

13. Donald D. Deschler, Ph.D., Jean B. Schumaker, Ph.D., and B. Keith Lenz, Ph.D., "Academic and Cognitive Interventions for LD Adolescents: Part I," *Learning Disability Quarterly* 17, no. 2, February 1984, 106–7.

14. "Social forces are undoubtedly at work, but maybe something biological is going on as well. For many kids, the onset of puberty brings alterations in the sleep-wake cycle . . . Dr. Mary Carskadon, a chronobiologist at Brown University School of Medicine in Providence, Rhode Island, believes that many teens need as much as 9 hours of sleep for maximum alertness." From "The Sleepy Teen Years," University of California at Berkeley *Wellness Letter,* August, 1995.

15. Priscilla Vail, *Smart Kids with School Problems* (New York: E.P. Dutton, 1987). Vail's book deals extensively with those impediments to the full benefit of a child's education.

16. K. Hurrelmann, U. Engel, B. Holler, and E. Nordlohne, "School, Family Conflicts and Psychosomatic Disorders," *Journal of Adolescence* 11, no. 3, September, 1988, 240.

17. William Damon. *Greater Expectations: Overcoming the Culture of Indulgence in America's Homes and Schools* (New York: Free Press, 1995), 74.

18. Martin E. P. Seligman, "Fall into Helplessness," *Psychology Today,* June, 1973, 65.

19. For a superb treatment of the parent-school alliance, see L. Eugene Arnold, ed. *Helping Parents Help Their Children* (New York: Brunner/Mazel Publishers, 1978) 363–78, "Teachers, Principals, and Parents: Guidance by Educators," by William Hetznecker, L. Eugene Arnold, and Arlene Phillips.

Conclusion

1. Marion Wright Edelman, *The Measure of Our Success: A Letter to My Children and Yours* (Boston: Beacon Press, 1992), 28.

2. The great French writer, André Malraux, tells a story of how, in 1940, he and a chaplain escaped the fascists. He reports on one of his long conversations and asked the chaplain:

"How long have you been hearing confessions?"

"About fifteen years."

"What has confession taught you about men?"

"Oh, confession teaches nothing, you know, because when a priest goes into the confessional he becomes another person—grace and all that. And yet . . . First of all, people are much more unhappy than one thinks . . . and then . . ."

He raised his brawny lumberman's arms in the starlit night: "And then, the fundamental fact is that there's no such thing as a grown-up person." From *Man's Fate* (New York: Random House, 1961), 242.

3. Mihaly Csikszentmihalyi, *Being Adolescent: Conflict and Growth in the Teenage Years* (New York: Basic Books, 1984), 163.

4. Jean L. Richardson, et al., "Relationship Between After-School Care of Adolescents and Substance Use, Risk Taking, Depressed Mood, and Academic Achievement," *Pediatrics,* 92(1): 32-38, 1993.

5. Geoffrey T. Holtz, *Welcome to the Jungle: The Why behind 'Generation X'* (New York: St. Martin's, 1995), 74.

6. Some students work to live, and the money earned helps the family. School often takes a back seat. Other students live to work, either because menial labor is more engaging than their present school-life, or because they feel like participants in the real world, or because the cash can take them places where they otherwise would not be able to go.

7. Robert Wright, "The Evolution of Despair," *Time* 28 August 1995, 50.

8. *Compuserve* magazine, March, 1994, 18.

9. E. B. White, *Stuart Little* (New York: Harper and Brothers, 1945), 155.

10. James Astman, "Speech to the Graduating Class of the Oakwood School, 1989.

11. Associated Press, "Teens Turn to Parents for Support," reported in *Christian Science Monitor,* June 16, 1995, 5.

12. Aeschylus, *The Tragedies of Aeschylus,* F.A. Paley, ed. (London: Whitaker, 1879), 336.

Recommended Reading

A briefly annotated list of sources—engaging reading by leading educators, social commentators, and psychologists.

Bell, Ruth and Leni Wildflower. *Talking with Your Teenager: A Book for Parents.* (New York: Random House, 1987). Effective strategies dealing with sexuality.

Bellah, Robert N. *Habits of the Heart: Individualism and Commitment in American Life.* (New York: Harper and Row, 1985). Social commentary about contemporary life.

Blake, Jeanne. *Risky Business: How to be AIDS-Smart and Stay Healthy: A Guide for Teenagers.* (New York: Workman Publishing, 1991). Very specific, clear information.

Bloom, Alan David. *The Closing of the American Mind.* (New York: Simon and Schuster, 1987). A powerful bestseller about the dumbing of America.

Bruns, Jerome H., D.A. Ed. *They Can But They Don't: Helping Students Overcome Work Inhibition.* (New York: Viking, 1992). A fascinating work, specific and clear, that sheds light on work-stoppages.

Carter, Carol. *Majoring in High School: Survival Tips for Students.* (New York: Noonday Press, Farrar, Straus, and Giroux, 1995). A clear, practical guide to strategies for successful coping. If your kids are up to it, this would be a helpful gift.

Damon, William. *The Moral Child.* (New York: The Free Press, 1988). A strong piece about authoritarian, authoritative, and permissive parenting.

Damon, William. *Greater Expectations: Overcoming the Culture of Indulgence in America's Homes and Schools.* (New York: Free Press), 1995. An attack on touchy-feely practices in parenting and teaching. Very worthwhile reading.

Debold, Elizabeth, Laurie Wilson, and Idelisse Malave. *Mother Daughter Revolution.* (Reading, Mass.: Addison-Wesley, 1993). Excellent treatment of the role of young women.

Dimoff, Timothy, and Steve Carper. *How To Tell If Your Kids Are Using Drugs.* (New York: Facts on File, Inc., 1992). Clear and helpful.

Edelman, Marian Wright. *The Measure of Our Success: A Letter to My Children and Yours.* (Boston: Beacon Press, 1992). Inspirational, thoughtful, emotional, substantial piece.

Elkind, David. *All Grown Up and No Place to Go: Teenagers in Crisis.* (Reading, Mass.: Addison-Wesley, 1984). Keep them busy and treat their emotional issues seriously—the important messages I got from this book.

Gardner, Howard. Frames of Mind: *The Theory of Multiple Intelligences.* (New York: Basic Books, 1983). Scintillating, in my opinion. A treatment of how kids are smart, rather than the treatments of how smart children are.

Gilligan, Carol. *A Different Voice: Psychological Theory and Women's Development.* (Boston: Harvard University Press, 1982). Simply put, a must. This is an important, late-twentieth century document.

Goleman, Daniel. *Emotional Intelligence.* (New York: Bantam Books, 1995). A mesmerizing treatment of the "new brain" and behavioral research in to the affective domain and its connection to intelligence. Any reader will find connections to one's own experience. An interesting document when one looks at one's own children.

Goodlad, John. *A Place Called School.* (New York: McGraw Hill, 1984). Another insider's view.

Hacker, Sylvia S. and Hacker, Randi. *What Every Teenager Really Wants to Know about Sex.* (New York: Carroll and Gray, 1993). Clear as a bell.

Harbeck, Karen, ed. *Coming Out of the Classroom Closet: Gay and Lesbian Students, Teachers, and Curricula.* (Binghamton, N.Y.: Harrington Park Press, 1992). Also clear as a bell. A thoughtful and specific treatment of the subject.

Hirsch, E.D. Cultural Literacy: *What Every American Needs to Know.* (New York: Vintage, 1988). This caused a storm of controversy because of its views toward getting students to learning something.

Holtz, Geoffey F. *Welcome to the Jungle: The Why Behind Generation X.* (New York: St. Martin's Griffin, 1995). A detailed, well-documented, interesting book about youth in their teens and twenties.

Hopson, Darlene Powell, M.D., and Derek S. Hopson, M.D. *Different and Wonderful: Raising Black Children in a Race-Conscious Society.* (New York: Fireside Books, 1992). Powerful, insightful, and serious. You may recognize your family here.

Keltner, Nancy, ed. *If You Print This, Please Don't Use My Name: Questions from Teens and Their Parents about Things That Matter.* (Davis, Calif.: Terra Nova Press, 1992). Many of your questions may be addressed here. An interesting format, too.

Kidder, Rushworth M. *How Good People Make Tough Choices.* (New York: William Morrow and Company, 1995). A superb book about the necessity for ethical fitness, the ability to make moral choices under pressure. Particularly exciting is the author's sense that many moral issues are debates between good versus good, rather than good versus bad. The former relationship allows for conversation; the latter eliminates it. Very readable.

Kohn, Alfie. *Punished by Rewards: The Trouble with Gold Stars, Incentive Plans, A's, Praise, and Other Bribes:* (Boston: Houghton Mifflin, 1993). A strong, well-documented treatment of the subject.

Kozol, Jonathon. *Amazing Grace: The Lives of Children and the Conscience of a Nation.* (New York: Crown, 1995). A telling description of the lives, the anecdotes, the feelings of vulnerability and hope amongst children living in the South Bronx. This book is moving and universal.

Kotlowitz, Alex. *There Are No Children Here: The Story of Two Boys Growing Up in the Other America.* (New York: Doubleday, 1992). Life in the projects, with lessons for us all.

Levine, Katherine G. *When Good Kids Do Bad Things.* (New York: Norton, 1991). Some interesting work here. Engaging reading on moral issues and adolescence.

Levine, Mel., M.D. *Keep a Head in School: A Student's Book about Learning Abilities and Learning Disorders.* (Cambridge, Mass.: Educators Publishing Service, 1990). Dr. Levine's work is consistently groundbreaking. He provides essential insights into learning disabilities and how students can cope with them successfully. Most anything he writes is a must for parents and educators.

Lickona, Dr. Thomas. *Raising Good Children.* (New York: Bantam, 1983). A must, with some telling step-by-step methodology here.

Lightfoot, Sara Lawrence. *The Good School: Portraits of Character and Culture.* (New York: Bantam, 1983). For those interested in the insides of schools, this is an extraordinary piece.

Mann, Judy. *The Difference: Growing Up Female in America.* (New York: Warner Books, 1994). A strong treatment of a subject worthy of our attention.

Muller, Ann. *Parents Matter: Parents' Relationships with Lesbian Daughters and Gay Sons.* (Tallahassee, Fla.: Naiad Press, 1987). More reinforcement for the notion that relationships with teenagers cannot be filled with rejection.

Nava, Michael and Robert Davidoff. *Created Equal: Why Gay Rights Matter to America.* (New York: St. Martin's Press, 1994). A political piece, an important document.

Pomeroy, Wardell B. *Girls and Sex.* 3d Edition (New York: Laurel-Leaf, 1991). Clear and evocative.

Postman, Neil. *The Disappearance of Childhood.* (New York: Vintage, 1994). Angry and thoughtful.

Rimm, Dr. Sylvia. *Why Bright Kids Get Bad Grades.* (New York: Crown, 1994). Some surprising information here. Very insightful.

Rodriguez, Luis J. *Always Running: La Vida Loca: Gang Days in L.A.* (Willimantic, Conn.: Curbstone Press, 1992). A beautifully written insider's view.

Sizer, Theodore. *Horace's Compromise: The Dilemma of the American High School.* (Boston: Houghton Mifflin, 1984). It will break your heart, but much of what Sizer is describing is taking place in America's schools.

Tannen, Deborah. *You Just Don't Understand: Women and Men in Conversation.* (New York: Ballantine, 1991). Clear, insightful, humorous. Be prepared to recognize yourself.

Vail, Priscilla I. *Smart Kids with School Problems.* (New York: E.P. Dutton, 1987). This is simply a brilliant book with insights for parents and teachers alike.

Warren, Andrea, and Jay Wiedenkeller. *Everybody's Doing It: How to Survive Your Teenagers' Sex Life (And Help Them Survive It, Too).* (New York: Penguin Books, 1993). Another insightful, clear book.

Wolf, Anthony E., Ph.D. *Get Out of My Life: But Could You Drive Me and Cheryl to the Mall?: A Parent's Guide to the New Teenager* (New York: Noonday, 1992). I loved this book. It is readable and substantial at the same time.

Bibliography

A list of the books used as source material for this book.

Aeschylus. *The Tragedies of Aeschylus,* F.A. Paley, ed. London: Whitaker, 1879.

Adler, Alfred. *Understanding Human Nature.* Greenwich, Conn: Fawcett Premier Book, 1954.

Arnold, Eugene L., ed. *Helping Parents Help Their Children.* New York: Brunner/Mazel, 1978.

Astman, James. *Monograph: A Dangerous Guide to the Forest: Education as a Moral Enterprise.* North Hollywood, California. The Oakwood School, 1987.

Balenky, Mary F., et al. *Women's Ways of Knowing.* New York: Basic Books, 1986.

Bell, Ruth and Leni Wildflower. *Talking with Your Teenager: A Book for Parents.* New York: Random House, 1987.

Bellah, Robert N. *Habits of the Heart: Individualism and Commitment in American Life.* New York: Perennial Library—Harper and Row, 1985.

Bettleheim, Bruno. *A Good Enough Parent: A Book on Child Rearing.* New York: A. Knopf, Inc., 1987.

Bing, Leon. *Smoked.* New York: Harper Collins, 1993.

Bing, Leon. *The Harper's Forum Book: What Are We Talking About?* 1991, *Harper's* magazine.

Blake, Jeanne. *Risky Business: How to be AIDS-Smart and Stay Healthy: A Guide for Teenagers.* New York: Workman Publishing, 1991.

Bloom, Alan David. *The Closing of the American Mind.* New York: Simon and Schuster, 1987.

Bowen-Woodward, Kathy, Ph.D. *Coping with a Negative Body Image.* New York: The Rosen Publishing Group, 1989.

Boyer, Ernest. *High School: A Report on Secondary Education in America.* The Carnegie Foundation for the Advancement of Teaching. New York: Harper and Row, Publishers, 1983.

Bradfield, Scott. *The History of Luminous Motion.* New York: Alfred A. Knopf, Inc. 1989.

Brick, Peggy. *In Seminars in Adolescent Medicine* 1, No. 2: New York: Thieme Medical Publishers, Inc., 1985.

Bruner, Jerome. *The Process of Education.* Cambridge, Mass.: Harvard University Press, 1963.

Brown, Lyn Mikel, and Carol Gilligan. *Meeting at the Crossroads: Women's Psychology and Girls' Development*. Harvard University Press, 1992.

Bruch, H. *Eating Disorders: Obesity, Anorexia Nervosa, and the Person Within*. New York: Basic Books, 1973.

Bruns, Jerome H., D.A. Ed. *They Can But They Don't: Helping Students Overcome Work Inhibition*. New York: Viking, 1992.

Bugliosi, Vincent, and Curt Gentry. *Helter Skelter*. New York: Bantam Books, 1976.

Caron, Ann F., Ed. D. *Don't Stop Loving Me: A Reassuring Guide for Mothers of Adolescent Daughters* New York: Henry Holt and Company, 1990.

Carter, Carol. *Majoring In High School: Survival Tips For Students*. New York: Noonday Press, Farrar Straus, and Giroux, 1995.

Cauwels, Janice M. *Bulimia: The Binge-Purge Compulsion*. New York: Doubleday and Company, 1983.

Chapman, Anne. *The Difference It Makes: A Resource Book on Gender for Educators*. Boston: National Association of Independent Schools, 1988.

Cisneros, Sandra. *The House on Mango Street,* New York: Vintage Books, 1989.

Coles, Robert. *The Spiritual Life of Children*. Boston: Houghton Mifflin Company, 1990.

Coles, Robert. *Children of Crisis: A Study of Courage and Fear*. Boston: Little, Brown, 1976.

Committee on Adolescence, Group for the Advancement of Psychiatry; *Normal Adolescence,* introduction by Katherine B. Oettinger. New York: Charles Scribner's Sons, 1968.

Conger, John Janeway. *Adolescence and Youth: Psychological Development in a Changing World*. New York: HarperCollins, 1991.

Csikszentmihalyi, Mihaly. *Being Adolescent: Conflict and Growth in the Teenage Years*. New York: Basic Books, 1984.

Csikszentmihalyi, Mihaly. *The Evolving Self: A Psychology for the Third Millennium*. New York: HarperCollins Publishers, 1993.

Csikzentmihalyi, Mihaly. *Flow: The Psychology of Optimal Experience*. New York: Harper and Row Publishers, 1990.

Csikzentmihalyi, Mihaly. *Talented Teenagers: The Roots of Success and Failure*. New York: Cambridge University Press, 1993.

Damon, William. *The Moral Child*. New York: The Free Press, 1988.

Damon, William. *Greater Expectations: Overcoming the Culture of Indulgence in America's Homes and Schools*. New York: Free Press, 1995.

Davitz, Lora and Joel Davitz. *How to Live almost Happily with a Teenager*. San Francisco: Harper and Row, 1982.

Debold, Elizabeth, Laurie Wilson, and Idelisse Malave. *Mother Daughter Revolution*. Reading, Mass.: Addison-Wesley, 1993.

Del Fattore, Joan. *What Johnny Shouldn't Read: Textbook Censorship in America*. New Haven, Conn.: Yale University Press, 1992.

Dewey, John. *The Child and the Curriculum*. Chicago: University of Chicago Press, 1956.

Dewey, John. *The Moral Writings of John Dewey*. Edited by James Gouinlock. Buffalo, N.Y.: Prometheus Books, 1994.

Dimoff, Timothy, and Carper, Steve. *How to Tell If Your Kids Are Using Drugs*. New York: Facts on File, Inc., 1992.

Donaldson, Margaret. *Children's Minds*. New York: W. W. Norton and Company, 1979.

DuPont, Robert L. Jr., M.D. *Getting Touch on Gateway Drugs: A Guide for the Family*. New York: American Psychiatric Press, 1984.

Eagen, Andrea Boroff. *Why Am I So Miserable If These Are the Best Years of My Life? A Survival Guide for the Young Woman*. Philadelphia: Lippincott, 1976.

Edelman, Marian Wright. *The Measure of Our Success: A Letter to My Children and Yours*. Boston: Beacon Press, 1992.

Elkind, David. *All Grown Up and No Place to Go: Teenagers in Crisis*. Reading, Mass.: Addison-Wesley, 1984.

Elkind, David. *Children and Adolescents; Interpretive Essays on Jean Piaget*. New York: Oxford University Press, 1970.

Elkind, David. *Hurried Child: Growing Up Too Fast Too Soon*. Reading, Mass.: Addison Wesley, 1981.

Elochness, Edward Monte, Jane Nelsen and Lynn Lott. *I'm on Your Side: Resolving Conflict with Your Teen-age Son or Daughter*. Rocklin, Calif.: Prima Publications, 1991.

Erichsen, Ann. *Anorexia Nervosa: The Broken Cycle*. London: Faber and Faber, 1987.

Erikson, Erik H. *Childhood and Society*. New York: W.W. Norton, 1950.

Erikson, Erik H. *Identity: Youth and Crisis*. New York: W.W. Norton, 1968.

Etzioni, Amitai. *The Spirit of Community: The Reinvention of American Society*. New York: Touchstone, 1993.

Evans, Glen and Farberow, Norman L., Ph.D. *The Encyclopedia of Suicide*. New York: Facts on File, 1988.

Fairchild and Hayward: *Now That You Know: What Every Parent Should Know about Homosexuality*. Boston: Harcourt, Brace, Jovanovich, 1979.

Faye, Martha. *Do Children Need Religion?: How Parents Today Are Thinking about the Big Questions*. New York: Pantheon, 1993.

Feldman, S. S., and Elliot, G. R., eds., *At the Threshold: The Developing Adolescent*. Cambridge, Mass.: Harvard University Press, 1990.

Fleming, Don Ph.D. *How to Stop the Battle with Your Teenager: A Practical Guide to Solving Everyday Problems*. New York: Prentice Hall, 1989.

Fontenelle, Don H., Ph.D. *Keys to Parenting Your Teenager*. New York: Barrons, 1992.

Freire, Paulo. *The Pedagogy of the Oppressed*. New York: Continuum, 1970.

Friedman, Samuel G. *Small Victories: The Real World of a Teacher, Her Students, and Their High School*. New York: Harper Perennial, 1990.

Gardner, Howard. *Frames of Mind: The Theory of Multiple Intelligences*. New York: Basic Books, 1983.

Gardner, Howard. *The Unschooled Mind: How Children Think and How Schools Should Teach*. New York: Basic Books, 1991.

Gardner, Dr. James E. *Understanding, Helping, Surviving the Turbulent Teens*. Sorrento Press, Inc. 1983.

Gardner, R. A. *The Parents' Book About Divorce*. New York: Doubleday and Co., Inc. 1977.

Giffin, Mary and Carol Felsenthal. *A Cry for Help: Exploring and Exploding the Myths about Teenage Suicide: A Guide for All Parents of Adolescents*. Garden City, N.Y.: Doubleday, 1983.

Gilligan, Carol. *A Different Voice: Psychological Theory and Women's Development*. Harvard University Press, 1982.

Gilligan, Carol, Nona P. Lyons, and Trudy J. Hanmer, eds. *Making Connections: The*

Relational Worlds of Adolescent Girls at Emma Willard School. Cambridge, Mass.: Harvard University Press, 1990.

Gilligan, Carol, Annie Rogers, and Deborah Tolman, eds. *Women, Girls, and Psychotherapy: Reframing Resistance.* New York, Harrington Park Press, 1991.

Ginott, Dr. Haim G. *Between Parent and Teenager.* New York: Avon Books, 1969.

Gleick, James. *Chaos: Making a New Science.* New York: Viking, 1988.

Goldberg, Natalie. *Long Quiet Highway.* New York: Bantam, 1993.

Goodlad, John. *A Place Called School.* New York: McGraw Hill, 1984.

Goleman, Daniel. *Emotional Intelligence.* New York: Bantam Books, 1995.

Gordon, Sol. *Sex Education and the Parents' Role.* New York: Public Affairs Committee pamphlet, 1977.

Grant, Gerald. *The World We Created at Hamilton High.* Cambridge, Mass.: Harvard University Press, 1988.

Green, Maxine. *Releasing the Imagination: Essays on Education, the Arts, and Social Change.* San Francisco: Jossey-Bass Publishers, 1995.

Greydanus, Donald E., M.D., F.A.A.P., Editor in Chief. *The American Academy of Pediatrics, Caring for Your Adolescent: Ages 12–21.*

Griffin, C., M. Wirthy, and A. Wirth. *Beyond Acceptance: Parents of Lesbians and Gays Talk about Their Experiences.* New York: St. Martin, Inc., 1990.

Grumet, Madeline R. *Bitter Milk: Women and Teaching.* Amherst: University of Massachusetts Press, 1988.

Hacker, Sylvia S. with Hacker, Randi. *What Every Teenager Really Wants to Know about Sex.* New York: Carroll and Gray, Publishers, 1993.

Hallowell, Edward M., M.D., and John J. Ratey, M.D. *Driven to Distraction: Recognizing and Coping with Attention Deficit Disorder from Childhood through Adulthood.* New York: Simon and Schuster: 1994.

Harbeck, Karen, ed. *Coming Out of the Classroom Closet: Gay and Lesbian Students, Teachers, and Curricula.* Binghamton, N.Y.: Harrington Park Press, 1992.

Hawley, Richard A. *The Purposes of Pleasure: A Reflection on Youth and Drugs.* Wellesley Hills, Mass.: Independent School Press, 1983.

Hechinger, Grace. *Teen-Age Tyranny.* New York: Morrow, 1963.

Hellman, Lillian. *Pentimento: A Book of Portraits.* New York: Signet, 1973.

Hipp, Earl. *Fighting Invisible Tigers: Stress Management Guide for Teens.* Minneapolis: Free Spirit Publishing, 1985.

Hirsch, E.D. *Cultural Literacy: What Every American Needs to Know.* New York: Vintage, 1988.

Holt, John. *Why Children Fail.* New York: Dell Publishing Company, 1964.

Holtz, Geoffey F. *Welcome to the Jungle: The Why Behind Generation X.* New York: St. Martin's, 1995.

hooks, bell. *Teaching to Transgress: Education as the Practice of Freedom.* New York: Routledge, 1994.

Hopson, Dr. Darlene Powell, and Dr. Derek S. Hopson. *Different and Wonderful: Raising Black Children in a Race-Conscious Society.* New York: Fireside Books, 1992.

Hurston, Zora Neale. *Their Eyes Were Watching God.* New York: Harper and Row Publishers, 1937, 1990.

Jackson, Philip W. *The Moral Life of Schools.* San Francisco: Jossey-Bass Publishers, 1993.

Jerald, A.T. *The Psychology of Adolescence.* 2nd ed. New York: MacMillan, 1963.

Johnson, Magic. *What You Can Do to Avoid AIDS.* New York: Times Books, 1992.

Kaestle, Carl F. *The Public Schools and the Public Mood.* New York: American Heritage, February, 1990.

Kagan, Jerome and Coles, Robert. *12 to 16: Early Adolescence.* New York: W. W. Norton and Company, Inc. 1972.

Kagan, Robert. *The Evolving Self.* Cambridge, Mass.: Harvard University Press, 1982.

Keltner, Nancy, editor. *If You Print This, Please Don't Use My Name: Questions from Teens and Their Parents about Things That Matter.* Davis, Calif.: Terra Nova Press, 1992.

Ketcham, Katherine and Ginny Lyford Gustafson. *Living on the Edge: A Guide to Intervention for Families with Drug and Alcohol Problems.* New York: Bantam Books, 1989.

Kidder, Rushworth M. *How Good People Make Tough Choices.* New York: William Morrow and Company, Inc., 1995.

Kilpatrick, William K. *Why Johnny Can't Tell Right from Wrong: Moral Illiteracy and the Case for Character Education.* New York: Touchstone Books, 1993.

Kirp, David L. *Learning by Heart: Aids and Schoolchildren in America's Communities.* New Brunswick, N.J.: Rutgers University Press, 1989.

Kohn, Alfie. *Punished by Rewards: The Trouble with Gold Stars, Incentive Plans, A's, Praise, and Other Bribes:* Boston: Houghton Mifflin, 1993.

Kotlowitz, Alex. *There Are No Children Here: The Story of Two Boys Growing Up in the Other America.* New York: Doubleday, 1992.

Kozol, Jonathon. *Savage Inequalities: Children in America's Schools.* New York: HarperPerennial, 1992.

Kozol, Jonathon. *Amazing Grace: The Lives of Children and the Conscience of a Nation.* New York: Crown Publishers, 1995.

Krell, N. *The Universal Experience of Adolescence.* University of London Press, 1969.

Kushner, Harold. *When All You've Ever Wanted Isn't Enough.* New York: Simon and Schuster, 1986.

Lang, Susan S. *Extremist Groups in America.* New York: Franklin Watts Co., 1990.

Levenkron, Steven. *The Best Little Girl in the World.* New York: Warner Books, 1978.

Levenkron, Steven. *Treating and Overcoming Anorexia Nervosa.* New York: Warner Books, 1982.

Levine, Katherine G. *When Good Kids Do Bad Things.* New York: Norton, 1991.

Levine, Mel., M.D. *Keep a Head in School: A Student's Book about Learning Abilities and Learning Disorders.* Cambridge, Mass.: Educators Publishing Service, Inc., 1990.

Levine, Saul V, *Radical Departures.* New York: Harcourt, Brace, Jovanovich, 1984.

Lickona, Thomas. *Educating for Character: How Our Schools Can Teach Respect and Responsibility.* New York: Bantam, 1992.

Lickona, Dr. Thomas. *Raising Good Children.* New York: Bantam, 1983.

Lidz, Theodore. *The Person: His Development through the Life Cycle.* New York: Basic Books, 1968.

Lightman, Alan. *Einstein's Dreams.* New York: Pantheon Books, 1993.

Lynn, R. N *12 to 16: Early Adolescence: Raising Sexually Healthy Children: A Loving Guide for Parents, Teachers and Care-Givers* New York: Rawson Associates, 1988.

Lightfoot, Sara Lawrence. *The Good School: Portraits of Character and Culture.* New York: Bantam, 1983.

Malraux, André. *Anti Memoirs.* New York: Bantam Books, 1967.

Mann, Judy. *The Difference: Growing Up Female in America.* New York: Warner Books, 1994.

Martz, Larry. *Making Schools Better: How Parents and Teachers across the Country Are Taking Action—and How You Can Too.* New York: Times Books, 1993.

Maurer, Harry, ed. *Sex: An Oral History.* New York: Viking, 1994.

Mauss, A. L, and Peterson, D. W. *Prodigals as Preachers: The Jesus Freaks and the Return to Respectability.* Paper presented at the Convention of the Society for the Scientific Study of Religion, San Francisco, 1993.

McCoy, Kathy, Ph.D. *The New Teenage Body Book.* New York: Body Press/Perigee, 1992.

Melton, J. Gordon. *Encyclopedic Handbook of Cults in America.* New York: Garland Publishing, Inc., 1986.

Monette, Paul. *Becoming a Man—Half a Life Story.* New York: Harcourt, Brace, Jovanovich, Publishers, 1992.

Nava, Michael and Robert Davidoff. *Created Equal: Why Gay Rights Matter to America.* New York: St. Martin's Press, 1994.

Muller, Ann. *Parents Matter: Parents' Relationships with Lesbian Daughters and Gay Sons.* Tallahassee, Fla.: Naiad Press, 1987.

Muus, Rolf E. *Theories of Adolescence,* Third Edition. New York: Random House, 1975.

Noam, Gil and Thomas Wren, eds. *The Moral Self: Building a Better Paradigm.* Cambridge, Mass.: MIT Press, 1993.

Noddings, Nel. *Caring: A Feminine Approach to Ethics and Moral Education.* Berkeley: University of California Press, 1984.

Noddings, Nel. *The Challenge to Care in Schools: An Alternative Approach to Education.* New York: Teachers College Press, 1992.

Offer, D., E. Ostrov, and K. Howard, *The Adolescent: A Psychological Self Portrait.* New York: Basic Books, 1981.

Packer, Alex J. *Bringing Up Parents.* Washington, D.C.: Acropolis Books, Inc., 1985.

Peck, M., N. L. Faberow, and R. E. Litman, eds. *Youth Suicide.* New York: Springer, 1985.

Piaget, J. *The Moral Judgment of the Child.* New York: Free Press, 1932/1965.

Pipher, Mary. *Reviving Ophelila: Saving the Selves of Adolescent Girls.* New York: Ballantine Books, 1994.

Pirsig, Robert. *Zen and the Art of Motorcycle Maintenance.* New York: William Morrow and Company, Inc., 1984.

Pomeroy, Wardell B. *Girls and Sex.* (3rd Edition) New York: Laurel-Leaf., 1991.

Postman, Neil. *The Disappearance of Childhood.* New York: Vintage, 1994.

Powell, Douglas R. *Families as Nurturing Systems: Support across the Life Span.* New York: Hayworth Press, 1991.

Powell, Arthur G., Eleanor Farra, and David K. Cohen, *The Shopping Mall High School: Winners and Losers in the Educational Marketplace.* Boston: Houghton Mifflin, 1985.

Poulin, A. Jr., editor: *Contemporary American Poetry,* Fourth Edition: Boston: Houghton Mifflin Co., 1985.

Rice, Philip F. *The Adolescent: Development, Relationships, and Culture.* Fifth Edition. Boston: Allyn and Bacon, 1987.

Richards, Arlene and Irene Willis. *How to Get It Together When Your Parents Are Coming Apart.* Summit, N.J.: Willard Press, 1976.

Riley Dorothy Winbrush, ed. *My Soul Looks Back, Less I Forget: A Collection of Quotations by People of Color.* New York: HarperCollins, 1993.

Rimm, Dr. Sylvia. *Why Bright Kids Get Bad Grades.* New York: Crown, 1994.

Riordon, Cornelius. *Girls and Boys in School: Together or Separate?* New York: Teachers College Press, 1990.

Roberts, Jillian. *I'd Rather Be in Philadelphia.* New York: Ballantine Books, 1992.

Rodriguez, Luis J. *Always Running: La Vida Loca: Gang Days in L.A.* Willimantic, Conn.: Curbstone Press, 1992

Rosemond, John. *Parent Power: A Common-Sense Approach to Parenting in the 1990s and Beyond.* Kansas City: A Universal Press Syndicate Company, 1990.

Rumney, Avis. *Dying to Please: Anorexia Nervosa and Its Cure.* Jefferson, N.C.: McFarland & Company, 1983.

Sadker, David and Myra Sadker. *Failing at Fairness: How America's Schools Cheat Girls.* New York: Charles Scribner's Sons, 1994.

Salinger, J.D. *Catcher in the Rye.* New York: Bantam Books, 1952.

Salk, Dr. Lee. *What Every Child Would Like His Parents to Know.* New York: Warner Paperback Library. 1973.

Seligman, Martin E. P. *Helplessness or Depression, Development, and Death.* San Francisco: W.H. Freeman, 1975.

Seligman, Martin E. P. *Learned Optimism.* New York: Random House, 1991.

Shapiro, Joseph R. *No Pity: People with Disabilities Forging a New Civil Rights Movement.* New York: Times Books, division of Random House, 1993, 14.

Sheehy, Gail. *Passages: Predictable Crises of Adult Life.* New York: Bantam Books, 1980.

Sheehy, Gail. *New Passages: Mapping Your Life across Time.* New York: Random House, 1995.

Sizer, Theodore. *Horace's Compromise: The Dilemma of the American High School.* Boston: Houghton Mifflin, 1984.

Sizer, Theodore. *Horace's School.* Boston: Houghton Mifflin, 1992

Somers, Leon. *Talking to Your Children about Love and Sex.* New York: Penguin Signet, 1990.

Spock, Benjamin, M.D. and Michael B. Rothenberg. *Baby and Child Care.* New York: Pocket Books, 1971.

Stone and Church, *Childhood and Adolescence,* 2nd edition, New York: Random House: 1968.

Sudar, H.S., A. B. Ford, and N. B. Rushworth, eds. *Suicide in the Young.* Boston: Wright, 1984.

Sze, William C., Ph.D. *Human Life Cycle.* New York: Jason Aronson, Inc., 1975.

Tannen, Deborah. *You Just Don't Understand: Women and Men in Conversation.* New York: Ballantine, 1991.

Thorne, Barrie. *Gender Play: Girls and Boys in School.* Rutgers University Press, 1993.

Vail, Priscilla I. *Smart Kids with School Problems.* New York: E.P. Dutton, 1987.

Verdral, Joynce. *My Teenager Is Driving Me Crazy.* New York: Ballantine, 1989.

Vigil, James Diego. Barrio *Gangs: Street Life and Identity in Southern California.* Austin: University of Texas Press, 1991.

Voss, Jacqueline, and Jay Gale. *A Young Woman's Guide to Sex.* Los Angeles, Calif.: The Body Press, 1986.

Winder, Alvin E., and David L. Angus. *Adolescence: Contemporary Studies.* New York: Van Nostrand Reinhold Company, 1968.

Warren, Andrea, and Jay Wiedenkeller. *Everybody's Doing It: How to Survive Your Teenagers' Sex Life (And Help Them Survive It, Too).* New York: Penguin Books, 1993.

Warschaw, Dr. Tessa Albert and Victoria Secunda. *Winning with Kids.* New York: Bantam Books, 1990.

Wender, Paul H., M.D. *The Hyperactive Child, Adolescent, and Adult: Attention Deficit Disorder through the Lifespan.* New York: Oxford University Press, 1987.

White, E.B. *Stuart Little.* New York: Harper and Bros., 1945.

Whitehead, Alfred North. *The Aims of Education.* New York: Free Press, 1929.

Wingerd, William N., and Gary R. Gruber. *Understanding and Enjoying Adolescence.* New York: Longman and Company, 1988.

Wolf, Anthony E., Ph.D. *Get Out of My Life: Could You Drive Me and Cheryl to the Mall?* New York: Noonday, 1992.

Wynn, Edward A. *Reclaiming Our Schools: A Handbook on Teaching Character, Academics, and Discipline:* New York: Macmillan Publishing Company, 1993.

Yellen, Andrew G., Ph.D. *The Art of Perfect Parenting and Other Absurd Ideas.* Northridge, Calif.: Yellen and Associates, 1993.

Zohar, Dana and Ian Marshall. *The Quantum Society: Mind, Physics, and a New Social Vision.* New York: William Morrow and Company, Inc, 1996, 326–27.

Index